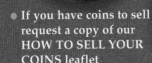

Editor
Deborah Lees

Art Editor
Sheradon Dublin

Consultant Editors
Mark Rasmussen
Richard West

Advertisement Manager
Jay Jones

Advertising Executive
Alan Dean

Production
Paul Lincoln

Associate Publisher
Niall Clarkson

An IPC Media annual published by IPC Country & Leisure Media Focus Network (part of the IPC Media Group of Companies) from: IPC Media, Focus Network, Leon House, 233 High Street, Croydon CR9 1 HZ.
Tel: 020 8726 8000
Fax: 020 8726 8299

Distributed by
MarketForce,
Kings Reach Tower,
Stamford Street,
London SE9 1LS.
Tel: 020 7633 3300

Pre-press by CTT; printed by Stones, Unit 10, Acre Estate, Wildmere Road, Banbury Oxon OX16 3ES.

BRITISH COINS

MARKET VALUES 2006

CONTENTS

SPECIAL FEATURES

LATEST MARKET PRICES – FULL LISTINGS
British Coin Prices

This Coenwulf gold penny sold for £230,000 setting a new world record

SELLING YOUR COINS & NOTES?

To satisfy overwhelming demand from our buyers Warwick and Warwick urgently require quality material of all types. We particularly need Great Britain, World and single country collections and accumulations of any size and in any condition from Fair to FDC.

The market for quality material has never been stronger and if you are considering the sale of your collection, now is the time to act.

FREE VALUATIONS

We will provide a free professional and without obligation valuation of your collection. Either we will make you a fair, binding private treaty offer, or we will recommend inclusion of your property in our next public auction.

FREE TRANSPORTATION

We can arrange insured transportation of your collection to our Warwick offices completely free of charge. If you decline our offer we ask you to cover the return carriage costs only.

FREE VISITS

Visits by our valuers are possible anywhere in the country or abroad, usually within 48 hours, in order to value larger collections. Please phone for details.

EXCELLENT PRICES

Our ever expanding customer base means we are in a position to offer prices that we feel sure will exceed your expectations.

ACT NOW

Telephone Richard Beale today with details of your property. E-mail or fax us if you prefer.

Get the experts on your side.

Warwick & Warwick

www.warwickandwarwick.com

Warwick & Warwick Ltd., Chalon House, Scar Bank, Millers Rd, Warwick CV34 5DB
Tel: 01926-499031 Fax: 01926-491906 E-mail: richard.beale@warwickandwarwick.com

The Royal Maundy

A ceremony that sees its origins in the days of Christ, Richard West investigates the advent of the giving of Maundy Money to the poor and looks at some of the designs depicted on these sought-after coins

On April 13, 2006, Maundy Thursday, 80 men and 80 women will each receive 80p worth of Maundy Money, it being The Queen's 80th birthday year. The ceremony is seeped in tradition, both in terms of gifts given by the monarch, and in its being held on Maundy Thursday. It was the day before his betrayal and crucifixion, Jesus gathered with his disciples, and washed their feet, giving them a new commandment 'that ye love one another'. This commandment gave the day its name of Maundy Thursday: the ritual of washing of feet still practised by some.

George IV obverse and reverse Maundy coin with the new positioning of the date through the middle divided by the number 4. The portrait of the King was designed by Benedetto Pistrucci

The King's Dole

The idea of the monarch helping the poor has a long history, the gifts being known variously as Alms, the King's Dole or Largesse. They took the form of food, clothing or money, often given on a daily basis, with special gifts at Christmas and Easter, or at specific occasions such as a Coronation. At times the preference was to give money, and later money replaced any gifts.

It is believed King Edward II (1307-1327) was the first monarch to wash the feet of those chosen from the poor and elderly on Maundy Thursday, a tradition continued up to the reign of James II (1685-1688). While the washing of feet ceased to be part of the Maundy Thursday ceremony from the 18th century (1736 is recorded) –

Elizabeth II obverse and reverse showing the Queen's portrait design by Mary Gillick

although it was revived in 2003 by the new Archbishop of Canterbury, Dr Rowan Williams – the act is very much remembered. In the days when the monarch performed the task, although the feet of those chosen had already been washed twice, the sensibilities of the monarch, both from the odour and any risk of infection, were protected by a nosegay. Today those participating are provided with nosegays made of spring flowers and herbs. The officials wear linen towels worn over the right shoulder and tied round the waist.

Giving of coins

The tradition of giving silver coins is said to have originated with St Augustine in 597AD at Canterbury. King John (1199-1216) gave gifts of money to the poor in 1213, 13p pence to each of the 13 men, representing Jesus and his 12 disciples. Edward II was the first monarch to take part in the ceremony, washing the feet of 50 poor men, while Edward III (1327-1377) washed feet and gave money. Over the years the monarch participated in the ceremony, so it became known as the Royal Maundy.

It is believed that it was Henry IV who first related the number of gifts to the age of monarch. In the reigns of Henry VII and VIII it became the practice to allow for an extra year, this being the 'year of grace' that it was believed God gave to the sovereign.

The gifts of money were accompanied by food and clothing, even the monarch's robes worn during the ceremony, but gradually the gifts became of money alone. At first only silver pennies were distributed, but in 1551 the threepence was added, and later the twopence and fourpence. Each recipient receives the gift in two purses, a white one containing the Maundy money, and a red one with money in lieu of food and clothing. This practice continues today, the sum given in lieu being £5.50.

Until the 18th century, the recipients were of the same sex as the monarch: then it was changed to include as many men and women as the monarch's age. A further change has been while the recipients were once chosen from the poor, now they are selected for outstanding Christian service to the church.

In many respects it was Charles II who took the greatest interest in the ceremony actually washing the feet despite it being a time of plague, while it was during his reign that the specific Maundy money was introduced. He also gave the alms dishes still used today to carry the purses, one known as the Maundy Dish, the other as the Fishes Dish.

The Maundy Money

Within *British Coins Market Values* are listed the sets of Maundy Money, starting in 1670 with the reign of Charles II (1660-1684). However, from the start of the reign in 1660 coinage was produced, undated, in one, two, three and four penny denominations, the obverse having the portrait of the King within an inner circle. Later a second set appeared, by Thomas Simon, which has the bust of the King extending to the edges of the coin, known as Undated Maundy Money or Simon's Maundy Money, although it was not used solely for Maundy purposes. As the years passed the coins changed from hammered to milled, with a 2d silver coin being produced, dated, in 1668, followed in 1670 by the 1d, 3d and 4d, and thus 1670 is the first year for the set of four coins.

Reverse of the silver Maundy 1d, 2d and 3d coins used in 2000. Note the crown and the oak wreath surrounding the date and numerals still exists

Different dies

The dies for the 1670 coins were produced by Jan Roettier, a Dutch artist whose work the King preferred to that of Simon. The obverse features the royal portrait, while the reverse has his monogram, the 'C', shown once on the 1d, with two, three or four intertwined on the 2d, 3d and 4d respectively.

For the reign of James II, the portrait was naturally changed, while the reverse features 'I', 'II', 'III' or 'IIII' to denote the denomination. The 'I' could be the denomination, or it could again by a monogram, for IACOBVS.

William and Mary's reign (William III and Mary II - 1689-1694) brought a change to the design of the reverse of the coins that has remained basically the same. Instead of a monogram, the four denominations are denoted by the numerals 1, 2, 3 and 4. The obverse naturally featured the busts of William and Mary.

The subsequent reigns of William III (1694-1702), Anne (1702-1714), George I (1714-1727)

Maundy coin with the BRITT OMN deleted from the circular inscription

and George II (1727-1760) saw only changes with the differing portraits. The Maundy money retained the original young bust of George II throughout his reign, even though it was changed on the everyday coinage. In the case of George I, II and III there was not space on the Maundy coins for the list of their titles.

George portraits

George III's reign (1760-1820) provides considerable interest, with changes to both the bust and the reverse. The first portrait used was of the young King by Richard Yeo, with the same reverse design introduced for the reign of William and Mary. However, the reverses for 1784 and 1786 have the numerals looking rather squat. In 1792 a new bust was used, by Lewis Pingo, again with the squat numerals on the reverse, changed again in 1795 back to the original reverse, still with Pingo's portrait on the obverse, although with some minor differences from that of 1792. Another new portrait came in 1817, this time by Benedetto Pistrucci, and while the reverse retained the original design with Arabic numerals, its inscription was amended to recognise the Union with Ireland, and that the King surrendered the title of King of France.

The reign of George IV (1820-1830) brought about a change in the design of the reverse of the coins that has been adopted ever since. While retaining the basic concept of the Arabic 1, 2, 3 or 4, the legend was moved to the obverse. The dies for the reverses were by Jean Baptiste Merlen. The one portrait of George IV was used throughout the reign even though the normal coinage saw a change in portrait.

1830-present

The portrait used for William IV (1830-1837) was by William Wyon, with the Merlen reverse. In 1831 a few proof sets were produced in gold.

For the long reign of Queen Victoria (1837-1901) three portraits were used. The first bust, known as the 'young head' was by William Wyon, replaced in 1888 by the 'jubilee head' by Joseph Edgar Boehem (the Golden Jubilee year was in fact 1887). The third portrait, used from 1893, is by Thomas Brock, and is known as the 'old head'. To coincide with the introduction of the 'jubilee head', a further slight alteration was made to the reverse, affecting the crown, resulting in the reverse which is still in use today.

A bust by G. W. DeSaulles was used through the reign of Edward VII (1901-1910). For George V (1910-1936) it was that by Bertram Mackennal, although a modification was made during the reign. It was also during this reign the silver content of the coins was altered (a change had also occurred during George III's reign).

Although Edward VIII (1936) did participate in the ceremony, the Maundy coins used for 1936 had the portrait of George V. The portrait used for the reign of George VI (1936-1952) was by T. Humphrey Paget. From 1949 a change was made to the inscription following India's independence. The reign also saw a change in the silver content.

For the present reign, only Mary Gillick's portrait has been used. From 1954 the legend 'BRITT OMN.' was omitted from all coinage.

The white and red Maundy purses. To purchase similar items go to www.maundymoney.com

Legal tender

With the change from 240 pennies to the pound to decimal currency, the denominations of the Maundy coins automatically became 'new pence'. All Maundy Money remains legal tender, not that anyone would use it, and so all the coins up to 1970 were re-valued as decimal pence.

During the reign of Queen Victoria the Maundy coins could be purchased by anyone, but this was stopped from 1909, limiting the quantity minted to the recipients.

In general the coins have been of sterling silver standard (92.5%), but in 1920 all silver coins were debased to 50%. The Coinage Act of 1946 again debased all silver coins to a cupro-nickel alloy, but it was decided that the Maundy Money should revert to 92% silver.

Today's ceremony

For over two centuries, the monarch did not attend the ceremony, and it was not until 1932 that George V took part personally. As far as possible, The Queen has attended the ceremony.

In the early days the ceremony might be held at places such as Windsor, Eton or Greenwich, while in the 18th and 19th centuries it was at the Chapel Royal in Whitehall. From 1891 Westminster Abbey was frequently used or St Paul's Cathedral. However, The Queen has made a point of taking the ceremony around the country, so Westminster Abbey was used almost every alternate year up to 1980, from then onwards a different cathedral has been used.

In 2006 each recipient will receive eight sets of coins. Additional sets are minted, which are available to a selected few. For example, those employed by the Royal Mint, over five years.

During the service it is the Lord High Almoner who serves on the monarch, while The Yeoman of the Guard carry the Maundy gifts. It ends with the Maundy prayer, recalling the act of humility of Christ over 2,000 years ago.

ACKNOWLEDGEMENTS

The Royal Mint, Royal Maundy (Pitkin Pride of Britain books) and The Royal Maundy by Dr B. Robinson.

The year in coins

Read on to find out the biggest sellers at the coin auctions held over the last 12 months and the state of the British coin market

In 2004/5 there have been times when so many major sales were competing for the attention of collectors that it was thought the great supply of material would swamp the market. However, there have been some spectacular prices realized at auction that continues to show the great strength in the market for British coins.

The year opened in appropriate style at COINEX 2004 with the offering by Spink of the first new Anglo-Saxon gold coin to be sold at auction for 100 years, a completely unrecorded gold penny or 'mancus' struck at London by the Mercian King Coenwulf, and in superb condition. The estimate of £100,000-125,000 was speculative and two American dealers fought the price up to £230,000, a new world record at auction for a British coin and the first to break the £200,000 barrier. In world terms this is quite a modest sum but the coin requires an export license, a factor which is understood to have deterred several contenders, and at the time of writing the Culture Minister, David Lammy, has placed a two-month export ban on the coin to enable British institutions to raise funds to keep it in Britain.

The same auction contained an offering of 100 picked coins from the Pimprez Hoard of silver pennies of Henry I and Stephen, found in 2002 at

A new world record was set when this unrecorded unique Coenwulf gold penny went for £230,000

Pimprez 50km north of Paris. The result was enormous interest and commensurate prices, a Henry I type XIV penny of Shrewsbury, an extremely rare mint for the reign, selling for £4,945, estimate £400-500, and a lovely Stephen Watford type penny of Wareham for £2,530, estimate £600-800.

COINEX 2004 also saw the St James's Auction, Auction 1, in association with Baldwin's. The highest price was £33,900, estimate £22,000-25,000, for a Henry VII Sovereign.

A fortnight later Auktion Leu 92, Zürich sold an attractive small group of English and Scottish gold coins including a Victoria 1870 pattern sovereign that sold for £18,000.

Morton & Eden's Autumn sale also indicated the trend for quality gold coins when a low estimate of £12,000-15,000 placed on an extremely fine 1644 Oxford triple unite attracted a bid of £37,950, a new auction record for a 'currency' triple unit. The same sale contained an extremely rare heavy noble of Edward IV. One of the famous Fishpool Hoard coins, this piece sold in 1968 for £10,000.

The 2005 season was kicked off by Dix Noonan Webb (DNW)'s quarterly Spring sale. This was followed by a double catalogue from Noble Numismatics Pty Ltd., Sydney, one catalogue being devoted to the extensive collection of William Lampard of Wellington, New Zealand. The Lampard sale realized $A1,186,000, estimate $A672,000, with all lots sold. Two weeks later American Numismatic Rarities sold the magnificent Louis E Eliasberg, Sr Collection of

Stephen Watford penny of Wareham in good very fine condition sold for £2,530 at Spink in 2004

This heavy noble coin from Edward IV reign was bid up to £14,000

world gold coins in New York.

The highlight of the season, however, was the extraordinary Samuel King collection of English gold coins, auctioned by Spink on May 5, 2005. 217 lots sold for £1,630,000. The highest price of £149,500, estimate £40,000-50,000, was for the famous 1703 VIGO five guineas of Queen Anne, a true 'world coin'. This piece had realized £42,900 in the Sharps Pixley sale in 1989.

Less than a week later, St James's Auctions offered Auction 2, a huge sale of 1004 lots, estimated at over £1 million. Of particular interest was a Charles I 'two-shilling' piece coined during the siege of Pontefract castle. Struck from shilling dies on an outsize flan, this coin should technically be called a 1 shilling and 8 pence piece but is so rare that it was unpriced in the catalogues and its presale value was uncertain. In the event it realized £24,150 as against perhaps £3,000 expected for an identical shilling on a normal flan.

On May 30, 2005 the Pre-Long Beach Auction, held by Ira & Larry Goldberg Coins & Collectibles Inc., Beverly Hills, contained the very extensive Cheshire Collection of 1264 lots. Graded and catalogued in the American style, but largely

Spink's sale on May 5, 2005 saw the highest price fetched for this 1703 VIGO five guineas of Queen Anne at £149,500

bought in London, this sale provided a useful guide to the world market. Very high prices were realized for individual items, noticeably £12,600 for a 1551 Edward VI silver crown, purchased in November 2004 at London Coin Auctions for £4,620.

Finally on June 2, 2005 Heritage World Coin Auctions, also at Long Beach, California, offered a single magnificent English coin as part of a general sale. The 'pattern' 1643 Charles I Oxford triple unite, is one of two known examples. Though probably a currency issue it is struck to a very high standard from an obverse die of unusually fine work. This example had last sold as part of the Selig Collection, Spink Auction 70, for £48,400 in 1989. Now on an estimate of £55,000-70,000, it sold for £235,000, another new world record for a British coin at auction.

Charles I lozenge-shaped two-shilling Pontefract besieged from 1648 realized £24,150 at St James's Auctions on May 11, 2005

Celtic Coinage

The market for Celtic coins remains a niche sector with more affinity with the contemporary Greek and Roman coinages than with the rest of the British series. None of the large collections, formed from new material discovered over the last couple of decades, have yet been offered for sale and price trends remain uncertain. A weakness is the lack of 'headline' prices in the Celtic market due to the continuing possibility that the rarity of certain types will be diluted by new finds. The highest price realized during the year was £5,200 in Classical Numismatic Group, Auction 67 for a well-centred Ambiani series A stater in above average condition. DNW Auction 65 contained a useful small group of 84 lots, realizing £39,000, with robust prices for the larger denominations and the prettier pieces.

English Hammered Gold

In many ways hammered gold is the flagship series of the British coinage. Not rare in absolute terms, it includes some of the most imposing and attractive denominations in the coinage such as the noble, sovereign, ship ryal and triple unite.

A Charles I Gold Triple Unite 1643 set a new world record when it fetched £235,000 in California in June 2005

The Samuel King collection contained some lovely examples including the excessively rare fine sovereign of Edward VI sold for £59,800, estimate £30,000-40,000. An excellent example of the famous George Noble of Henry VIII, the only tudor coin to depict St George and the dragon, sold for £26,450, estimate £10,000-12,000.

Not all hammered gold is expensive, excellent examples of the popular nobles of Edward III and Henry VI can be had in high grade for around £2,000 and the portrait gold coins of James I and Charles I in above average condition will cost just into four figures. Although undated, these coins have the added interest of a mint mark, placed at the beginning of the legend to signify the period during which they were struck.

The danger with hammered gold coins is that, being decorative and in very pure and thus soft metal, they have often been damaged. Mounted or repaired gold coins lose a considerable portion of their value.

English Hammered Silver

English hammered silver remains a vast and popular series. It encompasses some of the most famous names in English history – Alfred the Great, William the Conqueror, Richard III, Elizabeth I and the Civil War coinage of Charles I. Curiously interest in the early Saxon series seems to have subsided from the peak of 10 or 15 years ago and prices are now stable.

Spink Auction 172 obtained £1,725 for a normal non-portrait penny of Eadwig, estimate £800-1,000, and £1,000 for a common two-line type penny of Edward the Elder.

The short- and long-cross coinages still remain popular. The second portion of the Jeffrey Mass collection startled the room by breaking the £1,000 barrier for a Henry III long-cross penny. A class 2b coin of Norwich sold for £1,265. In the later medieval silver the emphasis is swinging back to type coins of the rarer reigns, Henry IV and Richard III. Richard III groats have now convincingly broken through the £1,000 level in VF grade and are rapidly approaching £1,500 in attractive condition. Tudor portrait coins have been extremely popular for several years and collectors are now being more selective. Both Henry VIII testoons and Edward VI crowns have proved difficult to sell if not in fine enough condition. Despite the enormous price of £41,500 realized for a magnificent Edward VI crown in the 2003 Slaney sale, none of the 30 examples offered at auction in the last year, with the exception of the Cheshire coin noted above, has sold for more than £4,000.

Charles I provincial and siege coinage remains extremely popular and is perhaps the one series where collectors are prepared to purchase coins in inferior condition in order to obtain an example. St James's Auction 1 realized £10,900 for a Carlisle siege shilling of 1645, on a small flan and weak in parts.

Milled Gold

For collectors of the milled gold series the year 2004/5 has brought an almost unimagined run of quality material to the market. Few could have predicted that over 200 five guinea pieces would be offered, selling from between £1,035 for an almost very fine but ex-jewellery example in Spink Auction 171 to almost £150,000 for the Samuel King 1703 VIGO. There was some concern that the market would be overwhelmed by this quantity but supply has created its own demand. The King collection also contained both varieties of the very important George III 1820 pattern £5. The 'normal' inscribed edge piece, just 25 known, was practically as struck and sold for £66,700, estimate £35,000-40,000. The plain edge variety, one of two known, the other being in the British Museum, in EF grade but slightly

George Noble of Henry VIII sold for £26,450 at Spink in 2005

scuffed sold for £43,700, estimate £30,000-40,000.

Sovereigns continue to be the most popular denomination in the milled gold series, and several collectors have been encouraged to sell and take advantage of the high-prices. No less than three very rare 1828 sovereigns have been offered at auction during the year. In contrast prices for the patterns and proofs have been mixed. The Cheshire Collection had a superb George III pattern two-guinea piece of 1773 in FDC condition, but was unwanted at £15,400.

Milled Silver

Milled silver is the workhorse series of the British coinage, and often the series in which collectors start their interest.

The Cheshire Collection contained an excellent run of currency and proof milled silver, and achieved some spectacular prices for the best, including an extraordinary £15,000 for a 'Dorrien and Magens' 1798 shilling. The same sale re-offered the only example of the very rare William III 1697 crown to survive in true EF condition.

Victorian milled silver remains very popular, with particular emphasis on the 1854 florin and shilling, as well as a resurgence of interest in the 20th century series in particular the George V 1934 crown. The mintage of 932 pieces makes this coin rare but far from unobtainable.

Charles I Carlisle besieged shilling 1645 crown above CR went for £10,900 at St James's Auction 1 in 2004

Copper and Bronze

The prices for copper and bronze coins have risen very sharply in the last decade, partly on the back of a lack of supply, but there is a feeling that these series, particularly the copper may be reaching a peak, with prices now too high to attract new collectors.

In 2004 an important private collection was dispersed privately and in May 2005 the very extensive copper section of the Cheshire collection suffered from lack of demand with a relatively high proportion unsold. The sad and unexpected death of Colin Cooke, one of the leading specialist dealers in this series has also taken away a driving force in the market.

£1,000 was realized for this King of Wessex, Edward the Elder two-line type Penny at Spink in March

Scottish Coins

The last few years has seen a considerable quantity of Scottish coins coming onto the market, to the extent that in some series, particularly the medieval Scottish prices have shown a slight decline. The Allen Barr collection sold by Mark Rasmussen had a comprehensive run of Scottish ryals and 60-shilling pieces of Mary Queen of Scots and James VI.

The most expensive Scottish gold coin sold during the last year was a fine, rare and popular guinea-sized 1701 William II Pistole, and Scotland's only issue of milled gold, that sold in the McDonald collection for £6,650.

Irish Coins

A wide range of Irish coins have been available in the last year, but prices have been mixed and it is difficult to discern any clear trends.

Mary Queen of Scots ryal from 1565 is one to watch as it usually sells for a low price

In October 2004 Baldwin's Auctions 38 sold a Henry VII late portrait issue groat, class 1, offered in Patrick Finn list 15 at £475, for £900, but the next lot, a Henry VII class 3 groat, listed at £350, could only attract a bid of £250.

This year Spink's traditional February *Irish Circular* contained an attractive small-type collection of Hiberno-Norse pennies including all the main series, that sold out almost immediately with multiple orders.

Two Lambert Simnel groats, both from the 2000 Dublin Millennial Collection, realized £1,300 and £1,650 apiece in a Dublin auction in February 2001. Re-offered in Baldwin's Auctions 40, they now swapped values and sold for £2,530 and £1,725.

Anglo-Gallic Coins

Very little Anglo-Gallic material has become available over the last year. A small group of high-quality gold in Munzen und Medaillen, Auction 95, Basel, October 2004 sold well above estimate, including an extremely fine Edward III Leopard d'or, third issue at £6,000 and a superb Edward the Black Prince Pavillion d'or, second issue of Bordeaux at £6,500. Neither are rare coins but the quality of strike and design found on Anglo-Gallic gold is to the market's taste.

GB Silver Crown of William III from 1697 with well-set colour sold for £13,250 at the Pre-long Beach auction in May 2005

Coin housekeeping

Here are some helpful hints, along with some of the best accessories on the market, that can help you keep your collection in good condition

ABOVE: Coin cabinets are produced and available from Peter Nichols in St. Leonards-on-Sea

Storage

Careful thought should be given to the storing of coins, for a collection which is carelessly or inadequately housed can suffer irreparable damage. Corrosion depends on the presence of water vapour, and therefore coins should not be stored in damp attics or spare bedrooms but, where possible, in evenly heated warm rooms.

We should also point out, that one must be very careful only to pick up coins by the edges, for sweaty fingerprints contain corrosive salt. The following are suitable methods of storage.

Wooden cabinets

A collection carefully laid out in a wood cabinet is seen at its most impressive. Unfortunately, the modern wooden cabinets, which are custom-built, especially for coins are not cheap. Their main advantages are the choice of tray and hole

sizes, and the fact that because the manufacturer is often himself a collector, he takes care to use only well-matured woods.

Among the makers of wood cabinets the best are Peter Nichols of St Leonards, East Sussex, please contact them on (tel: 01424 436682.)

If one cannot afford a new

ABOVE: Leuchtturm cleaning bath for brass, copper, silver and gold coins is available from the Duncannon Partnership in Reigate

cabinet, then a secondhand version may be the answer. These can sometimes be purchased at coin auctions, or from dealers, and can be very good value. However, it is not always easy to find one with the tray hole sizes to suit your coins.

Do-it-yourself cabinet makers should also be careful not to use new wood, which will contain corrosive moisture. In this case the best method would be to use wood from an old piece of furniture.

LEFT: Lindner Karat coin album supplied with 10 assorted pages, optional slipcase available. Album price £23.10

Albums, plastic cases, carrying cases and magnifiers

There are many of these on the market, and some of them are both handsome and inexpensive. There are also very attractive Italian and German-made, attaché type carrying cases for collectors, with velvet lining and different sizes of trays, and so on. These can be obtained

Lindner large coin carrying case, supplied with 10 assorted trays. Price £139.50

from a number of dealers, but Collectors' Gallery, 22 The Parade, St Mary's Place, Shrewsbury SY1 1DL (tel: 01743 272140) are the UK distributors.

We would also recommend the coin album, which claims to prevent oxidization. The coins are contained in cards with crystal-clear film windows so the collector can see both sides of the coins. The cards then slide into pages in an album, and might be a convenient method of storage, especially for new collectors.

Lindner Publications Ltd., Unit 3A, Hayle Industrial Park, Hayle, Cornwall TR27 5JR (tel: 01736 751910. Fax: 01736 751911) supplies very useful coin and collecting boxes, as well as albums. To find out more you can also visit the company's website at www.stampaccessories.net

A new extended range of Lighthouse coin accessories, including presentation and attaché carrying cases, are available from the Duncannon Partnership, 4 Beaufort Road, Reigate RH2 9DJ (tel: 01737 244222). Feel free to phone them for a brochure.

March 2005 saw Crystalair Compression packaging come to the UK market. These packs immobilize items between two layers of clear,

Envelopes

Plastic envelopes, being transparent, are very useful for exhibition, but we never recommend them for long-term storage purposes. They tend to make the coins 'sweat' which, with copper and bronze in particular, can lead to corrosion. Manilla envelopes are much more suitable since the paper is dry. Most collectors use them in conjunction with a cardboard box, which makes for simple, unobtrusive and inexpensive coin storage.

The best article we have seen on coin and medal storage was by Mr L R Green, who is Higher Conservation Officer at the Department of Coins and Medals at the British Museum. This appeared in the May 1991 issue of Spink's *Numismatic Circular*.

ABOVE: Lindner coin boxes available in standard clear format or smoked-glass format. 130 variations available. Standard clear box £14.95, smoked-glass box £15.50

inert, polyurethane film that molds to the object placed between it. These are perfect for storing and transporting valuable and delicate items such as lenses, coins, stamps and gems, that also need to be viewed. For details contact Lane Packaging Ltd., Headley Park 8, Headley Road East, Woodley, Reading RG5 4SA. (tel: 0118 944 2425) or log on to www.lanepackaging.com

In Central London, probably the best place to visit is Vera Trinder, 38 Bedford Street, London WC2 E9EU (tel: 020 7836 2365/6), who does appear to keep a very good stock.

Lastly, magnifiers can be obtained from the accessory dealers mentioned, as well as the stationers WHSmith and opticians.

Cleaning coins

In the course of each week coin dealers examine many coins, which some poor unfortunates have unwittingly ruined by cleaning. They are, therefore, usually the best people to ask about

A variety of attaché cases for keeping your coins are available from the Duncannon Partnership

A selection of Crystalair Compression Packs

the subject of cleaning coins.

One dealer told us of an expectant gentleman who offered his late father's collection of copper coins, which he had 'brightened up' the previous day, to be certain of a good offer. The dealer did not enjoy his customer's disappointment when he found himself unable to make any offers, but the coins had been cleaned with harsh metal polish.

We would always advise people never to clean coins unless they are very dirty or corroded. Do note that by 'dirt' we don't mean oxide which, on silver coins, can give a pleasing bluish tone favoured by collectors. The following instructions may be of some help, but do not, of course, apply to extremely corroded coins found in the ground, for if important, they are the province of a museum conservationist.

Gold coins
Gold should cause collectors few problems,

since it is subject to corrosion only in extreme conditions. For example, a gold coin recovered from a long spell in the sea might have a dull, rusty appearance. However, give it a bath in methylated spirits and this will usually improve a dirty gold coin. But here's one word of warning – gold coins should not be rubbed in any way.

Silver coins
Silver coins will discolour easily, and are susceptible to damp or chemicals in the atmosphere. Gentle brushing with a soft, non-nylon, bristle brush will clear loose dirt, but if the dirt is deep and greasy, a dip in ammonia and careful drying on cotton wool should work. There is no need to clean a coin that has a darkish tone.

Copper and bronze coins
There is no safe method of cleaning copper or bronze coins without actually harming them, and we would only recommend the use of a non-nylon, pure bristle brush to deal with dirt.

There is no way of curing the ailments peculiar to these metals, namely verdigris (green spots) or bronze disease (blackish spots) permanently, and we would advise collectors not to buy pieces in such condition, unless they are very inexpensive.

And remember looking after your coins could make you money in the future!

Museum collections

Needing inspiration for your coin collection or tips on the best way to displays your wares? Here's a round-up of the best museums in the UK

London, The British Museum

The display includes an enormous number of coins and objects used as money over the last 4,500 years. The first major British exhibition of British archaeology in over 20 years, 'Buried Treasure: Finding Our Past' – the result of a unique collaboration between The British Museum and four other major UK museums in Cardiff, Manchester, Newcastle and Norwich – will last until 2006. The exhibition will travel to each venue after London. From the Spring of 2006 until the Autumn there will be an exhibition at the Yorkshire Museum relating to Constantine the Great – this includes many items loaned by the British Museum The Keeper of Coins is: Mr Joe Cribb, British Museum, Great Russell Street, London WC1B 3DG. Tel: 020 7323 8404. Fax: 020 7323 8171. or E-mail: coins@thebritish-museum.ac.uk or visit www.thebritishmuseum.ac.uk

Edinburgh, National Museums of Scotland

The National Museums house the premier collection of Scottish coins and tokens, and significant collections of English, British, ancient and foreign material. The Scottish

ABOVE: The HSBC Money Gallery in The British Museum (picture: copyright, British Museum)

coins include the Coats collection, on which Edward Burns based his three-volume standard work, *The Coinage of Scotland*. Many coins of all periods and types made or used in Scotland are included, anyone wishing to view specific coins or series is welcomed by appointment. Curator of Numismatics is: Mr Nick Holmes, Royal Museum, Chambers Street, Edinburgh EH1 1JF. Tel: 0131 247 4061 E-mail: n.holmes@nms.ac.uk

Glasgow, Hunterian Museum

A permanent gallery devoted to numismatics is open at the Hunterian Museum featuring over 2,000 items. The Hunter Coin Cabinet contains the important 18th century collection of the eminent Scot and Royal physician, Dr William Hunter. The Curator of Coins is: Dr Donal Bateson, Hunterian Museum, University of Glasgow, Glasgow G12 8QQ. Tel: 0141 339 8855.

Cardiff, National Museum and Gallery

There is a general exhibition of coins and medals including many rare pieces. Two spectacular hoards are currently on show: The Bridgend Hoard (1994) of Roman coins circa AD310. The Tregwynt (Pembs) Civil War hoard of gold and silver coins will now form part of 'Buried Treasure: Finding Our Past' exhibition. The Assistant Keeper in charge of coins is: Mr EM Besly, Department of Archaeology and Numismatics, National Museum and Gallery, Cathays Park, Cardiff CF10 3NP. Tel: 02920 573291. E-mail: Edward.Besly@nmgw.ac.uk

Birmingham, Museum and Art Gallery

Birmingham Museum has one of the largest regional coin collections in England, with important groups of British Celtic, Saxon/Norman and medieval coins. Curator of Antiquities and Numismatics is: David Symons, Birmingham Museum and Art Gallery, Chamberlain Square, Birmingham B3 3DH. Tel: 0121 303 4201 or visit the website at www.bmag.org.uk

Cambridge, The Fitzwilliam Museum

The Department of Coins and Medals houses one of the greatest collections of Ancient Greek coins, and the Grierson collection of European medieval coins, currently being catalogued in 14 volumes. Recently the Museum has acquired the collection of Christopher Blunt, and the Dr William Conte collection of Norman coins. The Department's website gives access to the Corpus of Early Medieval Coin Finds (EMC), and the Sylloge of Coins of the British Isles (SCBI), which contain about 60,000 medieval coins, (go to www-cm.fitzmuseum.cam.ac.uk/coins/). The Keeper of Coins and Medals is: Dr Mark Blackburn, Fitzwilliam Museum, Trumpington Street, Cambridge CB2 1RB Tel: 01223 332915.

Oxford, The Ashmolean Museum

This museum is engaged in a plan to present its art and archaeology more effectively to a wider public. A Heritage Lottery Funding of £15m and support from the Linbury Trust have gone towards meeting the £50m required.
The galleries associated with Cockerell's fine original building, including Ancient Egypt, Greek and Roman Sculpture, and most of the Western Art galleries, will remain open. The plan will

ABOVE: The British Museum houses these coins from the Hoxne Hoard, buried in the 5th century and found in 1992

involve the demolition and rebuilding of the Heberden Coin Room. Information about coins for scholarly purposes should be still available. The museum will reopen at the end of 2008 and will include a major new Money Gallery, an environmentally controlled and highly secure Coin Store, a Coin Study Room for visitors, a Seminar Room for numismatic teaching and a Numismatic Library. Further information is available at http://www.ashmol.ox.ac.uk/ash/development/

York, Yorkshire Museum

This coin collection is particularly strong in Roman coinage, Northumbrian stycas, English hammered silver and trade tokens. Hoards and single finds from Yorkshire are particularly well represented. Please contact the Yorkshire Museum, Museum Gardens, Curator of Access – Archaeology Andrew Morrison, York YO1 7FR. Tel: 01904 687687. E-mail: andrew.morrison@ymt.org.uk

Belfast, Ulster Museum

This collection is not on display, sections are occasionally on show as part of historical exhibitions. To view the collection an appointment is needed. The museum acquired many of its Irish pieces from the Carlyon-Britton collection. Curator of coins is: Mr Robert Heslip, Ulster Museum, Botanic Gardens, Belfast BT9 5AB. Tel: 02890 383000.

Dublin, National Museum of Ireland

This museum has the most important collection of Irish coins and houses the former collection of the Royal Irish Academy. The collection includes important donations, recent important hoards, and the Dr Arthur Went collection of medals. The Curator of Coins is: Mr Michael Kenny, Keeper of the Art & Industrial Division, National Museum of Ireland, Collins Barracks, Benburb Street, Dublin 7, Eire. Tel: 0035 31677 7444.

Other important UK museums

Other museums with collections of British coins:–
■ Blackburn Museum, Museum Street, Blackburn, Lancashire (01254 667130).

■ City Museum, Queen's Road, Bristol BS8 1RL (01179 223571). Good on Bristol mint coins.
■ Royal Albert Memorial Museum, Queen Street, Exeter EX4 3RX (01392 665858).
■ Manx Museum, Douglas, Isle of Man (01624 675522). Excellent for Viking and Hiberno-Norse.
■ The Leeds Museum Resource Centre, Yeadon, Leeds (01132 146526).
■ Manchester Museum, The University, Manchester M13 (0161 275 2634).
■ Reading Museum, Blagrave Street, Reading, Berkshire (01189 399800).

A useful guide entitled: *Museums and Select Institutions in the UK and Ireland with holdings of numismatic material* has been formulated by Peter Preston-Morley, priced at £5. Many of our museums have co-operated with the British Academy to produce a series of books under the heading *Sylloge of Coins of the British Isles*, now running to 50 plus volumes. Below we list the ones which deal with coins in the British Isles.

1. Fitzwilliam Museum, Cambridge. *Ancient British and Anglo-Saxon Coins*, by P. Grierson.
2. Hunterian Museum, Glasgow. *Anglo-Saxon Coins*, by A.S. Robertson.
3. *The Coins of the Curitani*, by D. F. Allen.
4. Royal Collection of Coins and Medals, National Museum, Copenhagen. *Part 1, Ancient British and Anglo-Saxon Coins before Aethelred II*, by Georg Galster.
5. Grosvenor Museum, Chester. *Coins with the Chester Mint-Signature*, by E J E Pirie.
6. National Museum of Antiquities of Scotland, Edinburgh. *Anglo-Saxon Coins*, by R B K Stevenson.
7. British Museum. *Hiberno-Norse Coins*, by R H M Dolley.
8. *The Caroligian Coins in the British Museum*, by Michael Dolley and K F Morrison.
9. Ashmolean Museum, Oxford. *Part I, Anglo-Irish Coins, John-Edward III*, by M Dolley and W Seaby.
10. Ulster Museum. Belfast. *Part I, Anglo-Irish Coins, John Edward III*, by M Dolley and W Seaby.
11. Reading University. *Anglo-Saxon and Norman Coins*, by C E Blunt and M Dolley.
12. Ashmolean Museum, Oxford. *Part II, English Coins 1066-1279*, by D M Metcalf.

13. Royal Collection of Coins and Medals, National Museum, Copenhagen. *Part 111a, Anglo-Saxon Coins: Cnut, mints Axbridge to Lymne*, by Georg Galster.
14. *Part 111b, Cnut, mints Lincoln and London.*
15. *Part IIIc, mints Lynford to the end.*
16. *Collections of Ancient British, Romano and English Coins formed by Mrs Emery May Norweb*, by C E Blunt, F Elmore Jones & Commander R P Mack.
17. Midland Museums. *Ancient British Coins, and Coins of the British and Gloucestershire Mints*, by L V Grinsell, C E Blunt and M Dolley.
18. Royal Collection of Coins and Medals, National Museum, Copenhagen. *Part IV, Anglo-Saxon Coins from Harold and Anglo-Norman Coins*, by Georg Galster.
19. Bristol and Gloucester Museums. *Ancient British Coins and Coins of the British and Gloucestershire Mints*, by L V Grinsell, C E Blunt and M Dolley.
20. The R P Mack Collection. *Ancient British, Anglo-Saxon and Norman Coins*, by R P Mack.
21. Yorkshire Collections. *Coins from Northumbrian Mints c.895-1279; Ancient British and Later Coins from other Mints to 1279*, by E J E Pirie.
23. Ashmolean Museum, Oxford. *Part III, Coins of Henry VII*, by D M Metcalf.
24. West Country Museums. *Ancient British, Anglo-Saxon and Anglo-Norman Coins*, by A J H Gunstone.
25. *Anglo-Saxon, Anglo-Norman and Hiberno-Norse Coins in the National Museum, Helsinki and other Public Collections in Finland*, by T Talvio.
26. Museums in East Anglia. *Morley St Peter Hoard, and Anglo-Saxon, Norman and Angevin Coins, and Later Coins of the Norwich Mint*, by T H McK Clough.
27. Lincolnshire Collections. *Coins from Lincolnshire Mints and Ancient British and Later Coins to 1272*, by A J H Gunstone.
28. Cumulative Index of Volumes 1-20 of the Sylloge of Coins of the British Isles, by V Smart.
29. Mersey Country Museums. *Ancient British and Later Coins to 1279*, by M Warhurst.
30. *Ancient British, Anglo-Saxon and Norman Coins in American Collections*, by J D Brady.

Reading Material

If your numismatic library is looking a bit empty have a look through some of our suggested titles and where you're likely to find them

We have included the prices you can expect to pay, but since some of the books are long out of print they can only be obtained second-hand *(indicated in the list by SH in brackets)*.

Allen, Martin *The Durham Mint*. British Numismatic Society Special Publication No. 4. 2003. 222pp, 12 plates. £45. The first book to be published on the Durham Mint since 1780.

Bateson, J D *Coinage in Scotland*. 1997. 175pp, and well illustrated. £20. The most up-to-date narrative account of the coins in print.

Bateson, J D *Scottish Coins*. 1987. Shire Publications no.189. 32pp, and illustrated. £2. A useful little 'taster' to the subject. The Shire Publications are always good value.

Besly, E *Coins and Medals of the English Civil War*. 1990. 121pp, and beautifully illustrated. (SH)

Besly, E *Loose Change, a Guide to Common Coins and Medals*. Cardiff. 1997. 57pp, £6.95.

Blunt, C E Stewart, B H I H, Lyon, C S S *Coinage in 10th Century England*. 1989. 372pp, 27 plates. £60.

Buck, I *Medieval English Groats*. 2000. 66pp, illustrated. £15.

Byatt, D *Promises to Pay. The First Three Hundred Years of Bank of England Notes*. 1994. 246pp, beautifully illustrated. £35.

British Academy (Publisher) *Sylloge of Coins of the British Isles*. 50 volumes, many still in print.

Brooke, G C *English Coins*, Reprint Edition. London, 1966. 300pp, 72 plates. (SH). An important one-volume of English coinage.

Challis, C *A New History of the Royal Mint*. 1992. 806pp, 70 figures and maps. £95. A very substantial volume.

Coincraft's *Standard Catalogue of English and UK Coins*. 1999. 741pp, 5,000+ photos. £19.50.

Coincraft's *Standard Catalogue of the Coins of Scotland, Ireland, Channel Islands and Isle of Man*. 1999. 439pp, fully illustrated. £34.50.

Cooper, D *Coins and Minting*. 1996. Shire Publications 106. 32pp, and illustrated. £2.25. An excellent account of minting.

Cooper, D *The Art and Craft of Coinmaking*. 1988. 264pp, fully illustrated. £2.25. An excellent account of minting.

Dolley, M *Viking Coins in the Danelaw and Dublin*. 1965. 32pp, 16 plates. (SH). This and the next two are excellent introductory handbooks.

Dolley, M *Anglo-Saxon Pennies* – Reprint, 1970. 32pp, 16 plates. (SH).

Dolley, M *The Norman Conquest and English Coinage*. 1966. 40pp, illustrated. (SH).

Dowle, A and Finn, P *The Guide Book to the Coinage of Ireland*. 1969. (SH). The first standard catalogue of Irish, useful still for information on patterns and proofs and good bibliography.

Dyer, G P (Editor). *Royal Sovereign 1489-1989*. 1989. 99pp, fully illustrated. £30. An attractive book from the Royal Mint to coincide with the Sovereigns 500th anniversary.

Elias, E R D *The Anglo-Gallic Coins*. 1984. 262pp, fully illustrated. £20. Essential for collectors of this series.

Freeman, A *The Moneyer and Mint in the Reign of Edward the Confessor 1042-1066*. 2 parts, 1985. £40. A complete survey of the coinage of one reign.

Frey, A R *Dictionary of Numismatic Names*. Reprinted 1973. 311pp, and an additional 94pp of glossary of numismatic terms. (SH). The best numismatic diary, well worth searching for a second hand copy.

Grinsell, L V *The History and Coinage of the Bristol Mint*. Bristol Museum and Art Gallery publication. 1986. 60pp, fully illustrated. £5.

Grueber, H A *Handbook of the Coins of Great Britain and Ireland*. Revised edition, London, 1970. 272pp, 64 plates. (SH). A superb book.

Hobbs, Richard *British Iron Age Coins in the British Museum*. 1996. 246pp, 137 plates. £40. Invaluable. Listing over 4,500 pieces.

Holmes, Richard *Scottish Coins, a History of*

Small Change in Scotland. An invaluable guide to the identification of 'historic' small change. Edinburgh, 1998. 112pp, illustrated. £5.99.

de Jersey, P *Celtic Coinage in Britain*. Shire Publications, 1996. 56pp, illustrated. £4.99.

Linecar, H W A *British Coin Designs and Designers*. 1977. 146pp, fully illustrated. (SH).

Linecar, H W A *The Crown Pieces of Great Britain and the Commonwealth of Nations*. 1969. 102pp, fully illustrated. (SH). The only book dealing solely with all British crowns.

Linecar, H W A and Stone, A G *English Proof and Pattern Crown-Size Pieces, 1658-1960*. 1968. 116pp, fully illustrated. (SH). An important book.

Manville, H E and Robertson, T J *Encyclopedia of British Numismatics Vol.1. British Numismatic Auction Catalogues from 1710 to the Present*. 1986. 420pp, illustrated. £25.

Manville, H E Vol.2.1. *Numismatic Guide to British and Irish Periodicals 1731-1991*. 1993. 570pp, illustrated £60.

Manville, H E Vol.2.2. *Numismatic Guide to British and Irish Periodicals, 1836-1995*. 1997. 634pp, 31 illustrations. £60. Important reference.

Manville, A E *Tokens of the Industrial Revolution*, Foreign Silver Coins countermarked for use in Great Britain, c1787-1828. 308pp, 50 plates. £40. A highly important work.

Marsh, M A *The Gold Sovereign*, Jubilee edition. 2002. 136pp. £16.95.

Marsh, M A *The Gold Half-Sovereign*, 2nd edition. 2004. 119pp, 54 plates. £18.50.

Mass, J P *The J P Mass Collection. English Short Cross Coins, 1180-1247*. £50. 2,200 specimens from the author's collection. 2001.

McCammon, A L T *Currencies of the Anglo-Norman Isles. 1984.* 358pp, 1,000+ illustrations. £25. Essential for students and collectors.

Mucha, M *Hermitage Museum, St Petersburg, Part IV. English, Irish and Scottish Coins, 1066-1485.* 23 plates, 2005. £40.

North, J J *English Hammered Coins. Volume 1. Early Anglo-Saxon to Henry III, c.A.D.600-1272.* 1994. 320pp, 20 plates. £35; Volume 2. *Edward I to Charles II, 1272-1662.* 1993. 224pp, 11 plates. £30. Essential. A great reference for collectors.

North, J J and Preston-Morley, P J *The John G Brooker Collection - Coins of Charles 1.* (Sylloge of Coins of the British Isles, Number 33) £19.50.

O'Sullivan, W *The Earliest Irish Coinage, 1981.* 47pp, 4 plates. (SH) Deals with the Hiberno-Norse Coinage.

O'Sullivan, W *The Earliest Anglo-Irish Coinage.* 1964. 88pp, 10 plates. (SH). Deals with the coinage from 1185-1216. Reprint available at £5.

Peck, C W *English Copper, Tin and Bronze Coins in the British Museum, 1558-1958.* 1960. 648pp, 50 plates. (SH). Essential. The seminal work on the subject.

Rayner, P A *English Silver Coins Since 1649.* 254pp, illustrated, 3rd edition. 1992. £19.95. Essential. 3,000 coins listed, 400 illustrated. Deals with varieties, rarities, patterns and proofs and mintage figures.

Robinson, B *Silver Pennies and Linden Towels: The Story of the Royal Maundy.* 1992. 274pp, 118 illustrations. £29.95. A very important work on the subject, entertainingly presented.

Spink. *Standard Catalogue of*

British Coins. 41st edition. 2006. Fully illustrated. Price to be announced. After half a century still the first point of reference for collectors of English coins.

Spink and Son (Publishers, but edited by H.A. Linecar). *The Milled Coinage of England 1662-1946.* Reprinted 1976. 146pp, illustrated. (SH). A useful volume dealing with the gold and silver coinage and giving degrees of rarity; superseded on the silver by Rayner, but important for gold.

Spink. *Coins of Scotland, Ireland and the Islands.* 2nd edition. 2003. Fully illustrated. £25. An important addition to one's library.

Stewart, I H *The Scottish Coinage.* 2nd edition. 1967. 215pp, 22 plates. (SH). Long out of print, but still essential for the serious collector.

Sutherland, C H V *English Coinage, 600-1900.* 1973. 232pp, 108 plates. (SH). Beautifully written and the best narrative account of coinage.

Thompson, J D A *Inventory of British Coin Hoards, AD 600-1500.* 1956. 165pp, 24 plates. (SH)

Van Arsdell, R D *Celtic Coinage of Britain.* 1989. 584pp, 54 plates, 80 maps. £40. A pioneering work causing much debate; important for the illustrations alone.

THE GOLD SOVEREIGN

by MICHAEL A. MARSH
GOLDEN JUBILEE EDITION

CAMBRIDGE (Publications)

Withers, P and B *British Coin Weights.* A corpus of the coin-weights made for use in England, Scotland and Ireland. 1993. 366pp, illustrated. £95. For the serious student.

Withers, P and B *Farthings and Halfpennies, Edward I and II.* 2005. 60pp, illustrated. £10. Helpful series guide.

Withers, P and B *Farthings and*

Halfpennies, Edward III and Richard II. 2002. Illustrated. £10.

Withers, P and B R *Halfpennies and Farthings, Henry IV, V and VI.* 2003. 68pp, illustrated. £12.

Withers, P and B R *Halfpennies and Farthings, Edward IV – Henry VII.* 2004. 56pp, illustrated. £12.

Withers, P and B R *Small Silver, Henry VIII – The Commonwealth.* 2004. 56pp, illustrated. £12.

Withers, P and B R Irish *Small Silver, John – Edward VI.* 2004. 56pp, illustrated. £12.

Woodhead, P *The Herbert Schneider Collection of English Gold Coins. Part 1. Henry III-Elizabeth I.* 1996. 466pp, 83 plates. £60. A wonderful catalogue of the finest collection in private hands. This first volume describes and illustrated 890 coins, most in superb condition.

Woodhead, P *The Herbert Schneider Collection of English Gold Coins. Volume 2. 1603 to 20th Century.* 58 plates, 2002. Essential like volume 1, it describes and illustrates 674 coins.

Wren, C R *The Voided Long Cross Coinage, 1247-1279.* 1993. 80pp, illustrated. £9.

Wren, C R *The Short Cross Coinage 1180-1247.* 1992. 90pp, illustrated. £8.75. Two very good guides to identification with excellent drawings.

Williams, J *Money, a History.* 1997. 256pp, fully illustrated. £25. Accompanies the British Museum's HSBC Money Gallery opened in 1997.

Wilson, A and Rasmussen, M *English Pattern Trial and Proof Coins in Gold, 1547-1968.* 2000. 537pp, illustrated. £85. Covers a fascinating series and is likely to enhance interest in these collectable non-currency gold issues.

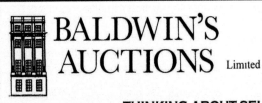
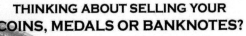

Tips for collecting

If you are new to the numismatic hobby or have just stumbled across an old family collection in the loft, here is some vital advice to get you started and put you in touch with the experts

How much is it worth?

There was a time when newcomers to coin collecting would ask the question 'What is it?' Nowadays, certainly the most common question dealers hear is 'What is it worth?' It is a sign of the times that history takes second place to value. The object of COINS MARKET VALUES is to try to place a value on all the coins produced in what is known geographically as the British Isles, in other words England, Wales, Scotland and Ireland, and the Channel Islands, as well as the Anglo-Gallic series.

This is a difficult task because many coins do not turn up in auctions or lists every year, even though they are not really rare. However, we make a stab at a figure so that you, the collector, can at least have an idea of what you will have to pay.

How to sell at auction

In England we are well served with a number of auction houses, giving the potential seller considerable choice. In London alone we have, in alphabetical order, Baldwins, Bonhams, Dix Noonan Webb, Morton and Eden Ltd. in association with Sotheby's, and Spink. There are also smaller companies up and down the country, such as Croydon Coin Auctions.

The best approach for the seller is first of all to compare all their catalogues and if possible attend the auctions so that you can see how well they are conducted. The type of auctioneer bringing down the gavel may changed your mind. Talk it over with their experts, for you may have special cataloguing requirements and you could find that one of the firms might look after them better than the others.

An obvious coin, like say an 1887 £5, requires little expertise and will probably sell at a certain price in almost any auction. However, if you require expert cataloguing of countermarked coins or early medieval, then you need to know what the company is capable of before you discuss a job rate.

You should remember though that, while it is not complicated to sell by auction, you may have to wait at least three or four months from the time you consign the coins to the auctioneers before

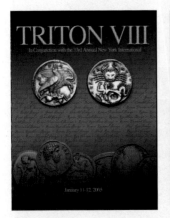

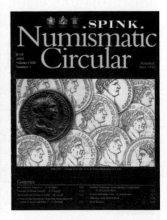

you receive any money. There are times when auctions manage to achieve very high prices, and other times when, for some inexplicable reason, they fail to reach even a modest reserve.

You should also bear in mind that the best deal in the long term is not always the lowest commission rate. Finally, auctioneers will usually charge you at least 10 per cent of the knock-down price, and you should bear in mind that some buyers may also be inhibited from paying a top price by a buyer's premium, generally all charging around 15 per cent.

Dealers

The function of a dealer is to have a stock of coins for sale at marked prices. However, they will naturally only wish to buy according to the ebb and flow of their stocks. It is also true to say that dealers infinitely prefer fresh material, and if you strike at the right time it is possible that you could achieve a better price than by waiting for auction, since of course you will receive the money immediately.

Generally speaking, both dealers and auctioneers will not make any charge for a verbal valuation, but you should allow for the dealer to be making a profit of at least 20 per cent.

Bullion coins

Relating to Kruggerrands, sovereigns, and so on, most newspapers carry the price of gold, which

is fixed twice daily by a group of leading banks. Anyone can buy sovereigns, and Krugerrands and other bullion coins, and it is better these days now that there is no VAT on top.

Normally, when you sell a bullion coin you expect the coin dealer to make a few pounds profit on each coin, but don't expect a good price for a mounted coin attached to a watch chain, which will not be worth anything like an undamaged item. Also, read up and learn more about the market.

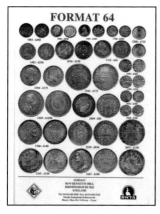

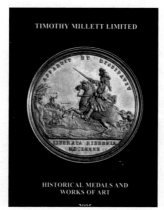

How to collect coins

You should obviously purchase your coins only from a reputable dealer. How can you decide on a reputable dealer? You can be sure of some protection if you choose one who is a member of the British Numismatic Trade Association or the International Association of Professional Numismatists. Membership lists of these organisations can be obtained from the respective secretaries:

• Mrs. Rosemary Cooke, PO Box 2, Rye, East Sussex TN31 7WE. (Tel/Fax: 01797 229988 or E-mail: bnta@lineone.net

• Jean-Luc Van Der Schueren, 14 Rue de la Bourse, B 1000 Brussels, Belgium. (Tel: 0032 2 513 3400; Fax: 0032 2 513 2528).

However, many dealers are not members of either organisation, and it does not mean that they are not honest and professional. The best approach is simply to find one who will unconditionally guarantee that the coins you buy from him are genuine and accurately graded.

As a general rule you should only buy coins in the best condition available, and on this subject you will at first have to rely on the judgement of the dealer you choose. However, remember it will not always be possible to find pieces in 'Extremely Fine' condition, for example, and it can sometimes be worth buying coins which are not quite 'Very Fine'.

In the case of great rarities, of course, you might well have to make do with a coin that is only Fine, or even Poor. If there are only six known specimens of a particular piece, and four are in museums, it seems pointless to wait 20 years for another one to be found in the ground. Over the last few years condition has become too important in many ways, and has driven away collectors, because obviously you cannot buy coins only in top condition, since in certain series that would rule out at least 50 per cent of the available specimens. It very much depends on the type of coin, the reign it comes from and so on, so please be realistic.

It is worth taking out subscriptions with auction houses so that you can receive copies of all their catalogues, because this is an excellent way to keep up with prices as well as the collections that are being offered.

However, one should not overlook the fact that a number of dealers produce price lists, which in many ways are most useful to the collector, because coins can then be chosen at leisure by mail order. It is also easier to work out what one can afford to buy than when in the hot-house atmosphere of the auction room.

The most famous list is Spink's *Numismatic Circular,* first published in 1892 and still going strong with 10 issues a year. It is more than a price list, being an important forum for numismatic debate and the reporting of new finds, etc., (annual subscription £18).

There are also many expert dealers who produce excellent lists; many of them advertise in this publication and obviously we cannot mention them all here, but a good cross section of those who list domestic coins, and not listed in any order of preference, is as follows:–

• A.H. Baldwin and Sons Ltd., 11 Adelphi Terrace, London WC2N 6BJ. Hammered and Milled.

• Lloyd Bennett, PO Box 2, Monmouth, Gwent NP5 3YE. Hammered, Milled, Tokens.

• B.J. Dawson, 52 St Helens Road, Bolton, Lancashire BL3 3NH. Hammered, Milled, Tokens, Medals.

• Dorset Coin Co. Ltd., 193 Ashley Road, Parkstone, Poole, Dorset BH14 9DL. All Coins and Banknotes.

• Format, 18-19 Bennetts Hill, Birmingham B2 5QJ. All British.

• Grantham Coins, PO Box 60, Grantham, Lincolnshire. Milled, good on Maundy.

• K.B. Coins, 50 Lingfield Road, Martin's Wood, Stevenage, Hertfordshire SG1 5SL. Hammered and Milled.

• Knightsbridge Coins, 43 Duke Street, St James, London SW1Y 6DD. Hammered and Milled

• Peter Morris, PO Box 223, Bromley, Kent BR1 4EQ. Hammered, Milled, Tokens.

• Spink & Son Ltd., 69 Southampton Row, Bloomsbury, London WC1B 4ET. Hammered and Milled.

• S.R. Porter, 18 Trinity Road, Headington Quarry, Oxford OX3 8QL. Milled and Hammered.

• Mark Rasmussen, PO Box 42, Betchworth, Surrey RH3 7YR. Hammered and Milled.

• Roderick Richardson, The Old Granary Antiques Centre, Kings Staithe Lane, Kings Lynn PE30 1LZ. Hammered and Milled.

• Chris Rudd, PO Box 222, Aylsham, Norfolk NR11 6TY. Specialist dealer in Celtic Coins.

• Classical Numismatics Group Inc. (Seaby Coins), 14 Old Bond Street, London W1X 4JL. Hammered, some Milled.

• Simmons & Simmons, PO Box 104, Leytonstone, London E11 1ND.

Societies

You should consider joining your local numismatic society, there being quite a number of these throughout the country. At the time of going to press there were over 50 across the UK. To find if there is one near you, get in touch with the British Association of Numismatic Societies: Mr. P.H. Mernick, c/o General Services, 42 Campbell Road, London E8 4DT (Tel: 020 8980 5672; E-mail: bans@mernicks.com; www.coinclubs.freeserve.co.uk).

The BANS organises annual congresses and seminars, and it is a good idea for the serious collector to consider attending one of these. Details are usually well publicised in the numismatic press.

Those collectors who wish to go a little further can apply for membership of the British Numismatic Society, and for their annual membership fee they receive a copy of the *British Numismatic Journal,* which incorporates details of current research and important articles, as well as book reviews.

Members can also borrow books

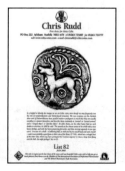

from its library in the Warburg Institute.

The Secretary of the British Numismatic Society is Lt. Cdr. C.R.S. Farthing RN, 10 Greenbanks Gardens, Wallington, Fareham, Hants PO16 8SF. (Tel: 01329 284661).

Coin Fairs

Whilst it is always important to visit museums to see coins, it is worth remembering that there is often a fine array on show at coin fairs around the country, and most dealers do not mind showing coins to would-be collectors, even if they cannot afford to buy them on the spot.

The BNTA COINEX show is now held at a new venue and will be held at the The Platinum Suite, Excel 1, Western Gateway, Royal Victoria Dock, London E16 1XI on September 30 to October 1 – for details call the BNTA Secretary on 01797 229988.

Howard and Frances Simmons, are organisers of the London Coin Fairs at the Holiday Inn, Bloomsbury, London (formerly the Post House, Bloomsbury). They will take place in February, May and November. Their telephone number is 020 8989 8097.

The Croydon team of Davidson/Monk organise the monthly shows at the Commonwealth Institute, Kensington, London W8. For more details ring 020 8656 4583 or 020 8651 3890.

Michael Veissid organises the monthly Midland Coin and Stamp Fair, on the second Sunday of every month. To find out about dates and times just call 01743 272140 or visit m.veissid@btinternet.com

There are also fairs held at York racecourse in January and July. For further information on these events ring 01793 513431.

Finally, for details of the very successful Irish coin show in Dublin, in February every year, held in conjunction with the Irish Numismatic Society, contact Michael Kelly (Tel: 003531 839 1082).

Coin Grading

IT IS MOST important that newcomers to collecting should get to know the various grades of condition before attempting to buy or sell coins.

The system of grading most commonly used in Britain recognises the following main classes in descending order of quality: Brilliant Uncirculated (B.Unc,BU), Uncirculated (Unc), Extremely Fine (EF), Very Fine (VF), Fine (F), Fair, Poor.

It is not surprising that beginners get confused at their first encounter with these grades. The word 'FINE' implies a coin of high quality, yet this grade turns out to be very near the bottom of the scale and is in fact about the lowest grade acceptable to most collectors of modern coinage in Britain.

American grading

It is not really necessary to go into the details of American grading here, since it is only on a very few occasions that a British collector will order the coins he wants directly from an American dealer. However, across the Atlantic their grading system is quite different from ours, and whilst it purports to be a lot more accurate, it is actually much more prone, in our opinion, to be abused, and we prefer the English dealers' more conservative methods of grading. American dealers use many more terms than we do, ranging from Mint State to About Good. The latter could be described as 'very heavily worn, with portions of lettering, date and legend worn smooth. The date may be partly legible'. In England we would simply say 'Poor'.

Numerical method

The other area which British collectors will find difficult to evaluate is the American numerical method of describing coins as, for example, MS 70, MS 65. The MS simply stands for Mint State and an MS 65 would be described as 'an above average Uncirculated coin which may be brilliant or lightly toned but has some surface marks'. The MS system seemed to be acceptable at first but there now appear to be two schools of thought in America and you will quite frequently see coins graded in the more traditional manner as well as the MS style in sale catalogues. Fortunately American grades have not come into use in this country, although dealers have followed the American manner of embellishing coin descriptions to make them more desirable, which is understandable and in many ways can be an improvement on the old method of saying simply that the coin is 'Fine', which, of course, might not do justice to it.

Full mint lustre

There are two schools of thought on the use of the terms Brilliant Uncirculated and Uncirculated. The former is often considered to be the most useful and descriptive term for coins of copper, bronze, nickel-brass or other base metals, which display what is known as 'full mint lustre'. When this term is being used it is often necessary in the same context to employ the grade Uncirculated to describe coins which have never been in circulation but have lost the original lustre of a newly minted coin. However, some dealers and collectors tend to classify as Uncirculated all coins which have not circulated, whether they are brilliant or toned, and do not use the term Brilliant Uncirculated.

Fleur de coin

Sometimes FDC (fleur de coin) is used to define top grade coins, but this really only applies to pieces in perfect mint state, having no flaws or surface scratches. With modern methods of minting, slight damage to the surface is inevitable, except in the case of proofs, and therefore Brilliant Uncirculated or Uncirculated best describe the highest grade of modern coins.

The word 'proof' should not be used to denote a coin's condition. Proofs are pieces struck on specially prepared blanks from highly polished dies and usually have a mirror-like finish.

Opinions differ

In all this matter of condition it might be said that the grade 'is in the eye of the beholder', and there are always likely to be differences of opinion as to the exact grade of a coin. Some collectors and dealers have tried to make the existing scale of definitions more exact by adding letters such as N (Nearly), G (Good, meaning slightly better than the grade to which the letter is added), A (About or Almost) and so on. To be still more accurate, in cases where a coin wears more on one side than the other, two grades are shown, the first for the obverse, the second for the reverse thus: GVF/EF.

Additional description

Any major faults not apparent from the use of a particular grade are often described separately. These include dents and noticeable scratches, discoloration, areas of corrosion, edge knocks, holes, on otherwise good quality pieces, and the like.

Middle range of grades

One should always look for wear on the highest points of the design, of course, but these vary from coin to coin. To present a comprehensive guide to exact grading one would have to illustrate every grade of every coin type in a given series, on the lines of the famous *Guide to the Grading of United States Coins*, by Brown and Dunn. This is a complete book in itself (over 200 pages) and obviously such a mammoth task could not be attempted in the space available here. Therefore, on the following page we present representative examples from three different periods in the British series, to illustrate the 'middle' range of coin conditions.

Still in mint state

We have already dealt with the grades BU and Unc; they both describe coins which are still in the state in which they left the Mint, and which have never passed into general circulation. They are likely to show minor scratches and edge knocks due to the mass handling processes of modern minting.

Fair and Poor

At the other end of the scale we have Fair, a grade that is applied to very worn coins which still have the main parts of the design distinguishable, and Poor which denotes a grade in which the design and rim are worn almost flat and few details are discernible.

Here we show (enlarged) examples of the grades EF, VF and F. On the left are hammered long cross pennies of Aethelred II; in the centre, from the later hammered series, are groats of Henry VIII; on the right are shillings of William IV.

Extremely Fine. This describes coins which have been put into circulation, but have received only the minimum of damage since. There may be a few slight marks or minute scratches in the field (flat area around the main design), but otherwise the coin should show very little sign of having been in circulation.

Very Fine. Coins in this condition show some amount of wear on the raised surfaces, but all other detail is still very clear. Here, all three coins have had a little wear as can be seen in the details of the hair and face. However, they are still in attractive condition from the collector's viewpoint.

Fine. In this grade coins show noticeable wear on the raised parts of the design; most other details should still be clear. The penny and the groat show a lot of wear over the whole surface. On the shilling the hair above the ear has worn flat.

Extremely Fine (EF)

Very Fine (VF)

Fine (F)

Abbreviations & Terms

used in the Market Price Guide section

* – Asterisks against some dates indicate that no firm prices were available at the time of going to press.

2mm – P of PENNY is 2mm from trident. On other 1895 pennies the space between is only 1mm.

AE – numismatic symbol for copper or copper alloys.

Arabic 1, Roman I – varieties of the 1 in 1887.

Arcs – decorative border of arcs which vary in number.

B (on William III coins) – minted at Bristol.

1866 shilling lettered BBITANNIAR in error

BBITANNIAR – lettering error.

Bank of England – this issued overstruck Spanish dollars for currency use in Britain 1804-1811.

black – farthings 1897-1918, artificially darkened to avoid confusion with half sovereigns.

briit – lettering error.

B. Unc, BU – Brilliant Uncirculated condition.

C (on milled gold coins) – minted at Ottawa (Canada).

C (on William III coins) – minted at Chester.

close colon – colon close to DEF.

crosslet 4 – having upper and lower serifs to horizontal bar of 4 (see plain 4).

cu-ni – cupro-nickel.

dashes (thus –) following dates in the price list indicate that some particular characteristic of a coin is the same as that last described. Two dashes mean that two characters are repeated, and so on.

debased – in 1920 the silver fineness in British coins was debased from .925 to .500.

diag – diagonal.

'Dorrien and Magens' – issue of shillings by a group of bankers. Suppressed on the day of issue.

DRITANNIAR – lettering error.

E (on William III coins) – minted at Exeter.

E, E* (on Queen Anne coins) – minted at Edinburgh.

Edin – Edinburgh.

EEC – European Economic Community.

EF (over price column) – Extremely Fine condition.

E.I.C. – East India Co (supplier of metal).

Elephant and castle

eleph, eleph & castle – elephant or elephant and castle provenance mark (below the bust) taken from the badge of the African ('Guinea') Company, which imported the metal for the coins.

Eng – English shilling. In 1937, English and Scottish versions of the shilling were introduced. English versions: lion standing on crown (1937-1951); three leopards on a shield (1953-66).

exergue – segment below main design, usually containing the date.

On this penny the exergue is the area containing the date

ext – extremely.

F – face value only.

F (over price column) – Fine condition.

(F) – forgeries exist of these pieces. In some cases the forgeries are complete fakes, in others where the date is rare the date of a common coin has been altered. Collectors are advised to be very cautious when buying any of these coins.

Fair – rather worn condition.

Fantasies – non-currency items, often just produced for the benefit of collectors.

far colon – colon father from DEF than in close colon variety.

FDC – Fleur de coin. A term used to describe coins in perfect mint condition, with no flaws, scratches or other marks.

fig(s) – figure(s).

fillet – hair band.

flan – blank for a coin or medal.

GEOE – lettering error.

Florin of Victoria with the design in the Gothic style

Gothic – Victorian coins featuring Gothic-style portrait and lettering.

guinea-head – die used for obverse of guinea.

H – mintmark of The Mint, Birmingham, Ltd.

hd – head.

hp, harp (early, ord etc.) – varieties of the Irish harp on reverse.

hearts – motif in top RH corner of Hanoverian shield on reverse.

illust – illustration, or illustrated.

im – initial mark.

inc, incuse – incised, sunk in.

inv – inverted.

JH – Jubilee Head.

The Jubilee Head was introduced on the coinage in 1887 to mark Victoria's Golden Jubilee

KN – mintmark of the Kings Norton Metal Co Ltd.

L.C.W. – Initials of Leonard Charles Wyon, engraver.

lge – large.

LIMA – coins bearing this word were struck from bullion captured by British ships from foreign vessels carrying South American treasure, some of which may have come from Peru (capital Lima).

1902 pennies showing the low horizon variety (A) and the normal horizon (B)

low horizon – on normal coins the horizon meets the point where Britannia's left leg crosses behind the right. On this variety the horizon is lower.
LVIII etc – regnal year in Roman numerals on the edge.
matt – type of proof without mirror-like finish.
M (on gold coins) – minted at Melbourne (Australia).
'military' – popular name for the 1813 guinea struck for the payment of troops fighting in the Napoleonic Wars.
mm – mintmark.
Mod eff – modified effigy of George V.
mule – coin struck from wrongly paired dies.
N (on William III coins) – minted at Norwich.

William III shilling with N (for Norwich mint) below the bust

no. – number.
obv – obverse, usually the 'head' side of a coin.
OH – Old Head.
ord – ordinary.
OT – ornamental trident.
P (on gold coins) – minted at Perth (Australia).
pattern – trial piece not issued for currency.

piedfort – a coin which has been specially struck on a thicker than normal blank. In France, whence the term originates, the Kings seem to have issued them as presentation pieces from the 12th century onwards. In Britain medieval and Tudor examples are known, and their issue has now been reintroduced by the Royal Mint, starting with the 20 pence piedfort of 1982.
plain (on silver coins) – no provenance marks in angles between shields on reverse.
plain 4 – with upper serif only to horizontal bar of 4 (see crosslet 4).
pln edge prf – plain edge proof.
plume(s) – symbol denoting Welsh mines as source of metal.
proof, prf – coin specially struck from highly polished dies. Usually has a mirror-like surface.
prov, provenance – a provenance mark on a coin (e.g. rose, plume, elephant) indicates the supplier of the bullion from which the coin was struck.
PT – plain trident.
raised – in relief, not incuse.
RB – round beads in border.
rev – reverse, 'tail' side of coin.
r – right.
r & p – roses and plumes.

Roses and plumes provenance marks

rose – symbol denoting west of England mines as source of metal.
RRITANNIAR – lettering error.
rsd – raised.
S (on gold coins) – minted at Sydney (Australia).
SA (on gold coins) – minted at Pretoria (South Africa).

Scottish shilling 1953-66

Scot – Scottish shilling. Lion seated on crown, holding sword and sceptre (1937-51); lion rampant, on shield (1953-66).
SS C – South Sea Company (source of metal).

1723 shilling bearing the South Sea Company's initials

SEC – SECUNDO, regnal year (on edge).
sh – shield(s).
sm – small.
'spade' – refers to spadelike shape of shield on George III gold coins.

'Spade' guinea, reverse

TB – toothed beads in border.
TER – TERTIO, regnal year (on edge).
trnctn, truncation – base of head or bust where the neck or shoulders terminate.
Unc – Uncirculated condition.
var – variety.
VF – Very Fine condition.
VIGO – struck from bullion captured in Vigo Bay.
VIP – 'very important person'. The so-called VIP crowns were the true proofs for the years of issue. Probably most of the limited number struck would have been presented to high ranking officials.
W.C.C. – Welsh Copper Co (supplier of metal).
wire type – figure of value in thin wire-like script.
W.W. – initials of William Wyon, engraver.
xxri – lettering error.
y, Y (on William III coins) – minted at York.
YH – Young Head.

Victoria Young Head Maundy fourpence

Treasure truths

On September 24, 1997 the Treasure Act 1996 came into being, replacing the old medieval law of treasure trove. This widened the definition of finds that are treasure, and under the new procedures, which are set out in the Code of Practice on the Act, the new Treasure Valuation Committee assists the Secretary of State for Culture to submit an annual report.

In the past, before an object could be declared 'treasure' and therefore be the property of the Crown, it had to pass three tests:– it had to be made substantially of gold or silver; it had to have been deliberately hidden with the intention of recovery; and its owner or the heirs had to be unknown. If then a museum wanted to keep the coins (or artefacts) the lawful finder normally received the full market value; if not the coins were returned to the finder.

The new Act removes the need to establish that objects were hidden with intention of being recovered; it also sets out the precious metal content required for a find to qualify as treasure; and it extends the definition of treasure.

'All coins that contain at least 10 per cent of gold or silver by weight of metal and that come from the same find, provided a find consists of at least two coins with gold or silver content of at least 10 per cent. The coins must be at least 300 years old at the time of discovery. In the case of finds consisting of coins that contain less than 10 per cent gold or silver there must be at least 10 such coins... Single coins will not be treasure, unless they are found in association with objects that are treasure, or unless there is exceptionally strong evidence that they were buried with the intention of recovery (for example, a single coin found in plough soil without any sign of a container would not provide such evidence)'.

As far as the more modern coins are concerned, such as finds of guineas or sovereigns, the Act reads as follows: 'Only objects that are less than 300 years old, that are made substantially of gold or silver, that have been deliberately hidden with the intention of recovery and whose owners or heirs are unknown will come into this category. In practice such finds are rare and the only such discoveries that have been made within recent years have been hoards of gold and silver coins of the eighteenth, nineteenth or twentieth centuries. Single coins found on their own will not qualify under this provision, unless there is exceptionally strong evidence to show that they were buried with the intention of recovery: for

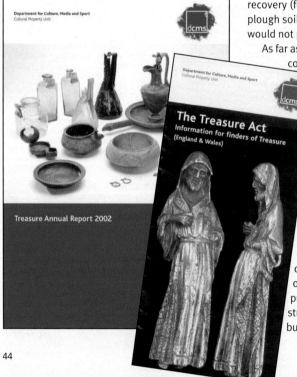

Department for Culture, Media and Sport
Cultural Property Unit

dcms

Treasure Annual Report 2002

Department for Culture, Media and Sport
Cultural Property Unit

dcms

The Treasure Act
Information for finders of Treasure
(England & Wales)

example, a single coin found in plough soil without any sign of a container would provide such. Therefore gold and silver objects that are clearly less than 300 years old need not be reported unless the finder has reason to believe that they may have been deliberately hidden with the intention of recovery'.

All this simplifies the task of coroners in determining whether or not a find is treasure, and it includes a new offence of non-declaration of treasure. It also states that lawful occupiers and landowners will have the right to be informed of finds of treasure from their land and they will be eligible for reward. Finally, following the Government's recent operational review of the Treasure Act. a decision was taken to extend the definition of 'Treasure' to include:–
a) any object (other than a coin), any part of which is base metal which, when found, is one of at least two base metal objects in the same find which are of Prehistoric date.
b) any object (other than a coin), which is of Prehistoric date, and any part of which is gold and silver.

A Treasure (designation) order was debated in parliament on Tuesday July 17, 2002, and came into force on January 1, 2003.

The Committee

The Treasure Trove Reviewing Committee was established in 1977 as an independent body, to advise Ministers on the valuation of treasure trove finds. Under the new Act that body has been replaced by the Treasure Valuation Committee.

Under the new arrangements the national museums will no longer submit valuations to the Treasure Valuation Committee, but instead the committee itself will commission valuation reports from expert advisers. All the interested parties (the finder, the landowner and the museum that intends to acquire the find) will be given the chance to comment on these valuations or indeed commission independent valuations of their own.

These reports are now delivered very quickly and there is no doubt that the new procedures are as transparently fair as it is possible to be. The latest published report, for the period 2001/2, deals with 214 finds and it is attractively illustrated throughout in colour.

At present the committee is chaired by Professor Norman Palmer, a leading authority on the law of treasure trove. The current committee consists of Professor Norman Palmer; Doctor Jack Ogden, National Association of Goldsmiths; Trevor Austin, President of the National Council for Metal Detecting; Doctor Arthur MacGregor, Curator of Antiquities at the Ashmolen Museum; Mrs. Mary Sinclair, a coin dealer – chiefly of the medieval period; and Thomas Curtis, a coin dealer specialising in ancient coins.

Information for finders & metal detectorists:
Copies of *The Treasure Act 1966, Code of Practice (England Wales) 1997*, can be obtained from the Department of National Heritage. This gives much useful information including a current list of coroners in the UK, and a list of coins commonly found that contain less than 10 per cent of gold or silver. It also gives advice on the care of finds, identification and storage, etc.

There is also a very useful leaflet entitled *The Treasure Act, information for finds of treasure*, which deals with everything in a question and answer way, for example:
What should I do if I find something that may be treasure?
How do I report a find of treasure?
What if I do not report a find of treasure?
How do I know that I
will receive a fair
price for my find?
Note: both these
publications can
presently be
obtained free of
charge from:
Department of
Culture, Media and
Sport, 2-4 Cockspur
Street, London SW1Y
5DH. Tel: 020 7211 6200.

Forgeries

Most collectors know that there have been forgeries since the earliest days of coin production, so it is only to be expected that some new forgeries appear on the scene every year. It seems that there is always someone willing to deceive the collector and the dealer. However, nowadays very few forgers end up making much money. As a result of the actions of the British Numismatic Trade Association, the trade is much more tightly knit than ever before, and anxious to stamp out new forgeries before they have a chance to become a serious menace.

They were last a matter of serious concern in the late 1960s and early 1970s, when an enormous number of 1887 £5 pieces and United States $20 manufactured in Beruit came on to the market. Also in the early 1970s the group of Dennington forgeries could have made a serious impact on the English hammered gold market, but for lucky early detection. (Unfortunately we have noticed a number of these are still in circulation, and so we will deal with them later in this article.) In the late 1970s a crop of forgeries of Ancient British coins came to light causing a panic in

ABOVE: Dennington forgeries: Edward III noble (top) and Mary Fine Sovereign.

academic and trade circles. This caused a lack of confidence in the trade and it has taken a number of years for everyone to feel happy that there was no further problem. The BNTA firmly pursues any mention of forgeries and one hopes that a new spate of copies of Anglo-Saxon coins from the West Country are not allowed to develop. They are being sold as replicas, but they are still deceptive in the wrong hands. Bob Forrest compiled a list of these and it was published by the IAPN *Bulletin of Forgeries* in 1995/6 Vol.20 No.2. He has now done an update of this which will be available at the end of the coming year.

The worrying forgeries

We mentioned earlier the Dennington forgeries. It is now many years since the trial of Anthony Dennington at the Central Criminal Court, where he was found guilty of six charges of 'causing persons to pay money by falsely pretending that they were buying genuine antique coins' *The Times*, July 10, 1969). A small number of these pieces are still in the trade, and since they have deceived some collectors and dealers, we've recorded them more fully here. These pieces appeared in the IBSCC Bulletin in August 1976.

1 *Henry III gold penny*
2 *Edward III Treaty period noble*
3 *Another, with saltire before King's name*
4 *Henry IV heavy coinage noble*
5 *Henry V noble, Class C*
(mullet at King's sword arm)
6 *Henry VI mule noble*
7 *Henry VI noble, annulet issue, London*
8 *Edward IV royal, Norwich*
9 *Another, York*
10 *Elizabeth I Angel*
11 *Mary Fine Sovereign 1553*
12 *James I unite, mintmark mullet*
13 *James I rose royal, 3rd coinage, mint mark lis*
14 *James I 3rd coinage laurel*
15 *Commonwealth unite 1651*
16 *Commonwealth half-unite 1651*
17 *Charles II touch piece*

One can only reiterate that these copies are generally very good and you must beware of them. The following points may be useful guidelines.

RIGHT: Modern cast copies of Anglo-Saxon pennies: Ceolwulf 1st above and Ceonwulf below.

■ The coins are usually slightly 'shiny' in appearance, and the edges are not good, since they have been filed down and polished.

■ They are usually very 'hard' to touch, whereas there is a certain amount of 'spring' in the genuine articles.

■ They usually feel slightly thick, but not always, not quite like an electrotype but certainly thicker than normal.

■ Although the Mary Fine sovereign reproduction is heavy, at 16.1986 gr, these pieces are usually lighter in weight than the originals so be careful.

As far as forgeries of modern coins are concerned, the most worrying aspects has been the enormous increase in well produced forgeries in the last 25 years.

They are so well produced that it is often impossible for the naked eye to detect the difference, and it has therefore become the job of the scientist and metallurgist. Many of these pieces have deceived dealers and collectors, although they do not seem to have caused too great a crisis of confidence. This increase in the number of modern counterfeits has been due to the enormous rise in coin values since the 1960s.

It is well known that the vast majority of these modern forgeries have emanated from the Middle East, as we suggested earlier, where it is not illegal to produce counterfeits of other countries' coins. It has proved to be very good business for a lot of these small forgers in Beruit, and one can only rely on the alertness of the coin trade so that reports are circulated quickly whenever a new forgery is spotted.

Unfortunately, the main problem is still that the forger has every encouragement to continue production of copies, when one thinks of the profit involved. At the time of writing, it only takes about £290 worth of gold to make an 1887-dated five pound piece of correct composition, valued at around £650. We cannot, therefore, be complacent.

There is not enough space here to tell you in detail what to look for, and anyway detecting forgeries requires specialist knowledge, a 508 list of faults would not help. If you turn to the catalogue section of COINS MARKET VALUES you will find that as far as British coins are concerned we have placed (F) beside a number of coins which we know have been counterfeited, and which frequently turn up. However, you should watch out for sovereigns, in particular, of which there are forgeries of every date from 1900 to 1932 and even recent dates such as 1957 and 1976.

A list follows of the pieces you should be particularly careful about, especially if you notice that they are being offered below the normal catalogue value. Most modern forgeries of, say, Gothic crowns, seem to be offered at prices which are 10 per cent or 20 per cent below the current market price. The moral is, do not automatically think you have a bargain if the price is low – it could be a forgery!

LEFT: A 'Behra' counterfeit of the 1950s. The last of a series bearing the dates 1902 to 1920, where the original pattern piece was a genuine SA sovereign of unknown date but post-1924. An attempt was made to remove the SA mint mark on the tool used to prepare the dies, but traces remained and were transferred to all the dies.

1738, 1739 two guineas
1793, 1798 guineas
(there could also be other dates)
1820 pattern two pounds
1839 five pounds
(in particular the plain edge variety)
1887 five pounds
1887 (two pounds (there seem to be many forgeries of these))
1893 five pounds, two pounds
1902 five pounds, two pounds
1911 five pounds, two pounds
1817, 1819, 1822, 1825, 1827, 1887, 1889, 1892, 1892M, 1908C, 1913C sovereigns; also every date from 1900 to 1932 inclusive, plus 1957, 1959, 1963, 1966, 1967, 1974, 1976 1847 Gothic crowns
1905 halfcrowns

Other safeguards against forgery

(a) The best method of protection against purchasing forgeries is to buy your coins from a reputable dealer who is a member of the British Numismatic Trade Association or the International Association of Professional Numismatists, or one who will unconditionally guarantee that all his coins are genuine.
(b) Legal tender coins, which include five and two pound pieces, sovereigns, half sovereigns and crowns, are protected by the Forgery and Counterfeiting Act, and it is the responsibility of the police to prosecute in cases where this Act has been contravened.
(c) If your dealer is unhelpful over a non-legal tender item, which you have purchased and which you think has been falsely described, you can take legal action under the Trades Description Act 1968. However, we should warn you that it can be a tedious and long-winded business, but if you want to proceed in this you should contact your local Trading Standards Office or Consumer Protection department.

The different types of forgery

There are many different forgeries, but essentially they can be divided into two main groups. First of all there are contemporary forgeries intended to be used as face-value money (as in the cases, some years ago, of the counterfeit 50p pieces, which worked in slot machines), and secondly forgeries intended to deceive collectors.

Contemporary forgeries, those pieces struck in imitation of currency coins, are obviously not a serious problem to numismatists. The recent ones cause more trouble to bank clerks, anyway, and are not of a good enough standard to deceive numismatic experts. In general, those produced in the Middle Ages were base (which was how the forger made a profit), consisting wholly of base metal or occasionally having a thin coating of the proper metal on the outside. Sometimes they were struck, but more often they were cast.

Whatever the problems they caused at the time of issue, they are now often as interesting

Counterfeit

Summer 2005

Journal of the Counterfeit Coin Club, Vol. 10, No. 2

(top) A counterfeit coin of Kelantan (a state in
northern Malaysia).
(bottom) Its genuine counterpart (AH1256)

ABOVE: Counterfeit Journal from 2005

as the regular coins of the period.
However, one can be less light-hearted about
copies which are made to deceive collectors.
The following five methods of reproduction
have been used:

1. Electrotyping. These copies would normally
deceive an expert.

2. Casting. Old casts are easily recognisable,
having marks made by air bubbles on the
surface, and showing a generally 'fuzzy' effect.
Much more of a problem are the modern cast
copies, produced by sophisticated 'pressure-
casting', which can be extremely difficult for all
but the most expert to distinguish from the
originals (more of this later).

3. The fabrication of false dies. With hammered
coins counterfeits are not difficult for an expert
to detect. However, the sophisticated die-
production techniques used in Beirut have
resulted in the worrying features of modern
gold and silver coins described later.

4. The use of genuine dies put to some illegal
use such as re-striking (a mintmaster in West
Germany was convicted in 1975 of that very
issue).

5 Alteration of a genuine coin. The most common
one being a George V penny. (Ask your dealer
how many George V pennies he has seen with the
date altered to 1933 – it does happen!)

Counterfeit Coin Club

There is a Counterfeit Coin Club that produces a
small quarterly journal. For membership details
write to its President: Ken Peters, 8 Kins Road,
Biggin Hill, Kent TN16 3XU (tel: 01959 573686)

Literature on forgery

The back numbers of Spink's *Numismatic
Circulars* and Seaby's *Coin and Medal Bulletins*
are useful sources of information on the forgeries
that have been recorded over the years.

The ISBCC (set up by an IAPN in 1975 by the
late Vincent Newman) also produced a series of
important forgery bulletins, mainly on modern
coins, but are now only to be found second-hand.

The IAPN themselves still produce very good
reports on forgeries for their own members.

The most useful work on hammered coins is
by L.A. Lawrence in the *British Numismatic Journal*
back in 1905! (*Forgery in relation to Numismatics.*
BNJ 1905-1907, a series of articles; occasionally it
can be found in one bound volume).

British Coin Prices

CELTIC COINAGE

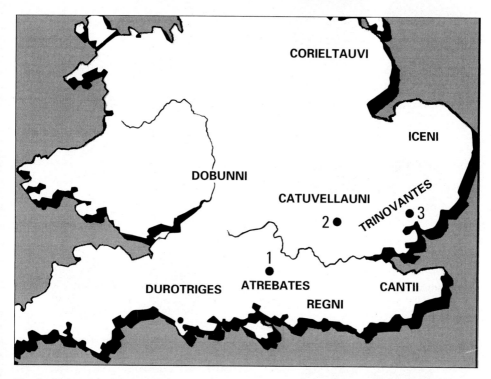

The distribution of the tribes in Britain based on the map in 'The coinage of Ancient Britain', by R.P. Mack, published by Spink and Son Ltd and B.A. Seaby Ltd.

Key to towns:
1. Calleva Atrebatum (Silchester)
2. Verulamium (St Albans)
3. Camulodunum (Colchester)

It is always difficult to produce a priced catalogue of coins, but none is more difficult than the early British series. The market has developed considerably since the publication of R.D. Van Arsdell's *Celtic Coinage of Britain,* which is an essential book for collectors (584 pages, 54 plates and many other illustrations, maps and diagrams).

A word of caution, though; quite a number of forgeries exist, some of relatively recent production, and unfortunately also numerous items from undeclared hoards are on the market, which makes it essential to buy from a reputable dealer.

We are very grateful for the help of Robert Van Arsdell since he produced the synopsis of the material which we have used. We have kept this very basic, and simply linked it up for easy reference with *The Coinage of Ancient Britain* by R. P. Mack, third edition, London 1975 (now out of print), and with the *British Museum Catalogue of British Iron Age Coins* by R. Hobbs, where it is possible. In the following lists Mack types are indicated by 'M' and BMC types by 'B'. The V numbers relate to the Van Arsdell catalogue. The existence of forgeries is indicated by **(F)**.

Gold staters without legends

AMBIANI	F	VF
Large flan type M1, 3, V10, 12	£400	£1750

Ambiani large flan type

Defaced die type M5, 7, V30, 33 ...	£300	£900
Abstract type M26, 30, V44, 46	£250	£650
Gallic War type M27, a, V50, 52 **(F)** ...	£135	£300

Gallic War gold stater

SUESSIONES		
Abstract type M34a, V85	£275	£800

VE MONOGRAM		
M82, a, b, V87 **(F)**	£275	£750

WESTERHAM		
M28, 29, V200, 202 , B1-24	£200	£450

Chute Gold Starter, V1205

CHUTE		
M32, V1205, B35-76 **(F)**	£145	£300

CLACTON		
Type I M47, V1458, B137-144	£300	£900
Type II M46, a, V30, 1455, B145-179	£325	£900

CORIELTAUVI		
Scyphate type M—, V—, B3187-93	£275	£750

CORIELTAUVI (N.E. COAST TYPE)		
Type I M50-51a, V800, B182-191 ...	£200	£450
Type II M52-57, S27, V804	£190	£425

Norfolk Wolf stater VA610-3

NORFOLK	F	VF
Wolf type M49, a, b, V610, B212-278	£175	£425

CORIELTAUVI		
South Ferriby Kite & Domino type, M449-450a, V.811, B3146-3186	£225	£525

Coritani (South Ferriby)

WHADDON CHASE		
M133-138, V1470-1478, B279-350 **(F)**	£200	£500
Middle , Late Whaddon Chase V1485-1509	£225	£600

Whaddon Chase stater

WONERSH		
M147, 148, V1522, B351-56	£350	£900

WEALD		
M84, 229, V144, 150, B2466-68	£450	£1450

ICENI		
Freckenham Type I M397-399, 403b, V620, B3384-95	£275	£600
Freckenham Type II M401, 2, 3a, 3c, V626, B3396-3419	£275	£575
Snettisham Type M—, V—, B3353-83	£300	£750

Iceni gold stater

ATREBATIC		
M58-61, V210-216, B445-76	£200	£425

Atrebatic stater

SAVERNAKE FOREST		
M62, V1526, B359-64	£225	£550
DOBUNNIC		
M374, V1005, B2937-40	£350	£850

Gold quarter staters without legends

AMBIANI	F	VF
Large flan type M2, 4, V15, 20 **(F)**	£225	£625
Defaced die type M6, 8, V35, 37	£200	£500
GEOMETRIC		
M37, 39, 41, 41A, 42, V65, 146, 69, 67	£75	£150
SUSSEX		
M40, 43-45, V143, 1225-1229	£75	£150
VE MONOGRAM		
M83, V87 **(F)**	£150	£350

Atrebatic quarter stater, Bognor Cog Wheel

ATREBATIC		
M63-67, 69-75, V220-256, B478-546	£135	£325

Caesar's trophy, quarter stater VA145

KENTISH		
Caesar's Trophy type V145	£125	£300

Gold staters with legends

COMMIUS	F	VF
M92, V350, B724-730	£350	£1000
TINCOMARUS		
M93, 93, V362, 363, B761-74	£450	£1250
VERICA		
Equestrian type M121, V500, B1143-58	£225	£575
Vine leaf type M125, V520, B1159-76	£250	£650

Verica gold stater

EPATICCUS	F	VF
M262, V575, B2021-23	£825	£2250
DUBNOVELLAUNUS		
In Kent M283, V176, B2492-98	£325	£825
In Essex M275, V1650, B2425-40 ...	£300	£800
EPPILLUS		
In Kent M300-1, V430, B1125-28 ...	£1250	£4000
ADDEDOMAROS (THREE TYPES)		
M266, 7, V1605, B2390-94 **(F)**	£200	£500
TASCIOVANUS		
Bucranium M149, V1680, B1591-1607 **(F)**	£325	£900

VOLISIOS DUMNOCOVEROS

Equestrian M154-7, V1730-1736, B1608-13	£300	£800
TASCIO/RICON M184, V1780, B1625-36	£525	£1350
SEGO		
M194, V1845, B1625-27	£1500	£4000
ANDOCO		
M197, V1860, B2011-14	£525	£1350

Tasciovanus Celtic Warrior

Cunobeline Gold Stater, V1910

CELTIC COINAGE

	F	VF
CUNOBELINE		
Two horses M201, V1910, B1769-71	**£675**	**£1750**
Corn ear M203 etc. V2010,		
B1772-1835 **(F)**	**£250**	**£550**

ANDOCO Stater

ANTED of the Dobunni		
M385-6, V1062-1066, B3023-27 **(F)**	**£450**	**£1200**
EISU		
M388, V1105, B3039-42 **(F)**	**£525**	**£1500**
INAM		
M390, V1140, B3056 **(F)**	extremely rare	
CATTI		
M391, V1130, B3057-60 **(F)**	**£375**	**£900**
COMUX		
M392, V1092, B3061-63 **(F)**	**£800**	**£2000**
CORIO		
M393, V1035, B3064-3133 ... ... ·	**£425**	**£1000**
BODVOC		
M395, V1052, B3135-42 **(F)**	**£700**	**£1850**

Bodvoc

VEP CORF		
M459-460, V940, 930, B3296-3300 **(F)**	**£425**	**£950**
DUMNOC TIGIR SENO		
M461, V972, B3325-27 **(F)**	**£700**	**£1600**
VOLISIOS DUMNOCOVEROS		
M463, V978, B3330-36	**£425**	**£1000**

Cunobeline quarter stater V.1913-1

Gold quarter staters with legends

TINCOMARUS		
Abstract type M95, V365	**£165**	**£350**
Medusa head type M97, V387,		
B811-24	**£200**	**£500**
Tablet type M101-4, V387-390,		
B825-79	**£125**	**£275**

Tincommius Medusa head gold quarter stater

	F	VF
EPPILLUS		
CALLEVA M107, V407, B986-1015 ...	**£125**	**£275**

Eppillus CALLEVA type

VERICA		
Horse type M111-114, V465-468,		
B1143-46	**£120**	**£250**
TASCIOVANUS		
Horse type M152-3, V1690,1692,		
B1641-1650	**£120**	**£250**
CUNOBELINE		
Various types, B1836-55 from	**£125**	**£275**

Silver coins without legends

DUROTRIGES		
Silver stater M317, V1235,		
B2525-2731 **(F)**	**£45**	**£135**
Geometric type M319, V1242,		
B2734-79	**£35**	**£100**
Starfish type M320, V1270,		
B2780-81	**£60**	**£200**

Starfish Unit

DOBUNNIC		
Face M374a, b, 5, 6, 8, V1020,		
B2950-3000	**£35**	**£100**
Abstract M378a-384d, V1042,		
B3012-22	**£30**	**£90**

Corieltauvi, showing boar and horse

CORIELTAUVI		
Boar type M405a, V855, B3194-3250	**£65**	**£175**
South Ferriby M410 etc, V875	**£50**	**£120**

Iceni Unit, V730

ICENI	F	VF
Boar type M407-9, V655-659, B3440-3511	£25	£75
Wreath type M414, 5, 440, V679, 675, B3763-74	£25	£80
Face type M412-413e, V665, B3536-55	£85	£275

QUEEN BOUDICA

	F	VF
Face type M413, 413D, V790, 792, B3556-3759	£50	£175

Silver coins of Boudica (left) and Commius (right)

COMMIUS

	F	VF
Head left M446b, V355, 357, B731-58	£45	£150

Silver coins with legends

EPPILLUS	F	VF
CALLEVA type M108, V415, B1016-1115	£45	£130

EPATICCUS		
Eagle type M263, V580, B2024-2289	£30	£90
Victory type M263a, V581, B2294-2328	£35	£100

Verica, Lion type unit V505

VERICA

	F	VF
Lim type M123, V505, B1332-59 ...	£40	£135

Silver unit, Epaticcus

CARATACUS

Eagle Type M265, V593, B2376-2384 (**F**)	£125	£350

TASCIOVANUS

Equestrian M158, V1745, B1667-68	£85	£275
VER type M161, V1699, B1670-73 ...	£85	£275

CUNOBELINE

Equestrian M216-8, 6, V1951, 1953, 2047, B1862	£95	£300
Bust right M236, VA2055, B1871-73	£85	£275

ANTED of the Dobunni

M387, V1082, B3032-38	£65	£160

EISU

M389, V1110, B3043-55	£50	£150

CELTIC COINAGE

BODVOC
M396, V1057, B3143-45 **(F)** £125 £400

ANTED of the Iceni
M419-421, V710, 711, 715,
B3791-4009 ... ... £30 £70

ECEN
M424, V730, B4033-4215 ... ... £25 £65

EDNAM
M423, 425b, V740, 734, B4219-4281 £30 £65

ECE
M425a, 426, 7, 8, V761, 764,
762, 766, B4348-4538 ... ... £25 £60

AESU
M432, V775, B4558-72 ... ... £50 £125

PRASUTAGUS
King of the Iceni (husband of Boudica),
B4577-4580 ... ... £600 £1750

ESUP ASU
M4566, VA924, B3272 ... ... £75 £275

VEP CORF
M460b, 464, V394, 950, B3277-3382,
B3305-3314 ... ... £50 £110

DUMNOC TIGIR SENO
M462, V974 B3328-3329 ... ... £175 £500

VOLISIOS DUMNOCOVEROS
M463a, V978, 980, B3339 ... ... £175 £500

ALE SCA
M469, V996 ... ... £150 £425

Bronze, base metal coins without legends

POTIN	F	VF
Experimental type M22a, V104	£40	£90

Potin coin class II

	F	VF
Class I M9-22, V122-131	£30	£80
Class II M23-25, V136-139	£30	£80
Thurrock Types V1402-1442	£40	£125

ARMORICAN	F	VF
Billon stater	£30	£100
Billon quarter stater	£50	£135

DUROTRIGES		
Bronze stater M318, V1290	£20	£50
Cast type M332-370, V1322-1370 ...	£35	£110

NORTH THAMES		
M273, 274, 281, V1646 1615, 1669	£35	£110

NORTH KENT		
M295, 296, V154	£65	£250

Bronze coins with legends

DUBNOVELLAUNUS in Essex		
M277, 8, V1665, 1667	£60	£200
TASCIOVANUS		
Head, beard M168, 9, V1707	£50	£175
VERLAMIO M172, V1808	£45	£175
Head, VER M177, V1816	£60	£225
Boar, VER M179, V1713	£50	£200
Equestrian M190, V1892	£85	£350
Centaur M192, V1882	£110	£450

ANDOCO		
M200, V1871	£70	£250

CUNOBELINE		
Victory, TASC M221, V1971	£40	£175
Victory, CUN M22, a, V1973	£45	£185
Winged animal, M225, V2081	£45	£185

Cunobeline bronze with Centaur reverse

Head, beard, M226, 9, V2131, 2085	£40	£165
Panel, sphinx, M230, V1977	£45	£185
Winged beast, M231, V1979	£45	£170
Centaur, M242, V2089	£40	£165
Sow, M243, V2091	£40	£165
Warrior, M244, V2093	£35	£150
Boar, TASC, M245, V1983	£50	£185
Bull, TASC M246, V2095	£40	£150
Metal worker, M248, V2097	£40	£165
Pegasus, M249, V2099	£35	£125
Horse, CAMV, M250, V2101	£45	£185
Jupiter, horse, M251, V2103	£45	£185
Janus head, M252, V2105	£50	£200
Jupiter, lion, M253, V1207	£40	£165
Sphinx, fig, M260, a, V2109	£45	£175

ENGLISH HAMMERED
Gold from 1344 and Silver from *circa* 600

Prices in this section are approximately what collectors can expect to pay for the commonest types of the coins listed; for most other types prices will range upwards from these amounts. Precise valuations cannot be given since they vary from dealer to dealer and, in any case, have to be determined by consideration of a number of factors e.g., the coin's condition (which is of prime importance in deciding its value).

For more detailed information refer to English Hammered Coins, Volumes 1 and 2, by J. J. North and published by Spink and Son Ltd. Any serious collectors should also obtain The Herbert Schneider Collection, Volume One, English Gold Coins 1257-1603, published by Spink and Son, 1996 and Volume Two English Gold Coins 1603 to 20th century, published by Spink and Son, 2002.

GOLD COINS
The Plantagenet Kings

Henry III gold penny

HENRY III 1216-1272

	F	VF
Gold Penny		

This specimen sold for £159,500 (including buyers premium) at a Spink auction on 9 July 1996. ext. rare

Edward III quarter noble

EDWARD III 1327-77
Third coinage

		F	VF
Florins or Double leopard		ext. rare	
Half florins or leopard...		ext. rare	
Quarter florins or helms		ext. rare	
Nobles	from	£1250	£3000
Half nobles	from	£1000	£3000
Quarter nobles		£400	£900

Fourth coinage
Pre-treaty with France (i.e. before 1315) with French title

	F	VF
Nobles	£575	£1250
Half nobles...	£425	£900
Quarter nobles	£200	£500

Transitional treaty period, 1361. Aquitaine title added

	F	VF
Nobles	£575	£1500
Half nobles	£325	£750
Quarter nobles	£185	£400

Edward III 1327-1377, Half noble, Transitional Treaty

Treaty period 1361-9 omit FRANC

	F	VF
Nobles, London	£525	£1300
Nobles, Calais		
(C in centre of rev.)	£600	£1450
Half nobles, London	£375	£850
Half nobles, Calais	£625	£1500
Quarter nobles, London	£200	£450
Quarter nobles, Calais...	£225	£500

Post-treaty period 1369-77 French title resumed

	F	VF
Nobles, London	£600	£1450
Nobles, Calais		
(flag at stern or C in centre)	£625	£1500
Half nobles, London	£1000	£3000
Half nobles, Calais	£950	£2500

There are many other issues and varieties in this reign. These prices relate to the commoner pieces.

Richard II London half noble

RICHARD II 1377-99

	F	VF
Nobles, London	£725	£1600
Nobles, Calais		
(flag at stern)	£750	£1750
Half nobles, London	£850	£2250

HAMMERED GOLD

	F	VF
Half nobles, Calais		
(flag at stern)	£1250	£3250
Quarter nobles, London	£450	£850

There are many different varieties and different styles of lettering.

HENRY IV 1399-1413
Heavy coinage

	F	VF
Nobles (120grs) London	£4000	£13500
Nobles, Calais (flag at stern)	£4500	£15000
Half nobles, London	£4000	*
Half nobles, Calais	£4500	*
Quarter nobles, London	£1000	£2500
Quarter nobles, Calais	£1250	£3250

Light coinage

	F	VF
Nobles (108grs)	£1450	£3750
Half nobles	£2000	£5000
Quarter nobles	£525	£1100

Henry V noble

HENRY V 1413-22

	F	VF
Nobles, many varieties, from	£675	£1450
Half nobles	£625	£1300
Quarter nobles	£300	£650

This reign sees an increase in the use of privy marks to differentiate issues.

Henry VI noble, Annulet issue

HENRY VI 1422-61
Annulet issue (1422-27)

	F	VF
Nobles, London	£600	£1350
Nobles, Calais (flag at stern)	£650	£1650
Nobles, York	£800	£2250
Half nobles, London	£425	£1100
Half nobles, Calais	£750	£2000
Half nobles, York	£925	£2750
Quarter nobles, London	£200	£475
Quarter nobles, Calais	£225	£550
Quarter nobles, York	£250	£650

Henry VI, Quarter-Noble, Annulet issue

Rosette-mascle issue 1427-30 ... ...

	F	VF
Nobles, London	£1000	£2750
Nobles, Calais	£1250	£3000
Half nobles, London	£1350	£3500
Half nobles, Calais	£1500	£4000
Quarter nobles, London	£575	£1250
Quarter nobles, Calais	£650	£1500

Pinecone-mascle issue 1430-4

	F	VF
Nobles, London	£900	£2500
Half nobles, London	£1750	£5000
Quarter noble	£750	£1750

Henry VI quarter noble, leaf-mascle

Leaf-mascle issue 1434-5

Nobles	£2000	£5500
Half nobles	£1850	£5250
Quarter nobles	£875	£2000

Leaf-trefoil issue 1435-8

Nobles	£1850	£5250
Quarter noble	£950	£1850

Trefoil issue 1438-43

Nobles	£2250	£6000

Henry VI Gold Noble, Pinecone-mascle, London

Leaf-pellet issue 1445-54

Nobles	£2250	£6000

Cross-pellet issue 1454-60

Nobles	£2500	£7000

EDWARD IV 1st reign 1461-70
Heavy coinage 1461-64/5

Nobles (108grs)	£2500	£7000
Quarter noble		ext. rare

Edward IV noble, heavy coinage

Light coinage 1464-70

	F	VF
Ryals or rose nobles (120grs),		
London	£600	£1350
Flemish copy	£375	£750

Edward IV Light Coinage 1464-70, Ryal, York

	F	VF
Ryals, Bristol (B in waves)	£675	£1650
Ryals, Coventry (C in waves))	£1350	£3000
Ryals, Norwich (N in waves)	£1450	£3250
Ryals, York (E in waves)	£650	£1600
Half ryals, London	£475	£1100
Half ryals, Bristol (B in waves) ...	£725	£1750
Half ryals, Coventry (C in waves) ...	£2750	£7500
Half ryals Norwich (N in waves) ...	£2500	£6500
Half ryals, York (E in waves)	£475	£1250
Quarter ryals	£300	£650
Angels	£4500	*

Edward IV angel, first reign

	F	VF
HENRY VI (restored) 1470-71		
Angels, London	£1000	£2750
Angels, Bristol (B in waves)	£1350	£4000
Half angels, London	£2000	£5000
Half angels, Bristol (B in waves) ...	£3500	*
EDWARD IV 2nd reign 1471-83		
Angels, London	£500	£1000
Angels, Bristol (B in waves)	£1750	£4000
Half angels, some varieties	£450	£975
EDWARD IV or V 1483		
mm halved sun and rose		
Angels	£1850	£6000
Half angels	£3000	*
RICHARD III 1483-85		
Angel, reading **EDWARD,** *mm* boar's		
head on obverse, halved sun and		
rose on reverse	£4500	£10000
Angels, reading **RICHARD or RICAD**	£1750	£4500
Half angels	£4000	*

Gold Angel, mm boar's head on obverse, and halved sun and rose on reverse

The Tudor Monarchs

Henry VII sovereign

	F	VF
HENRY VII 1485-1509		
Sovereigns of 20 shillings (all ext.		
rare) from	£12500	£35000
Ryals	£10000	£30000
Angels, varieties, different *mm* from	£475	£1200
Half angels	£425	£975

HAMMERED GOLD

Henry VII 1485-1509, Angel with Mint Mark pheon

HENRY VIII 1509-47

First coinage 1509-26

	F	VF
Sovereigns of 20 shillings *mm* crowned portcullis only	£5250	£15000
Angels (6s 8d) ... ... from	£475	£1200
Half angels	£450	£1000

Second coinage 1526-44

	F	VF
Sovereigns of 22s 6d, various *mm* ...	£5000	£14500
Angels (7s 6d)	£725	£1850
Half angels *mm* lis	£825	£2000
George-nobles *mm* rose	£4250	£16500
Half-George noble	£6000	*
Crowns of the rose *mm* rose	£4500	*
Crowns of the double-rose		
HK (Henry and Katherine of Aragon)	£450	£975
HA (Henry and Anne Boleyn) ...	£800	£2250
HI (Henry and Jane Seymour) ...	£525	£1250
HR (HENRICUS REX)	£475	£1000
Halfcrowns of the double-rose		
HK	£425	£975
HI	£525	£1250
HR	£625	£1350

Third coinage 1544-47

	F	VF
Sovereigns of 20s, London ... from	£3250	£9000
Sovereigns of 20s, Southwark	£3000	£8500
Sovereigns of 20s, Bristol	£3750	£11000
Half sovereigns, London	£650	£1650
Half sovereigns, Southwark	£675	£1650
Half sovereigns, Bristol	£875	£2750

*Henry VIII Angel, 3rd coinage with mint mark lis
(shown slightly enlarged)*

	F	VF
Angels	£475	£1000
Half angels	£450	£1000
Quarter angels	£425	£950
Crowns, HENRIC 8, London	£450	£1000
Crowns, Southwark	£525	£1250
Crowns, Bristol	£500	£1200

	F	VF
Halfcrowns, London	£375	£900
Halfcrowns, Southwark	£450	£950
Halfcrowns, Bristol	£475	£1250

EDWARD VI 1547-53

Posthumous coinage in name of Henry VIII (1547-51)

	F	VF
Sovereigns, London	£4500	£12500
Sovereigns, Bristol	£5250	£13500
Half sovereigns, London	£575	£1650
Half sovereigns, Southwark	£525	£1500
Crowns, London	£500	£1250
Crowns, Southwark	£525	£1350
Halfcrowns, London	£475	£1000
Halfcrowns, Southwark	£450	£975

Coinage in Edward's own name
First period 1547-49

	F	VF
Half sovereigns, Tower, read EDWARD 6	£1350	£4000

*Edward VI sovereign, posthumous coinage
(not actual size)*

	F	VF
Half sovereigns, Southwark	£1250	£3750
Crown	£2500	*
Halfcrowns	£2000	*

Second period 1549-50

	F	VF
Sovereigns	£3000	£9000
Half sovereigns, uncrowned bust London	£3250	*
Half sovereigns, SCUTUM on obv. ...	£1250	£3500
Half sovereigns, Durham House MDXL VII	£4500	*
Half sovereigns, crowned bust, London	£1100	£3000
Half sovereigns, half-length bust, Durham House	£4250	*
Crowns, uncrowned bust	£1200	£3000
Crowns, crowned bust	£1100	£2750
Halfcrowns, uncrowned bust	£1200	£3000
Halfcrowns, crowned bust	£975	£2500

*Edward VI fine sovereign of 30s third period with mint
mark ostrich head*

Edward VI Sovereign of 20 Shillings. Third Period

Third period 1550-53
'Fine' sovereigns of 30s, king
	F	VF
enthroned	£14500	£37500
Sovereigns of 20s, half-length figure ...	£2250	£6500
Half sovereigns, similar to last	£1350	£3250
Crowns, similar but SCUTUM on rev ...	£1200	£3000
Halfcrowns, similar	£1350	£3500
Angels	£5250	£16500
Half angel	ext. rare	

MARY 1553-4
Sovereigns, different dates, some
	F	VF
undated, some *mms*	£2850	£7250
Ryals, dated MDUI (1553)	£9500	£32500
Angels, *mm* pomegranate	£1100	£2850
Half angels	£2750	£6500

Mary Gold Sovereign of 1553

PHILIP AND MARY 1554-8	F	VF
Angels, *mm* lis	£2750	£7000
Half angels	£6500	*

Philip and Mary angel

Elizabeth I 1558-1603
Hammered issues
'Fine' sovereigns of 30s, different
	F	VF
issues from	£2750	£7500
Ryals	£7500	£22500
Angels, different issues	£650	£1650
Half angels	£600	£1500
Quarter angels	£525	£1250

Elizabeth I quarter angel

Pounds of 20 shillings, different	F	VF
mint marks from	£1450	£4000
Half pounds, different issues	£1100	£2750
Crowns —	£900	£2000
Halfcrowns —	£750	£1850

Elizabeth I hammered halfcrown

Milled issues
Half pounds, one issue but different
marks	£1850	£5250
Crowns —	£1650	£4500
Halfcrowns —	£1850	£5500

The Stuart Kings

James I gold Spur-ryal

James I Thistle crown

3rd coinage 1619-25

	F	VF
Rose-ryals, varieties	£2000	£5500
Spur-ryals	£2750	£8500
Angels	£1000	£2750
Laurels, different busts	£450	£925
Half Laurels	£350	£750
Quarter laurels	£200	£475

JAMES I 1603-25

1st coinage 1603-4

	F	VF
Sovereigns of 20 shillings two bust	£1350	£4000
Half sovereigns	£2000	£6000
Crowns	£1350	£3750
Halfcrowns	£625	£1250

2nd coinage 1604-19

	F	VF
Rose-ryals of 30 shillings	£1750	£4500
Spur-ryals of 15 shillings	£3000	£9000
Angels	£750	£2000
Half angels	£1850	£5000
Unites, different busts	£475	£1000
Double crowns —	£350	£750
Britain crowns —	£225	£500

James I laurel

CHARLES I 1625-49

Tower Mint 1625-42

Initial marks: lis, cross calvary, negro's head, castle, anchor, heart, plume, rose, harp, portcullis, bell, crown, tun, triangle, star, triangle in circle

*James I
Rose-ryal of
30 shillings*

	F	VF
Halfcrowns —	£185	£400
Thistle crowns, varieties	£225	£575

Charles I Unite, Tower Mint, 1625-43

Angels, varieties	£1750	£4000
Angels, pierced as touchpieces	£725	£1650
Unites –	£525	£1200
Double Crowns –	£400	£850
Crowns –	£200	£450

Charles I Double Crown, Tower Mint with mint mark heart

Tower Mint under Parliament 1642-9   **F**   **VF**
Initial marks: (P), (R), eye, sun, sceptre

	F	VF
Unites, varieties	£750	£2000
Double crowns –	£600	£1250
Crowns –	£325	£700

Briot's milled issues 1631-2
Initial marks: anemone and **B**, daisy and **B, B**

Angels	£3250	£8000
Unites	£1800	£5750
Double crowns	£1450	£4250
Crowns	£2000	£6500

Coins of provincial mints
Bristol 1645

Unites	£10000	£35000
Half unites		ext. rare

Chester 1644

Unites	£12500	£37500

Exeter 1643-44

Unites	£12500	£37500

Oxford 1642-46

Triple unites, from	£6500	£16500
Unites from	£1350	£3500
Half unites from	£1000	£2850

Truro 1642-43

Half unites		ext. rare

Shrewsbury 1644

Triple unites and unites		ext. rare

Worcester 1643-44

Unites	£13500	£40000

Charles I Oxford triple unite, 1643

Siege pieces 1645-49	F	VF
Pontefract besieged 1648-49		
Unites **(F)**		ext. rare

Commonwealth 1650 gold unite

COMMONWEALTH 1649-60

Unites *im* sun	£1100	£2750
– *im* anchor	£2250	£6500
Double crowns *im* sun	£750	£1650
– *im* anchor	£2000	£5250
Crowns *im* sun	£600	£1400
– *im* anchor	£2000	£5000

Commonwealth crown

CHARLES II 1660-85
Hammered Coinage 1660-62

Charles II gold unite

Unites, two issues from	£1250	£3000
Double crowns –	£900	£2250
Crowns –	£1000	£2500

SILVER COINS

In this section column headings are mainly F (Fine) and VF (Very Fine), but for pennies of the early Plantagenets - a series in which higher-grade coins are seldom available - prices are shown under the headings Fair and F. Again it should be noted that throughout the section prices are approximate, for the commonest types only, and are the amounts collectors can expect to pay - not dealers' buying prices. Descriptions of some early Anglo-Saxon coins are, of necessity, brief because of pressure on space. Descriptions such as 'cross/moneyer's name' indicate that a cross appears on the obverse and the moneyer's name on the reverse. For more details see Standard Catalogue of British Coins published by Spink and Son Ltd., and English Hammered Coins, Volumes 1 and 2 by J. J. North, published by Spink and Son Ltd.. (A new edition of Volume 2 was published in 1991 and a new edition of Volume 1 was published in 1994).

Anglo-Saxon Sceats and Stycas

Examples of Sceats

EARLY PERIOD c 600-750	F	VF
Silver sceats ... ...from	£50	£150

A fascinating series with great variation of styles of early art. Large numbers of types and varieties.

NORTHUMBRIAN KINGS c 737-867		
Silver sceats c 737-796 ...from	£85	£250
Copper stycas c 810-867 ...from	£20	£45

Struck for many kings. Numerous moneyers and different varieties. The copper styca is the commonest coin in the Anglo-Saxon series.

ARCHBISHOPS OF YORK c 732-900		
Silver sceats ... ...from	£75	£185
Copper stycas ... ...from	£20	£50

From here onwards until the reign of Edward I all coins are silver pennies unless otherwise stated

Kings of Kent

HEABERHT c 764	F	VF
Monogram/cross		ext. rare

One moneyer (EOBA).

ECGBERHT c 765-780		
Monogram/cross	£875	£2650

Two moneyers (BABBA and UDD)

EADBERHT PRAEN 797-798		
EADBERHT REX/moneyer	£1000	£3250

Three moneyers

Penny of Eadberht Praen

CUTHRED 789-807	F	VF
Non-portrait, various designs from	£575	£1500
Bust right	£625	£1650

Different moneyers, varieties etc.

BALDRED c 825		
Bust right	£900	£3000
Cross/cross	£675	£1750

different types and moneyers

Baldred penny, bust right

ANONYMOUS c 823		
Bust right	£750	£2250

Different varieties and moneyers.

Archbishops of Canterbury

JAENBERHT 766-792	F	VF
Various types (non-portrait) from	£850	£2500

AETHELHEARD 793-805		
Various types (non-portrait) from	£750	£2000

WULFRED 805-832		
Various groups (portrait types) from	£675	£1850

CEOLNOTH 833-870		
Various groups (portrait types) from	£525	£1250

Ceolnoth penny

AETHERED 870-889	F	VF
Various types (portrait, non-portrait)	£1500	£5000
PLEGMUND 890-914		
Various types (all non-portrait) from	£575	£1500

Kings of Mercia

Offa portrait penny

OFFA 757-796	F	VF
Non-portrait from	£450	£1000
Portrait from	£850	£2500
Many types and varieties		

Cynethryth (wife of Offa) portrait penny

CYNETHRYTH (wife of Offa)		
Portraits	£1750	£5500
Non-portrait	£950	£2750
COENWULF 796-821		
Various types (portrait, non-portrait)from	£400	£850

Coenwulf portrait penny

CEOLWULF 1821-823		
Various types (portrait)	£675	£1650
BEORNWULF 823-825		
Various types (portrait)	£750	£2250

Beornwulf penny

LUDICA 825-827		
Two types (portrait) (F)	£2500	£7000
WIGLAF 827-829, 830-840		
Two groups (portrait, non-portrait)	£1750	£5250
BERHTWULF 840-852		
Two groups (portrait, non-portrait)	£800	£2500

HAMMERED SILVER

Berhtwulf penny

BURGRED 852-874	F	VF
One type (portrait), five variants	£165	£400
CEOLWULF II 874-c 877		
Two types (portrait))	£1500	£4000

Kings of East Anglia

BEONNA c 758	F	VF
Silver sceat	£475	£1250
AETHELBERHT LUL (died 794)		
Portrait type (F)		ext. rare

Eadwald penny

EADWALD c 796	F	VF
Non-portrait types	£750	£2250
AETHELSTAN I c 850		
Various types (portrait, non-portrait)	£325	£850
AETHELWEARD c 850		
Non-portrait types	£450	£1200
EADMUND 855-870		
Non-portrait types	£275	£650

Viking Invaders 878-954

ALFRED	F	VF
Imitations of Alfred pennies and halfpennies from (Many different types, portrait and non portrait)	£325	£750
ANGLIA		
AETHELSTAN II 878-890		
Cross/moneyer	£950	£3000
OSWALD (Unknown in history except from coins)		
A/cross	£1200	£3750
ST EADMUND		
Memorial coinage, various legends etc.	£125	£300
Many moneyers.		
Halfpenny, similar	£425	£1000

HAMMERED SILVER

St Eadmund memorial penny

	F	VF
ST MARTIN OF LINCOLN c 925		
Sword/cross	£1750	£5000
AETHELRED c 870		
Temple/cross	£1500	£4000
YORK		
SIEVERT-SIEFRED-CNUT c 897		
Crosslet/small cross	£125	£250
Many different groups and varieties		
Halfpenny, similar	£425	£900
EARL SIHTRIC (unknown)		
Non-portrait	£1750	£5000
REGNALD c 919-921		
Various types, some blundered	£1250	£4250
SIHTRIC I 921-927		
Sword/cross	£1650	£5000
ANLAF GUTHFRITHSSON 939-941		
Raven/cross	£1650	£5000
Cross/cross	£1500	£4500
Flower/cross	£1750	£5250
ANLAF SIHTRICSSON 941-944, 948-952		
Various types	£1350	£4000
SIHTRIC II c 942-943		
Shield/standard	£1500	£4500
REGNALD II c 941-943		
Cross/cross	£1650	£5000
Shield/standard	£1750	£5250
ERIC BLOODAXE 948, 952-954		
Cross/moneyer	£2250	£7000
Sword/cross	£2500	£8000

St Peter of York halfpenny

	F	VF
ST PETER OF YORK c 905-927		
Various types ... ...from	£225	£500
Halfpenny, similar	£525	£1200

Kings of Wessex

	F	VF
BEORHTRIC 786-802		
Two types (non-portrait)		ext. rare
ECGBERHT 802-839		
FOUR GROUPS (portrait, non-portrait)	£850	£2750
Mints of Canterbury, London, Rochester, Winchester		

Aethelwulf Portrait Penny, Canterbury

	F	VF
AETHELWULF 839-858		
Four phases (portrait, non-portrait)	£350	£950
from Mints of Canterbury, Rochester (?)		
AETHELBERHT 858-866		
Two types (portrait) ... ...from	£350	£900
Many moneyers.		
AETHELRED I 865-871		
Portrait types ... ...from	£375	£1000
Many moneyers.		
ALFRED THE GREAT 871-899		
Portrait in style of Aethelred I ...	£450	£1200
Four other portrait types commonest being those		
with the London monogram reverse	£950	£2500
Halfpennies	£425	£900

Alfred the Great Penny, London monogram on reverse

	F	VF
Non-portrait types ... ...from	£375	£750
Many different styles of lettering etc.		
Halfpennies	£375	£750
EDWARD THE ELDER 899-924		
Non-portrait types:		
Cross/moneyer's name in two lines	£200	£450
Halfpennies as previous	£700	£1750

Rare penny of Edward the Elder with building on reverse

	F	VF
Portrait types:		
Bust/moneyer's name	£625	£1750
Many types, varieties and moneyers.		
Types featuring buildings, floral		
designs, etc	£1250	£4000
Many types, varieties and moneyers.		

Kings of all England

Aethelstan 924-939, Penny, building type reverse

Non-portrait types:

Cross/moneyer's name in two lines	£225	£500
Cross/cross	£250	£650

Portrait types:

bust/moneyer's name in two lines	£675	£2000
Bust/small cross	£575	£1500

Many other issues, some featuring buildings as illustrated above. There are also different mints and moneyer's names.

Aethelstan portrait penny with small cross on reverse

EADMUND 939-46

Non-portrait types:

Cross or rosette/moneyer's name in two lines	£225	£600
Silver halfpenny, similar	£675	£1500

Eadmund penny, two-line type

Portrait types:

Crowned bust/small cross	£625	£1500
Helmeted bust/cross crosslet ...	£850	£2500

Many other issues and varieties; also different mint names and moneyers.

EADRED 946-55

Non-portrait types:

Cross/moneyer's name in two lines	£200	£450
Silver halfpenny similar	£625	£1400
Rosette/moneyer's name	£275	£650

HAMMERED SILVER

Eadred penny, portrait type

Portrait types:

	F	VF
Crowned bust/small cross	£575	£1500

Again many variations and mint names and moneyers.

HOWEL DDA (King of Wales), died c948

Small cross/moneyer's name in two lines (GILLYS)	ext. rare

EADWIG 955-59

Non-portrait types:

Cross/moneyer's name ... from	£325	£800
Many variations, some rare.		
Silver halfpennies, similar	£875	£2250

Portrait types:

Bust/cross ... ... from	£2250	£7000

EADGAR 959-75

Non-portrait types:

Cross/moneyer's name ... from	£165	£375
Cross/cross ... ... from	£165	£375
Rosette/rosette ... ... from	£225	£525
Halfpennies ... ... from	£875	£2500

Eadgar, 959-957, Non Portrait Penny, Winchester

Portrait types

Pre-Reform	£675	£1850
Halfpenny, diademed bust/London monogram	£675	£1850
Reform (c.972)	£750	£2000

Many other varieties.

EDWARD THE MARTYR 975-78

Portrait types:

Bust left/small cross	£825	£2250

Many different mints and moneyers.

AETHELRED II 978-1016

Aethelred II 978-1016, Penny, Last small cross type

First small cross ... ... from	£425	£1250
First hand ... ... from	£110	£275
Second hand ... ... from	£110	£275
Benediction hand ... .,. from	£675	£1850

HAMMERED SILVER

	F	VF
CRUX ... ... from	£95	£190

Aethelred II CRUX type penny

Aethelred II , Long Cross penny

		F	VF
Long Cross		£100	£210
Helmet		£115	£275
Agnus Dei		£3500	*

Other issues and varieties, many mint names and moneyers.

Aethelred II long cross penny

CNUT 1016-35
		F	VF
Quatrefoil ... ... from		£90	£185

Cnut quatrefoil type penny

		F	VF
Pointed helmet ... ... from		£75	£150

Cnut pointed helmet type penny

		F	VF
Small cross ... ... from		£70	£135
Jewel cross ... ... from		£425	£975

Other types, and many different mint names and moneyers.

HAROLD I 1035-40
		F	VF
Jewel cross ... ... from		£240	£600

	F	VF
Long cross with trefoils ... from	£225	£550
Long cross with fleurs-de-lis from	£225	£550

Many different mint names and moneyers.

HARTHACNUT 1035-42
	F	VF
Jewel cross, bust left	£825	£2650
– bust right	£750	£2350
Arm and sceptre types	£725	£1750
Different mint names and moneyers.		
Scandinavian types struck at Lund	£225	£550

EDWARD THE CONFESSOR 1042-66
	F	VF
PACX type ... ... from	£165	£500
Radiate crown/small cross from	£85	£200
Trefoil quadrilateral	£90	£200
Small flan ... ... from	£75	£175
Expanding cross types ... from	£95	£225

Edward the Confessor Penny, Expanding Cross Type

	F	VF
Helmet types	£100	£250
Sovereign/eagles	£110	£265
Hammer cross	£90	£220

Edward the Confessor Hammer Cross Penny

	F	VF
Bust facing	£85	£190
Cross and piles	£85	£200
Large bust, facing, with sceptre	£950	£3250

Other issues, including a unique gold penny; many different mint names and moneyers.

HAROLD II 1066
	F	VF
Crowned head left with sceptre	£525	£1200

Harold II Penny, bust left with sceptre

	F	VF
Similar but no sceptre	£625	£1350

Harold II, bust left, without sceptre

	F	VF
Crowned head right with sceptre	£1250	£4000

The Norman Kings

WILLIAM I 1066-87

	F	VF
Profile/cross fleury ... ...from	£275	£650
Bonnet ... ...from	£200	£450
Canopy ... ...from	£300	£750
Two sceptres ... ...from	£225	£575
Two stars ... ...from	£200	£450
Sword ... ...from	£325	£775

William I profile/cross fleury penny

	F	VF
Profile/cross and trefoils ...from	£350	£900
PAXS ... ...from	£200	£400

WILLIAM II 1087-1100

William II, cross voided type penny

	F	VF
Profile ... ...from	£575	£1350
Cross in quatrefoil ... ...from	£500	£1200
Cross voided ... ...from	£500	£1200
Cross pattee over fleury ...from	£525	£1250
Cross fleury and piles ... ...from	£575	£1500

Henry I penny; small bust/cross and annulets

HENRY I 1100-1135

	F	VF
Annulets ... ...from	£425	£1000
Profile/cross fleury ... ...from	£275	£750
PAX ... ...from	£275	£725
Annulets and piles ... ...from	£325	£800
Voided cross and fleurs ... ...from	£650	£1750
Pointing bust and stars ... ...from	£950	£2750
Quatrefoil and piles ... ...from	£325	£800
Profile/cross and annulets from	£1350	£3500
Cross in quatrefoil ... ...from	£625	£1500

Henry I, full face/cross fleury penny

HAMMERED SILVER

	F	VF
Full face/cross fleury	£200	£550
Double inscription	£575	£1350
Small bust/cross and annulets	£425	£1000
Star in lozenge fleury	£400	£975
Pellets in quatrefoil	£200	£500
Quadrilateral on cross fleury ...	£150	£350
Halfpennies	£1350	£3500

STEPHEN 1135-54

	F	VF
Cross moline (Watford) ...from	£200	£550

Stephen 'Watford' Penny

	F	VF
Cross moline PERERIC	£575	£1500
Voided cross and mullets	£250	£600

Stephen Penny, voided cross pattée with mullets

	F	VF
Profile/cross fleury	£350	£950
Voided cross pommée (Awbridge)	£250	£625

There are also a number of irregular issues produced during the Civil War, all of which are very rare. These include several extremely rare and attractive pieces bearing the names of Empress Matilda and barons, such as Eustace Fitzjohn and Robert de Stuteville.

The Plantagenet Kings

HENRY II 1154-89

	Fair	F

Henry II Cross and Crosslets (Tealby) Penny

	Fair	F
Cross and crosslets ('Tealby' coinage)	£110	£275

The issue is classified by bust variants into six groups, struck at 32 mints.

Henry II Short Cross Penny 1b

HAMMERED SILVER

	F	VF
Short cross pennies	**£55**	**£135**

The 'short cross' coinage was introduced in 1180 and continued through successive reigns until Henry III brought about a change in 1247. HENRICVS REX appears on all these coins but they can be classified into reigns by the styles of the busts and lettering. We recommend a copy of C.R. Wren's illustrated guide The Short Cross Coinage 1180-1247, *as the best guide to identification.*

Richard I, 1189-1199, Short Cross Penny

RICHARD I 1189-99
Short cross pennies	**£65**	**£150**

JOHN 1199-1216
Short cross pennies	**£55**	**£135**

John Short Cross Penny

HENRY III 1216-72
Short cross pennies	**£25**	**£60**
Long cross pennies no sceptre	**£25**	**£50**
Long cross pennies with sceptre	**£20**	**£50**

Henry III, Long Cross Penny, no sceptre

Henry III, Long Cross Penny with sceptre

The 'long cross' pennies, first introduced in 1247, are divided into two groups: those with sceptre and those without. They also fall into five basic classes, with many varieties. We recommend C.R. Wren's, The Voided Long Cross Coinage, 1247-79 *as the best guide to identification.*

Edward I, 1st coinage, Long Cross penny

	F	VF

EDWARD I 1272-1307
1st coinage 1272-78
Long cross pennies ... ...from	**£25**	**£75**

similar in style to those of Henry III but with more realistic beard.

Edward I Penny, London

New coinage 1278-1307
Groats	£1650	£6000
Pennies, various classes, mints from	£20	£50
Halfpennies – ... ...from	£25	£60
Farthings – ... ...from	£25	£60

Edward I Farthing, London

Any new collector wishing to become serious about this area should obtain a copy of Edwardian English Silver Coins 1279-1351. Sylloge of coins of the British Isles 39 (The JJ North collection)

EDWARD II 1307-27
Pennies, various classes, mints from	£40	£60
Halfpennies ... ...from	£45	£105
Farthings ... ...from	£35	£75

EDWARD III 1327-77
1st and 2nd coinages 1327-43
Pennies (only 1st coinage) various types and mints	£200	£525
Halfpennies, different types and mints	£20	£50
Farthings	£30	£75

3rd coinage 1344-51 (Florin Coinage)
Pennies, various types and mints	£25	£75
Halfpennies –	£20	£45
Farthings	£30	£70

Edward III 1327-77, Groat Treaty Period

4th coinage 1351-77

	F	VF
Groats, many types and mints from	£50	£175

Edward III halfgroat Post-Treaty

		F	VF
Halfgroats –	... ...	£35	£125
Pennies –	... ...	£20	£75
Halfpennies, different types	...	£25	£80
Farthings, a few types	... ...	£85	£250

Henry IV halfpenny

RICHARD II 1377-99

	F	VF
Groats, four types from	£350	£1200

Henry VI Annulet issue halfgroat

	F	VF
Halfgroats	£275	£800
Pennies, various types, London	£200	£550
Pennies, various types, York ...	£60	£225
Pennies, Durham	£150	£450
Halfpennies, three main types ...	£30	£85
Farthings, some varieties	£100	£300

HENRY IV 1399-1413

	F	VF
Groats, varieties ... ...from	£1450	£6000
Halfgroats –	£475	£1200
Pennies –	£250	£750
Halfpennies	£185	£525
Farthings –	£625	£1750

Henry V Groat

HENRY V 1413-22

		F	VF
Groats, varieties	... ...from	£150	£450
Halfgroats	... ...	£125	£375
Pennies	... ...	£35	£95
Halfpennies	... ...	£25	£80
Farthings	... ...	£175	£575

HENRY VI 1422-61
Annulet issue 1422-1427

		F	VF
Groats	... ...	£50	£120
Halfgroats	... ...	£30	£95
Pennies	... ...	£20	£80
Halfpennies	... ...	£20	£50
Farthings	... ...	£90	£225

Rosette-Mascle issue 1427-1430

		F	VF
Groats	... ...	£50	£125
Halfgroats	... ...	£40	£100
Pennies	... ...	£35	£90
Halfpennies	... ...	£20	£50
Farthings	... ...	£125	£350

Pinecone-Mascle 1430-1434

		F	VF
Groats	... ...	£50	£120
Halfgroats	... ...	£35	£90
Pennies	... ...	£30	£95
Halfpennies	... ...	£20	£50
Farthings	... ...	£125	£350

Leaf-Mascle issue 1434-1435

		F	VF
Groats	... ...	£120	£325
Halfgroats	... ...	£100	£300
Pennies	... ...	£65	£150
Halfpennies	... ...	£30	£75

Leaf-Trefoil 1435-1438

		F	VF
Groats	... ...	£70	£200
Halfgroats	... ...	£65	£165
Pennies	... ...	£60	£150
Halfpennies	... ...	£25	£60
Farthings	... ...	£125	£350

Trefoil 1438-1443

		F	VF
Groats	... ...	£85	£250
Halfgroats	... ...	£150	£350
Halfpennies	... ...	£25	£75

Trefoil-Pellet 1443-1445

		F	VF
Groats	... ...	£135	£400

Henry VI Groat, Leaf-Pellet issue

Leaf-Pellet 1445-1454

		F	VF
Groats	... ...	£70	£200
Halfgroats	... ...	£70	£175
Pennies	... ...	£40	£100
Halfpennies	... ...	£20	£50
Farthings	... ...	£135	£375

Unmarked 1445-1454

	F	VF
Groats	£425	£1200
Halfgroats	£325	£750

Cross-Pellet 1454-1460

Groats	£110	£300
Halfgroats	£275	£650
Pennies	£50	£120
Halfpennies	£30	£80
Farthings	£150	£425

Lis-Pellet 1454-1460

Groats	£225	£700

These are many different varieties, mintmarks and mints in this reign. These prices are for commonest prices in each issue.

EDWARD IV 1st Reign 1461-1470
Heavy coinage 1461-4

Groats, many classes, all London	£150	£350
Halfgroats, many classes, all London	£225	£500
Pennies, different classes. London, York and Durham	£135	£350
Halfpennies, different classes, all London	£40	£100
Farthings. London	£175	£500

Edward IV Groat. Light Coinage

Light coinage 1464-70

Groats, many different issues, varieties, *mms* and mints from	£45	£140
Halfgroats, ditto	£40	£125
Pennies, ditto	£30	£80
Halfpennies, ditto	£25	£70
Farthings Two issues	£225	£650

Henry VI (restored), Groat, London

HENRY VI (restored) 1470-71

Groats, different mints, *mms* from	£150	£450
Halfgroats – from	£225	£550
Pennies – from	£200	£525
Halfpennies – from	£90	£225

EDWARD IV 2nd reign 1471-83

	F	VF
Groats, different varieties, mints etc	£60	£150
Halfgroats	£35	£110
Pennies	£30	£90
Halfpennies	£25	£75

EDWARD IV or V 1483

mm halved sun and rose

Groats	£825	£2500
Pennies	£850	£3000
Halfpennies	£175	£500

RICHARD III 1483-85

Groat, reading **EDWARD,** *mm* boar's head on obverse, halved sun and

rose on reverse	£1250	£3250

Groats, reading **RICARD,** London and York mints, various combinations of

mms	£475	£1200
Halfgroats	£675	£1650
Pennies, York and Durham (London mint unique)	£175	£475
Halfpennies	£150	£400
Farthing	£850	£2500

PERKIN WARBECK, PRETENDER'

Groat, 1494 [cf. BNJ XXVI, p. 125]	£950	£3000

The Tudor Monarchs
HENRY VII 1485-1509
Facing bust issues:

Henry VII Groat London open crown type

Groats, all London

Open crown without arches ...	£110	£325
Crown with two arches unjewelled	£95	£225
Crown with two jewelled arches	£70	£175
Similar but only one arch jewelled	£60	£150
Similar but tall thin lettering ...	£70	£175
Similar but single arch, tall thin lettering	£80	£200

Halfgroats, London

Open crown without arches, tressure unbroken	£225	£650
Double arched crown	£45	£120

	F	VF
Unarched crown	£40	£100
Some varieties and different *mms.*		
Halfgroats, Canterbury		
Open crown, without arches ...	£40	£110
Double arched crown	£35	£90
Some varieties and different *mms.*		
Halfgroats, York		
Double arched crown	£40	£120
Unarched crown with tressure		
broken	£40	£110
Double arched crown with keys		
at side of bust	£35	£110
Many varieties and different mms.		
Pennies, facing bust type		
London	£150	£425
Canterbury, open crown	£225	£500
– arched crown	£60	£150
Durham, Bishop Sherwood		
(S on breast)	£60	£150
York	£45	£120
Many varieties and mms.		
Pennies, 'sovereign enthroned' type		
London, many varieties	£45	£120
Durham –	£40	£100
York –	£35	£90
Halfpennies, London		
Open crown	£45	£125
Arched crown	£30	£80
Crown with lower arch	£25	£65
Some varieties and mms.		
Halfpennies, Canterbury		
Open crown	£70	£175
Arched crown	£60	£125
Halfpennies, York		
Arched crown and key below bus	£65	£135
Farthings, all London	£175	£600
Profile issues:		
Testoons im lis, three different		
legends	£6500	£15000

Henry VII profile issue testoon

Groats, all London
Tentative issue (double band to

	F	VF
crown)	£185	£525

Henry VII Groat, Tentative issue

	F	VF
Regular issue (triple band to		
crown)	£120	£375
Some varieties, and *mms*		
Halfgroats		
London	£90	£275
– no numeral after king's name	£375	£900
Canterbury	£75	£225
York, two keys below shield ...	£70	£200
– XB by shield	£275	£750

HENRY VIII 1509-47
With portrait of Henry VII
1st coinage 1509-26

	F	VF
Groats, London	£120	£350
Groats, Tournai	£475	£1250
Groats, Tournai, without portrait	£1750	*
Halfgroats, London	£110	£300
Halfgroats, Canterbury, varieties	£70	£185
Halfgroats, York, varieties	£65	£175
Halfgroats, Tournai	£675	£2000
Pennies, 'sovereign enthroned'		
type, London	£50	£135
Pennies, Canterbury, varieties ...	£65	£185
Pennies, Durham, varieties ...	£40	£100
Halfpennies, facing bust type,		
London	£30	£70
Canterbury	£65	£175
Farthings, portcullis type, London	£250	£600

Henry VIII second coinage groat,
with Irish title HIB REX

With young portrait of Henry VIII
2nd coinage 1526-44

	F	VF
Groats, London, varieties, *mms*	£85	£285
Groats, Irish title, HIB REX	£275	£800
Groats, York *mms*	£95	£325
Halfgroats, London *mms*	£50	£135
Halfgroats, Canterbury *mms* ...	£45	£135
Halfgroats, York *mms*	£45	£135
Pennies 'sovereign enthroned' type		
London, varieties, *mms*	£35	£120
Canterbury, varieties, *mms* ...	£75	£225
Durham –	£35	£110
York	£175	£525

Henry VIII, Halfpenny, 2nd Coingage, London

	F	VF
Halfpennies, facing bust type		
London, varieties, *mms*	£25	£75
Canterbury	£40	£100
York	£65	£175
Farthings, portcullis type	£300	£700

HAMMERED SILVER

With old bearded portrait 3rd coinage 1544-47 Posthumous issues 1547-51	F	VF
Testoons (or shillings)		
London (Tower mint), varieties,		
mms	£700	£2400
Southwark, varieties, *mms* ...	£725	£2500
Bristol, varieties, *mms*	£825	£3000
Groats, six different busts,		
varieties, *mms*		
London (Tower mint)	£90	£325
Southwark	£90	£325
Bristol	£100	£350
Canterbury	£95	£300
London (Durham House)	£185	£500
York	£80	£250

Henry VIII third coinage groat

Halfgroats, only one style of bust (except York which has two), varieties, mms		
London (Tower mint)	£70	£200
Southwark	£80	£250
Bristol	£80	£250
Canterbury	£60	£175
York	£65	£185
London (Durham House)	£375	£900

Henry VIII Penny, 3rd Coinage Tower

Henry VIII Penny, 3rd Coinage, Bristol

Pennies (facing bust) varieties, mms		
London (Tower mint)	£40	£125
Southwark	£50	£150
London (Durham House)	£425	£1000
Bristol	£60	£165
Canterbury	£40	£120
York	£40	£120
Halfpennies (facing bust) varieties, mms		
London (Tower mint)	£40	£110
Bristol	£75	£225
Canterbury	£45	£125
York	£40	£110

EDWARD VI 1547-53 1st period 1547-49		
Shillings, London (Durham House),		
mm bow, patterns (?)		ext. rare
Groats, London (Tower),		
mm arrow	£800	£2500
Groats, London (Southwark),		
mm E, none	£750	£2250
Halfgroats, London (Tower),		
mm arrow	£425	£1000
Halfgroats, London (Southwark),		
mm arrow, E	£400	£950
Halfgroats, Canterbury, mm none	£345	£800
Pennies, London (Tower),		
mm	£350	£1000
Pennies, London (Southwark),		
mm E	£375	£1100
Pennies, Bristol,		
mm none	£325	£900
Halfpennies, London (Tower),		
mm uncertain	£350	£900
Halfpennies, Bristol, mm none	£325	£850

Edward VI 2nd period shilling. Tower mint with mintmark Y.

Edward VI, Shilling, 2nd period Canterbury with mintmark t.

2nd period 1549-50		
Shillings, London (Tower) various		
mms	£135	£525
Shillings, Bristol, mm TC	£750	£2250
Shillings, Canterbury, mm T or t	£165	£600
Shillings, London (Durham House),		
mm bow, varieties	£150	£550

3rd period £550-53		
Base silver (similar to issues of 2nd period)		
Shillings, London (Tower),		
mm lis, lion, rose	£150	£525
Pennies, London (Tower),		
mm escallop	£65	£180
Pennies, York, mm mullet	£60	£180
Halfpennies, London (Tower) ...	£175	£500

	F	VF

Fine Silver
Crown 1551 mm Y, 1551-53
mm tun **£700** **£1800**

Edward VI Halfcrown 1551, walking horse

	F	VF
Halfcrown, walking horse, 1551, mm Y	**£600**	**£1500**
Halfcrowns, galloping horse, 1551-52, mm tun	**£600**	**£1500**

Edward VI 1552 halfcrown galloping horse

	F	VF
Halfcrowns, walking horse, 1553, mm tun	**£975**	**£3500**
Shillings, mm Y, tun	**£110**	**£375**
Sixpences, London (Tower), mm y, tun	**£125**	**£500**
Sixpences, York, mm mullet ...	**£185**	**£650**
Threepences, London (Tower), mm tun	**£200**	**£675**
Threepences, York mm mullet ...	**£400**	**£1100**
Pennies, sovereign type	**£975**	**£3500**
Farthings, portcullis type	**£1250**	*

Mary Groat

Mary Portrait Penny

	F	VF
MARY 1553-54		
Groats, mm pomegranate	**£120**	**£400**
Halfgroats, similar	**£750**	**£2500**
Pennies, rev VERITAS TEMP FILIA ...	**£625**	**£2000**
Pennies, rev CIVITAS LONDON	**£625**	**£2000**
PHILIP AND MARY 1554-58		
Shillings, full titles, without date	**£325**	**£1100**
– also without XII	**£350**	**£1250**
– dated 1554	**£325**	**£1100**
– dated 1554, English titles ...	**£350**	**£1250**
– dated 1555, English titles only	**£325**	**£1200**
– dated 1554, English titles only also without XII	**£425**	**£1400**
– 1555, as last	**£650**	*
– 1554 but date below bust ...	**£1500**	*
– 1555 but date below bust ...	**£1500**	*
– 1555 similar to previous but without ANG	**£2000**	*
Sixpences, full titles, 1554	**£350**	**£1200**
– full titles, undated	ext rare	
– English titles, 1555	**£350**	**£1350**
– similar but date below bust, 1554	**£650**	*
– English titles, 1557	**£325**	**£1200**
– similar, but date below bust, 1557	**£1000**	*
Groats, mm lis	**£125**	**£400**
Halfgroats, mm lis	**£375**	**£1200**

Philip and Mary Shilling, 1554 and full titles

	F	VF
Pennies, mm lis	**£400**	**£1350**
Base pennies, without portrait	**£75**	**£225**

HAMMERED SILVER

	F	VF
ELIZABETH I 1558-1603		
Hammered coinage, 1st issue 1558-61		
Shillings ELIZABETH		
Wire-line circles	£425	£1600
Beaded inner circles	£150	£625
ET for Z	£100	£350

Edward VI shilling greyhound countermark (reign of Elizabeth), and Elizabeth I hammered groat

Groats		
Wire-line inner circles	£135	£550
Beaded inner circles	£75	£250
ET for Z	£50	£200
Halfgroats		
Wire-line inner circles	£135	£500
Beaded inner circles	£45	£135

Elizabeth I Penny, wire-line inner circle

Pennies		
Wire-line inner circles	£200	£700
Beaded inner circles	£30	£80
Countermarked shillings of Edward VI, 1560-61		
With portcullis mark (Current for 4½d) **(F)**	£2000	*
With greyhound mark (current for 2½d) **(F)**	£2500	*

Hammered coinage, 2nd issue 1561-82

	F	VF
Sixpences, dated 1561-82	£65	£180
Threepences, 1561-82	£45	£125
Halfgroats, undated	£50	£165
Threehalfpences, 1561-62, 1564-70, 1572-79, 1581-82	£40	£110
Pennies, undated	£25	£85
Threefarthings, 1561-62, 1568, 1572-78, 1581-82	£75	£185

Elizabeth I Halfcrown, 1601

Hammered coinage, 3rd issue 1583-1603

	F	VF
Crowns, im **1**	£1250	£3000
Crowns, im **2**	£1500	£4500
Halfcrowns, im **1**	£700	£1750
Halfcrowns, im **2 (F)**	£1750	£6000
Shillings ELIZAB	£85	£325
Sixpences, 1582-1602	£55	£175
Halfgroats, E D G ROSA etc	£25	£70
Pennies	£25	£70
Halfpennies, portcullis type ...	£25	£75

There are many different mintmarks, such as lis, bell, lion etc., featured on the hammered coins of Elizabeth I, and these marks enable one to date those coins which are not themselves dated. For more details see J.J. North's English Hammered Coinage, *Volume 2.*

Elizabeth I Miled Coinage, Sixpence, 1562

Milled Coinage

Shillings		
large size	£350	£1000
Intermediate	£250	£650
Small	£225	£550
Sixpences		
1561	£100	£350
1562	£85	£325
1563-64, 1566	£90	£325
1567-68	£85	£300
1570-71	£275	£850
Groats, undated	£150	£500
Threepences, 1561, 1562-64 ...	£110	£350
Halfgroats	£175	£550
Threefarthings ... ... ext.rare		*

The Stuart Kings

JAMES I 1603-25

	F	VF
1st coinage 1603-04		
Crowns, rev EXURGAT etc	£850	£2750
Halfcrowns –	£950	£3250
Shillings, varieties	£85	£300
Sixpences, dated 1603-04,		
varieties	£60	£200
Halfgroats, undated	£25	£75
Pennies –	£20	£60

James I Sixpence, 1603

2nd coinage 1604-19

	F	VF
Crowns rev QVAE DEVS etc ...	£750	£2500
Halfcrowns –	£1200	£3500

James I 2nd coinage shilling

	F	VF
Shillings, varieties	£75	£250
Sixpences, dated 1604-15,		
varieties etc.	£50	£175
Halfgroats, varieties	£20	£50
Pennies	£20	£50
Halfpennies	£15	£45

James I Shilling, 3rd Coinage

3rd coinage 1619-25

	F	VF
Crowns	£600	£1500
– Plume over reverse shield ...	£750	£2000
Halfcrowns	£225	£675
– Plume over reverse shield ...	£350	£1000

James I halfcrown with plume over shield on reverse

	F	VF
Shillings	£85	£300
– Plume over reverse shield ...	£175	£675
Sixpences dated 1621-24	£65	£200
Halfgroats	£20	£50
Pennies	£15	£40
Halfpennies	£15	£35

James I sixpence of 1622

CHARLES I 1625-1649
Tower Mint 1625-1643
Crowns
(Obv. King on horseback. Rev. shield)

	F	VF
1st horseman/square shield		
im lis, cross calvary	£675	£1750
As last/plume above shield		
im lis, cross calvary, castle ...	£1000	£2750
2nd horseman/oval shield		
im plume, rose harp.		
Some varieties, from	£600	£1450
3rd horseman/round shield		
im bell, crown, tun, anchor,		
triangle, star, portcullis, triangle		
in circle. Some varieties, from	£600	£1450

Halfcrowns
(Obv. King on horseback. Rev. shield)

*Charles I
Tower halfcrown:
first horseman*

HAMMERED SILVER

	F	VF
1st horseman/square shield		
im lis, cross calvary, negro's head, castle, anchor.		
Many varieties, from	£200	£600
2nd horseman/oval shield		
im plume, rose, harp, portcullis.		
Many varieties, from	£100	£325
3rd horseman/round shield		
im bell, crown, tun, portcullis, anchor, triangle, star		
Many varieties, from	£75	£200
4th horseman/round shield		
im star, triangle in circle	£60	£150

Charles I
Tower Halfcrown,
mintmark
triangle

Shillings

	F	VF
1st bust/square shield		
***im* lis, cross calvary**		
Some varieties	£100	£400
2nd bust/square shield		
im cross calvary, negro's head, castle, anchor, heart, plume		
Many varieties, from	£85	£375
3rd bust/oval shield		
im plume, rose	£60	£225
4th bust/oval or round shield		
im harp, portcullis, bell, crown, tun		
Many varieties, from	£50	£175
5th bust/square shield		
im tun, anchor, triangle		
Many varieties, from	£45	£175
6th bust/square shield		
im anchor, triangle, star, triangle in circle		
Some varieties, from	£40	£150

Sixpences
(early ones are dated)

	F	VF
1st bust/square shield, date above		
1625 *im* lis, cross calvary		
1626 *im* cross calvary	£90	£325
2nd bust/square shield, date above		
1625, 1626 *im* cross calvary		
1626, 1627 *im* negro's head		
1626, 1628 *im* castle		
1628, 1629 *im* anchor		
1629 *im* heart		
1630 *im* heart, plume	£100	£400

	F	VF
3rd bust/oval shield		
im plume, rose	£65	£225
4th bust/oval or round shield		
im harp, portcullis, bell, crown, tun	£45	£150

Charles I Tower sixpence mm bell

	F	VF
5th bust/square shield		
im tun, anchor, triangle		
Many varieties, from	£50	£200
6th bust/square shield		
im triangle, star	£50	£185
Halfgroats		
Crowned rose both sides		
im lis, cross calvary, blackamoor's head	£25	£75
2nd bust/oval shield		
im plume, rose	£25	£80
3rd bust/oval shield		
im rose, plume	£25	£80
4th bust/oval or round shield,		
im harp, crown, portcullis, bell, tun, anchor, triangle, star		
Many varieties from	£20	£50
5th bust/round shield		
im anchor	£30	£90
Pennies		
Uncrowned rose both sides		
im one or two pellets, lis, negro's head	£20	£50
2nd bust/oval shield		
im plume	£25	£75
3rd bust/oval shield		
im plume, rose	£20	£50
4th bust/oval shield		
im harp, one or two pellets, portcullis, bell, triangle	£15	£45
5th bust/round shield		
im one or two pellets, none	£15	£45
Halfpennies		
Uncrowned rose both sides		
im none	£15	£40

Tower Mint, under Parliament 1643-48

Crowns
(Obv. King on horseback, Rev. shield)

	F	VF
4th horseman/round shield		
im (**P**), (**R**), eye sun	£700	£1750
5th horseman/round shield		
im sun, sceptre	£800	£1850

Halfcrowns
(Obv. King on horseback, Rev. shield)

	F	VF
3rd horseman/round shield		
im (**P**), (**R**), eye sun	£50	£200
im (**P**), foreshortened horse	£175	£550
5th horseman (tall)/round shield		
im sun, sceptre	£75	£225

Charles I Parliament shilling, mm eye

Sixpence of Broit's 2nd milled issue

	F	VF
Briot's hammered issues 1638-39		
im: anchor, triangle over anchor		
Halfcrowns	£750	£1850
Shillings	£350	£900

	F	VF
Shillings (revs. all square shield)		
6th bust (crude)		
im (**P**), (**R**), eye, sun	£45	£165
7th bust (tall, slim)		
im sun, sceptre	£50	£200
8th bust (shorter, older)		
im sceptre	£65	£275
Sixpences (revs. all square shield)		
6th bust		
im (**P**), (**R**), eye sun	£75	£225
7th bust		
im (**R**), eye, sun, sceptre ...	£65	£200
8th bust, (crude style)		
im eye, sun	£125	£375
Halfgroats		
4th bust/round shield		
im (**P**), (**R**), eye sceptre ...	£20	£70
7th bust (old/round shield)		
im eye, sun, sceptre	£20	£70
Pennies		
7th bust/oval shield		
im one or two pellets	£25	£75

*Charles I
Crown
of Exeter*

PROVINCIAL MINTS

York 1642-44		
im: lion		
Halfcrowns, varieties from	£275	£750
Shillings –	£225	£600
Sixpences –	£250	£675
Threepences	£65	£175

Aberystwyth 1638-42		
im: open book		
Halfcrowns, varieties from	£850	£3000
Shillings –	£375	£1000
Sixpences –	£325	£800
Groats –	£60	£175

Charles I Briot's crown

Aberystwyth groat

Briot's 1st milled issued 1631-32		
im: flower and **B**		
Crowns	£750	£1850
Halfcrowns...	£425	£1350
Shillings	£325	£700
Sixpences	£125	£375
Halfgroats	£60	£125
Pennies	£65	£165

Briot's 2nd milled issue 1638-39		
im: anchor, anchor and B, anchor and mullet		
Halfcrowns	£275	£800
Shillings	£150	£425
Sixpences	£75	£200

Threepences –	£45	£125
Halfgroats –	£50	£150
Pennies –	£70	£200
Halfpennies	£175	£500

Aberystwyth – Furnace 1647-48		
im: crown		
Halfcrowns from	£1850	£5000
Shillings	£2500	*

HAMMERED SILVER

	F	VF
Sixpences	£1250	£2750
Groats	£250	£575
Threepences	£225	£500
Halfgroats	£275	£800
Pennies	£675	£1850

Shrewsbury 1642
mm: plume without band

Pounds, varieties from	£2000	£4500
Halfpounds –	£850	£2000
Crowns –	£850	£2250
Halfcrowns –	£525	£1400
Shillings –	£875	£2250

Oxford 1642-46
mm: plume with band

Pounds, varieties from	£1850	£4500
Halfpounds –	£800	£2000
Crowns –	£750	£2000
Halfcrowns –	£250	£750
Shillings –	£275	£800
Sixpences –	£225	£700
Groats –	£135	£350
Threepences –	£100	£250
Halfgroats –	£110	£300
Pennies –	£185	£500

Bristol 1643-45
im: Bristol monogram, acorn, plumelet

Halfcrowns, varieties from	£350	£850

Charles I halfcrown of York with mm lion

Shillings –	£300	£800
Sixpences –	£250	£675
Groats –	£175	£450
Threepences –	£175	£475
Halfgroats –	£275	£650
Pennies –	£425	£950

Charles I sixpence, Bristol 1644

A, B, and plumes issues
Associated with Thomas Bushell; previously assigned to Lundy

Halfcrowns, varieties from	£925	£2750

	F	VF
Shillings –	£400	£1200
Sixpences –	£225	£600
Groats –	£200	£500
Threepences –	£175	£450
Halfgroats –	£475	£1000

Truro 1642-43
im: rose, bugle

Crowns, varieties	£350	£850
Halfcrowns –	£900	£2500
Shillings –	£3000	*

Bristol shilling 1644

Exeter 1643-46
im Ex, rose, castle

Halfpounds		ext. rare
Crowns, varieties	£400	£850
Halfcrowns	£300	£700
Shillings	£350	£850
Sixpences	£325	£750
Groats	£125	£300
Threepences	£125	£300
Halfgroats –	£250	£650
Pennies	£350	£950

Worcester 1643-4
im: castle, helmet, leopard's head, lion, two lions, lis, rose, star

Halfcrowns, many varieties ...	£750	£2000

Salopia (Shrewsbury) 1644
im: helmet, lis, rose (in legend)

Halfcrowns, many varieties ...	£850	£2250

Worcester or Salopia (Shrewsbury)
im: bird, boar's head, lis, castle, cross, and annulets, helmet, lion, lis, pear, rose, scroll

Shillings, varieties	£950	£2750
Sixpences	£825	£2250
Groats	£575	£1350
Threepences	£325	£750
Halfgroats	£525	£1250

'HC' mint (probably Hartlebury Castle, Worcester 1646)
im: pear, three pears

Halfcrowns	£1500	£3500

Chester 1644
im: cinquefoil, plume, prostrate gerb, three gerbs

Halfcrowns, varieties	£750	£2500
Shillings	£1350	*
Threepences	£850	£2000

Welsh Marches mint? 1644

	F	VF
Halfcrowns...	£800	£1750

Welsh Marches mint, halfcrown

SIEGE PIECES
Carlisle besieged 1644-45

	F	VF
Three shillings	£5750	£13500
Shillings (**F**)	£4500	£9000

Newark besieged many times
(surrendered May 6, 1646)

	F	VF
Halfcrowns, 1645-46 (**F**)	£700	£1500

Newark Besieged, Shilling, dated 1645

	F	VF
Shillings, 1645-46, varieties (**F**)	£500	£1100
Ninepences, 1645-46	£475	£950
Sixpences	£525	£1250

Pontefract besieged 1648-49

	F	VF
Two shillings, 1648	£5250	£15000
Shillings, 1648, varieties	£1350	£3250

Ponefract Besieged 1648, Siege Shilling

Scarborough besieged 1644-45
Many odd values issued here, all of which are
extremely rare. The coin's value was decided by
the intrinsic value of the piece of metal from which
it was made.

HAMMERED SILVER

	F	VF

Examples: 5s 8d, 2s 4d, 1s 9d, 1s 3d, 7d etc. (**F**).
Collectors could expect to pay at least **£6250** or
more in F and **£15000** in VF for any of these.

COMMONWEALTH 1649-60

	F	VF
Crowns, *im* sun 1649,51-54, 56 ...	£725	£1500
Halfcrowns, *im* sun 1649, 1651-6	£250	£600
—*im* anchor 1658-60	£850	£2250

Commonwealth Shilling, 1651

	F	VF
Shillings, *im* sun 1649, 1661-87	£150	£350
—*im* anchor 1658-60	£575	£1350

A superb 1651 sixpence

	F	VF
Sixpences, *im* sun 1649, 1651-7	£125	£325
—*im* anchor 1658-6	£475	£1000
Halfgroats undated	£30	£90
Pennies undated	£25	£70
Halfpennies undated	£25	£70

CHARLES II 1660-85
Hammered coinage 1660-62

	F	VF
Halfcrowns, three issues ... from	£250	£675
Shillings— ... ... from	£150	£475

Charles II hammered issue shilling

	F	VF
Sixpences—	£135	£400
Fourpences, third issue only ...	£30	£80
Threepences— ... ... from	£30	£70
Twopences, three issues from	£25	£65
Pennies— ... ... from	£25	£65

'ROYAL' AND 'ROSE' BASE METAL FARTHINGS

Until 1613 English coins were struck only in gold or silver — the monarchy considered that base metal issues would be discreditable to the royal prerogative of coining. However, silver coins had become far too small, farthings so tiny that they had to be discontinued. So to meet demands for small change James I authorised Lord Harington to issue copper farthing tokens. Subsequently this authority passed in turn to the Duke of Lennox, the Duchess of Richmond and Lord Maltravers. It ceased by order of Parliament in 1644.

	Fair	F	VF	EF
JAMES I **Royal farthing tokens**				
Type 1 Harington (circa 1613). Small copper flan with tin-washed surface, mint-mark between sceptres below crown	£10	£30	£75	£150
Type 2 Harington (circa 1613). Larger flan, no tin wash	£15	£15	£40	£90
Type 3 Lennox (1614-25). IACO starts at 1 o'clock position	£3	£10	£25	£75
Type 4 Lennox (1622-25). Oval flan, IACO starts at 7 o'clock	£8	£25	£65	£140
CHARLES I **Royal farthing tokens**				
Type 1 Richmond (1625-34). Single arched crown	£2	£8	£25	£65
Type 2 Transitional (circa 1634). Double arched crown	£6	£20	£50	£125
Type 3 Maltravers (1634-36). Inner circles	£3	£10	£30	£75
Type 4 Richmond (1625-34). As Type 1 but oval	£8	£25	£60	£140
Type 5 Maltravers (1634-36). Double arched crown	£10	£30	£70	£120
Rose farthing tokens (rose on reverse)				
Type 1 Small thick flan	£3	£10	£30	£80
Type 2 Same, but single arched crown	£2	£7	£25	£75
Type 3 Same, but sceptres below crown	£10	£25	£50	£90

James I Harington farthings, types 1, 2 and 3 (left to right)

Charles I Richmond, Maltravers and Rose farthings (left to right)

MILLED COINAGE from 1656

Again it must be stressed that the prices shown in this guide are the approximate amounts collectors can expect to pay for coins — they are not dealers' buying prices. Information for this guide is drawn from auction results and dealers' lists, with the aim of determining firm valuations. Prices still vary enormously from sale to sale and from one dealer's list to another. Allowance must also be made for the variance in the standards of grading. The prices given here aim at a reasonable assessment of the market at the time of compilation, but they are not the product of computers, which would, in any case, provide only average (not necessarily accurate) prices. It is not possible to forecast such values because of the erratic fluctuations that can occur, not only in boom conditions but also during times of economic uncertainty, and an annual catalogue of this type cannot be up to date on the bullion prices of common sovereigns, for example. If you are buying or selling bullion gold coins, refer to current quotations from bullion dealers.

With some denominations in the silver and copper series, column headings indicating condition change at the beginning of the lists of George III coins. The condition (grade) of a coin is of great importance in determining its market value. Notes on grading and on abbreviations etc. used in these price guides appear elsewhere in this publication.

Cromwell gold patterns

These were struck by order of Cromwell, with the consent of the Council. The dies were made by Thomas Simon, and the coins were struck on Peter Blondeau's machine. The fifty shillings and the broad were struck from the same dies, but the fifty shillings has the edge inscription PROTECTOR LITERIS LITERAE NUMMIS CORONA ER SALUS, while the broad is not so thick and has a grained edge. No original strikings of the half broad are known, but some were struck from dies made by John Tanner in 1738. All three denominations are dated 1656.

Oliver Cromwell gold half broad 1656

	F	VF	EF	Unc
Fifty shillings	*	£20000	£35000	*
Broad	*	£4750	£11000	£16000
Half broad	*	£4500	£8000	*

Five guineas

CHARLES II	F	VF	EF	Unc
1668-78 pointed end to trnctn of bust ...	£1750	£2750	£8000	*
1668, 69, 75—eleph below bust	£1750	£2750	£8000	15000
1675-8—eleph & castle below bust	£1750	£2750	£8000	*
1678-84 rounded end to trnctn	£1750	£2250	£7000	*
1680-4—eleph & castle	£1875	£3000	£8000	*
JAMES II				
1686 sceptres in wrong order on rev ...	£1750	£2750	£8500	*
1687-8 sceptres correct	£1750	£2750	£8500	*
1687-8 eleph & castle	£1750	£3000	£8500	*
WILLIAM AND MARY				
1691-4 no prov mark	£1900	£3000	£7500	*
1691-4 eleph & castle	£2000	£3250	£8000	*
WILLIAM III				
1699-1700 no prov mark	£1750	£2500	£7500	*
1699 eleph & castle	£1850	£2900	£8000	*
1701 new bust 'fine work'	£1750	£2500	£7000	£9000

Charles II 1676 five guineas, elephant and castle

George II 1729 five guineas

Charles II 1664 two guineas elephant below bust

James II 1687 two guineas

ANNE	F	VF	EF	Unc
Pre-Union with Scotland				
1703 VIGO below bust	*	*	£60000	*
1705-6 plain below	£2000	£3750	£9500	*
Post-Union with Scotland				
1706	£1750	£3000	£9500	£17500
1709 Larger lettering, wider shield and				
crowns	£1750	£3000	£8500	*
1711, 1713-4 broader bust	£1750	£3000	£9500	*

Pre-Union reverses have separate shields (top and right) for England and Scotland. Post-Union reverses have the English and Scottish arms side by side on the top and bottom shields.

GEORGE I	F	VF	EF	Unc
1716, 17, 20, 26	£2000	£3500	£14000	*

GEORGE II	F	VF	EF	Unc
1729, 31, 35, 38, 41 YH	£1700	£2250	£5750	£7500
1729 E,I,C, below head	£1700	£2500	£6250	£8000
1746 OH, lima below	£1700	£2750	£6250	£8500
1748, 53 plain below	£1700	£2750	£6250	£8500

GEORGE III	F	VF	EF	Unc
1770, 73, 77 patterns only	*	*	£35000	£70000

Two guineas

CHARLES II	F	VF	EF	Unc
1664, 5, 9, 71 pointed end to trnctn	£875	£1850	£6500	*
1664 elephant below	£875	£1850	£6500	*
1675-84 rounded end to trnctn	£800	£1750	£5000	£9500
1676, 78, 82-84 eleph & castle below bust	£900	£2000	£6750	*
1678 elephant below				ext. rare

JAMES II	F	VF	EF	Unc
1687	£900	£2500	£7000	*
1688/9	£1000	£2750	£8000	*

WILLIAM AND MARY	F	VF	EF	Unc
1691, 3, 4 eleph & castle	£950	£1850	£6000	*
1693, 4 no prov mark	£850	£1750	£5250	£7500

WILLIAM III	F	VF	EF	Unc
1701	£1000	£2750	£4750	*

ANNE	F	VF	EF	Unc
(none struck before Union)				
1709, 11, 13, 14	£750	£1750	£3250	£6000

GEORGE I	F	VF	EF	Unc
1717,20,26	£700	£1500	£3250	£4750

GEORGE II	F	VF	EF	Unc
1734, 5, 8, 9,YH (**F**)	£500	£750	£2000	£3500
1739, 40 intermediate head (**F**)	£550	£800	£2250	£3000
1748, 53 OH	£575	£875	£2500	£3500

GEORGE III	F	VF	EF	Unc
1768, 73, 77 patterns only	*	*	£14000	£20000

Guineas

CHARLES II	F	VF	EF	Unc
1663 pointed trnctn	£625	£2250	£7500	*
1663—eleph	£625	£2250	£7500	*
1664 trnctn indented	£625	£2250	£6500	*
1664—eleph	*	*ext. rare		*

GUINEAS

Charles II 1663 guinea elephant below bust

Anne 1713 guinea

George III 1768 guinea

	F	VF	EF	Unc
1664-73 sloping pointed trnctn	£650	£1650	£5000	*
1664, 5, 8 — eleph	£800	£2250	£5750	*
1672-84 rounded trnctn	£525	£1375	£4250	*
1674-84 — eleph & castle	£750	£2000	£6500	*
1677, 8 — eleph			ext. rare	

JAMES II
	F	VF	EF	Unc
1685, 6 1st bust	£475	£1200	£3000	£5750
1685 — eleph & castle	£500	£1250	£3750	*
1686-8 2nd bust	£500	£1200	£3000	£5750
1686-8 — eleph & castle	£500	£1250	£3500	*

WILLIAM AND MARY
	F	VF	EF	Unc
1689-94 no prov mark	£500	£1250	£4000	£6000
1689-94 eleph & castle	£525	£1500	£4250	*
1692 eleph	£700	£1750	£4750	*

WILLIAM III
	F	VF	EF	Unc
1695, 6 1st bust	£400	£850	£2850	£4000
1695, 7 — eleph & castle	*	*	*	*
1697-1701 2nd bust	£350	£850	£2850	*
1698-1701 — eleph & castle	£650	£2250	*	*
1701 3rd bust 'fine work'	£500	£1000	£4000	*

ANNE
Pre-Union[1]
	F	VF	EF	Unc
1702, 1705-7 plain below bust	£450	£850	£3000	£5000
1703 VIGO below	£3750	£8000	£20000	*

Post Union[1]
	F	VF	EF	Unc
1707, 8 1st bust	£425	£750	£1650	£2950
1707 — eleph & castle	£650	£1750	£4250	*
1707-9 2nd bust	£425	£850	£1650	£2950
1708-9 — eleph & castle	£700	£1650	£4500	*
1710-1714 3rd bust	£425	£650	£1650	£2500

[1]See note in prices of five guinea pieces for Anne.

GEORGE I
	F	VF	EF	Unc
1714 1st head PR. EL. (Prince Elector) in rev legend	*	£1750	£3000	£4500
1715 2nd head, tie with two ends	£325	£750	£1750	£3000
1715 3rd head, hair not curling round trnctn	£275	£650	£1800	£2850
1716-23 4th head, tie with loop	£250	£600	£1800	£2850
1721, 2 — eleph & castle	*		ext. rare	
1723-7 5th head, smaller, older bust	£275	£650	£1800	£2850
1726 — eleph & castle	£800	£2500	*	*

GEORGE II
	F	VF	EF	Unc
1727 1st YH, small lettering	£700	£1250	£3250	£4500
1727, 8 — larger lettering	£475	£1000	£3000	*
1729-32 2nd YH (narrower)	£400	£825	£2750	*
1729, 31, 2 — E.I.C. below	£475	£1250	£3250	£4500
1732-8 — larger lettering	£320	£700	£2250	£3000
1732 — — E.I.C. below	£600	£1250	£3500	*
1739, 40, 43 intermediate head	£300	£625	£1950	£2650
1739 — E.I.C. below	£500	£850	£3250	*
1745, 6 — larger lettering	£285	£625	£2000	*
1745 — LIMA below	£1500	£3000	£5250	*
1747-53, 5, 6, 8, 9, 60, OH	£300	£525	£1500	£2500

GEORGE III
	F	VF	EF	Unc
1761, 1st head	£600	£1500	£3000	£4000
1763, 4, 2nd head	£300	£850	£2250	*
1765-73, 3rd head	£225	£375	£900	£1500
1774-9, 81-6, 4th head	£175	£300	£625	£900
1789-99, 5th head, 'spade' rev (F)	£165	£275	£500	£750
1813, 6th head, rev shield in Garter ('Military guinea')	£425	£850	£1500	£2000

William and Mary 1691 half guinea

William III 1695 half guinea

George I 1719 half guinea

George I half guinea, 1725

George II 1756 half guinea

George III 1788 half guinea with 'spade' type shield on reverse

George I 1718 quarter guinea

Half Guineas

CHARLES II	F	VF	EF	Unc
1669-72 bust with pointed trnctn	£500	£925	£3250	*
1672-84 rounded trnctn...	£500	£925	£3500	*
1676-8, 80, 82-4 — eleph & castle	£550	£1200	£4000	*

JAMES II				
1686-8 no prov mark	£425	£900	£2650	*
1686 eleph & castle	£1250	*	*	*

WILLIAM AND MARY				
1689 1st busts	£650	£1500	£3250	*
1690-4 2nd busts	£600	£1200	£3750	*
1691-2 — eleph & castle	£650	£1275	£4000	*
1692 — eleph				ext. rare

WILLIAM III				
1695 no prov mark	£200	£550	£1850	£2750
1695, 6 eleph & castle	£425	£825	£2500	*
1697-1701 larger harp on rev	£250	£600	£2000	*
1698 — eleph & castle	£350	£750	£2500	*

ANNE				
Pre-Union[1]				
1702, 5 plain below bust	£425	£1200	£3250	*
1703 VIGO below	£3250	£7500	£15000	*
Post-Union[1]				
1707-14 plain	£250	£600	£1750	£2500

[1]See note in prices of five guineas for Anne.

GEORGE I				
1715, 17-24, 1st head...	£200	£450	£1000	£2000
1721 eleph & castle...	*	*	*	*
1725-7, smaller older head...	£175	£375	£900	£2000

GEORGE II				
1728-39 YH	£325	£650	£1750	*
1729-32, 9 — E.I.C. below	£450	£1200	£2750	*
1740, 3, 5, 6, intermediate head	£375	£800	£2250	*
1745 — LIMA below	£1250	£2500	£4750	*
1747-53, 5, 6, 58-60 OH	£250	£425	£1100	£1650

GEORGE III				
1762, 3, 1st head	£400	£875	£2250	*
1764-6, 8, 9, 72-5, 2nd head	£200	£400	£850	£1250
1774, 5, 3rd head	£600	£1500	£2750	*
1775-9, 81, 83-6, 4th head	£110	£200	£400	£800
1787-91, 93-8, 1800, 5th head	£100	£165	£325	£450
1801-3, 6th head	£90	£135	£275	£450
1804, 6, 8-11, 13, 7th head	£80	£135	£250	£400

Third guineas

GEORGE III	F	VF	EF	Unc
1797-1800 1st head	£60	£85	£200	£300
1801-3 — date close to crown on reverse	£60	£85	£200	£300
1804, 6, 8-11, 2nd head	£60	£80	£200	£300

Quarter guineas

GEORGE I	F	VF	EF	Unc
1718	£70	£150	£275	£425

GEORGE III	F	VF	EF	Unc
1762	£70	£150	£275	£425

COINS MARKET VALUES

Britannias
(See under Decimal Coinage)

Five pounds

	F	VF	EF	Unc
GEORGE III				
1820 pattern (F)	*	*	*	£50000
GEORGE IV				
1826 proof	*	*	£7000	£10000
VICTORIA				
1839 proof with 'Una and				
the Lion' rev (F)	*	*	£16000	£25000
1887 JH (F)	£375	£475	£600	£900
1887 proof	*	*	£1450	£2750
1887 proof no B.P.	*	*	£1500	£3000
1893 OH (F)	£400	£600	£875	£1500
1893 proof	*	*	£1500	£2850
EDWARD VII				
1902 (F)	£350	£450	£550	£850
1902 proof	*	*	£600	£850
GEORGE V				
1911 proof (F) ...	*	*	£950	£1500
GEORGE VI				
1937 proof	*	*	*	£725

ELIZABETH II
In 1984 the Royal Mint issued the first of an annual issue of Brilliant Uncirculated £5 coins. These bear the symbol 'U' in a circle to the left of the date on the reverse to indicate the standard of striking.

1981 proof	£400
1984	£400
1985	£425
1986	£425
1987 new effigy	£425
1988	£425
1989 500th anniversary of the sovereign, BU ...	£450
1990 Queen Mother's 90th birthday, proof	£575
1990	£435
1991	£450
1992	£450
1993 Coronation, proof	£700
1993	£475
1994	£500
1995	£535
1996 Queen's 70th Birthday, proof	£645
... ... BU	£575
1997 Golden Wedding, proof	£650
1997	£535
1998 Prince Charles 50th Birthday, proof	£600
1998 New Portrait	£535
1999 Diana Memorial, proof	£600
1999 Millennium, proof	£600
1999	£450
2000 Millennium, proof	£495
2000 Queen Mother Centenary, proof	£495
2000	£450
2001 Victorian Anniversary, proof	£525
2001 as above, reverse frosting, proof	£750
2001	£400
2002 Golden Jubilee, proof	£600
2002 Shield reverse, proof	£600
2002 Queen Mother memorial	£600
2003 Coronation Jubilee, proof	£560
2004 Entente Cordial, proof	£560

Two pounds

	F	VF	EF	Unc
GEORGE III				
1820 pattern (F)	*	*	£7500	£13500

George III 1820 pattern two pounds

	F	VF	EF	Unc
GEORGE IV ...				
1823 St George				
on reverse (F)	£375	£500	£750	£1500
1826 proof, shield				
reverse	*	*	£2250	£3750

William IV 1831 proof two pounds

	F	VF	EF	Unc
WILLIAM IV				
1831 proof	*	*	£3750	£6000
VICTORIA				
1887 JH (F) ...	£185	£220	£325	£425
1887 proof	*	*	£650	£1100
1893 OH (F) ...	£220	£300	£425	£700
1893 proof	*	*	£750	£1250
EDWARD VII				
1902 (F)	£175	£225	£325	£400
1902 proof	*	*	£300	£375
GEORGE V				
1911 proof (F)	*	*	*	£500

1937 proof two pounds

	F	VF	EF	Unc
GEORGE VI				
1937 proof ...	*	*	*	£425

TWO POUNDS

ELIZABETH II	F	VF	EF	Unc
1983 proof				£225
1986 Commonwealth Games, proof				£225
1987 proof				£250
1988 proof				£250
1989 500th anniversary of the sovereign, proof				£275
1990 proof				£250
1991 proof				£250
1993 proof				£250
1994 gold proof				£425
1994 gold proof 'mule'				£750
1995 VE day gold proof				£375
1995 50th Anniversary of UN, proof				£300
1996 European Football Championship				£350
1997 Bimetal gold proof				£350
1998 New portrait, proof				£300
1999 Rugby World Cup...				£300
2000 proof				£275
2001 Marconi, proof...				£295
2002 Shield reverse, proof				£300
2003 DNA bi-colour proof				£295
2004 Locomotive proof				£325
2005 2nd W.War proof				£325

Sovereigns

GEORGE III	F	VF	EF	Unc
1817 (F) £165		£300	£875	£1375
1818 ... ...£185		£350	£900	£1500
1819 ... ...£12500		£25000	£55000	*
1820 ... ...£165		£325	£900	£1375

GEORGE III
Type Laureate head/St George

	F	VF	EF	Unc
1821 ... ...£150		£275	£875	£1500
1821 proof ... ...*		*	£1500	£3000
1822 (F) £150		£275	£875	£1500
1823 ... ...£275		£1000	£3250	*
1824 ... ...£150		£275	£875	£1500
1825 ... ...£250		£800	£2500	*

Type bare head/shield

	F	VF	EF	Unc
1825 (F) ...	£180	£295	£775	£1350
1826	£180	£295	£775	£1375
1826 proof	*	*	£1200	£2500
1827 (F)	£180	£295	£800	£1300
1828 (F)	£1250	£3000	£10000	*
1829	£180	£295	£775	£1375
1830	£180	£295	£775	£1375

WILLIAM IV

	F	VF	EF	Unc
1831	£200	£375	£900	£1500
1831 proof	*	*	£1500	£2750

William IV 1831 proof sovereign

		F	VF	EF	Unc
1832 (F)		£200	£300	£850	£1500
1833		£200	£325	£850	£1600
1835		£200	£300	£850	£1500
1836		£200	£300	£850	£1500
1837		£200	£300	£850	£1600

VICTORIA
Type 1, YH obv, shield rev

	F	VF	EF	Unc
1838	£90	£375	£800	£1750

Victoria 1839 proof sovereign

	F	VF	EF	Unc
1839	£125	£500	£1200	£2500
1839 proof	*	*	£1200	£3000
1841	£800	£1650	£4500	*
1842	*	*	£150	£350
1843	*	*	£150	£350
1843 narrow shield	£2500	£4000	*	*
1844	*	*	£165	£325
1845	*	*	£165	£325
1846	*	*	£165	£325
1847	*	*	£165	£325
1848	*	*	£165	£325
1849	*	*	£165	£325
1850	*	*	£165	£325
1851	*	*	£165	£325
1852	*	*	£165	£325
1853	*	*	£150	£300

Victoria 1853 sovereign, shield on reverse

	F	VF	EF	Unc
1853 proof	*	*	£4000	£6500
1854	*	*	£150	£325
1855	*	*	£150	£325
1856	*	*	£150	£325
1857	*	*	£150	£325
1858	*	*	£165	£350
1859	*	*	£125	£275
1859 'Ansell' ...	£200	£700	£2750	*
1860	*	*	£165	£350
1861	*	*	£150	£300
1862	*	*	£150	£300
1863	*	*	£150	£300
1863 die number below wreath on rev	*	*	£150	£250
1863 '827' on truncation ...	£2000	£3500	*	*
1864 die no. ...	*	*	£140	£250
1865 die no. ...	*	*	£140	£250
1866 die no. ...	*	*	£140	£250
1868 die no. ...	*	*	£140	£250
1869 die no. ...	*	*	£140	£250
1870 die no. ...	*	*	£140	£250
1871 die no. ...	*	*	£140	£225
1871 S (Sydney mint) below wreath	*	*	£120	£600
1872	*	*	£120	£200
1872 die no. ...	*	*	£120	£175
1872 M (Melbourne mint) below wreath	*	*	£110	£350
1872 S	*	*	£250	£900
1873 die no. ...	*	*	£140	£225
1873 S	*	*	£110	£600
1874 die no. ...	£700	£1750	£4000	*
1874 M	*	*	£150	£700
1875 S	*	*	£125	£600
1877 S	*	*	£100	£450

	F	VF	EF	Unc
1878 S	*	*	£95	£450
1879 S	*	*	£95	£450
1880 M	£200	£850	£1450	£2500
1880 S	*	*	£110	£800
1881 M	*	*	£125	£800
1881 S	*	*	£100	£450
1882 M	*	*	£95	£450
1882 S	*	*	£95	£450
1883 M	*	£150	£450	£1500
1883 S	*	*	£100	£450
1884 M	*	*	£100	£450
1884 S	*	*	£100	£400
1885 M	*	*	£100	£400
1885 S	*	*	£100	£400
1886 M	£400	£1750	£2750	£5000
1886 S	*	*	£100	£450
1887 M	£275	£500	£1750	£3750
1887 S	*	*	£100	£575

Type II. YH obv, St George and Dragon rev

	F	VF	EF	Unc
1871	*	*	£80	£120
1871 S below head	*	£80	£250	£600
1872	*	*	£90	£150
1872 M below head	*	£100	£400	£1750
1872 S	*	*	£150	£500
1873	*	*	£80	£125
1873 M	*	*	£125	£500
1873 S	*	*	£175	£600
1874	*	*	£100	£125
1874 M	*	*	£175	£600
1874 S	*	*	£125	£600
1875 M	*	*	£100	£400
1875 S	*	*	£125	£400
1876	*	*	£100	£175
1876 M	*	*	£100	£400
1876 S	*	*	£125	£500
1877 M	*	*	£100	£400
1878	*	*	£100	£350
1878 M	*	*	£100	£350
1879	*	£200	£950	*
1879 M	*	*	£90	£400
1879 S	*	*	£450	£1650
1880	*	*	£100	£125
1880 M	*	*	£100	£350
1880 S	*	*	£100	£450
1881 M	*	*	£175	£500
1881 S	*	*	£100	£450
1882 M	*	*	£100	£400
1882 S	*	*	£100	£300
1883 M	*	*	£100	£350
1883 S	*	*	£120	£1000
1884	*	*	£80	£150
1884 M	*	*	£100	£300
1884 S	*	*	£100	£300
1885	*	*	£85	£150
1885 M	*	*	£100	£300
1885 S	*	*	£100	£275
1886 M	*	*	£100	£300
1886 S	*	*	£100	£350
1887 M	*	*	£100	£400
1887 S	*	*	£100	£250

Jubilee head coinage

	F	VF	EF	Unc
1887 **(F)**	*	*	£60	£90
1887 proof	*	*	£325	£500
1887 M on ground below dragon	*	*	£100	£250
1887 S on ground below dragon	*	*	£200	£675
1888	*	*	*	£90
1888 M	*	*	*	£350
1888 S	*	*	*	£275
1889	*	*	*	£90
1889 M	*	*	*	£200

SOVEREIGNS

	F	VF	EF	Unc
1889 S	*	*	*	£200
1890	*	*	*	£90
1890	*	*	*	£90
1890 S	*	*	*	£200
1891	*	*	*	£90
1891 M	*	*	*	£200
1891 S	*	*	*	£200
1892	*	*	*	£90
1892 M	*	*	*	£200
1892 S	*	*	*	£200
1893 M	*	*	*	£200
1893 S	*	*	*	£300

Old head coinage

	F	VF	EF	Unc
1893	*	*	*	£85
1893 proof	*	*	£375	£600
1893 M	*	*	*	£200
1893 S	*	*	*	£135
1894	*	*	*	£85
1894 M	*	*	*	£125
1894 S	*	*	*	£125
1895	*	*	*	£85
1895 M	*	*	*	£125
1895 S	*	*	*	£125
1896	*	*	*	£85
1896 M	*	*	*	£110
1896 S	*	*	*	£135
1897 M	*	*	*	£110
1897 S	*	*	*	£110
1898	*	*	*	£85
1898 M	*	*	*	£100
1898 S	*	*	*	£135
1899	*	*	*	£85

1898 Victoria Old Head sovereign

	F	VF	EF	Unc
1899 M	*	*	*	£100
1899 P (Perth mint) on ground below dragon	*	*	*	£750
1899 S	*	*	*	£125
1900	*	*	*	£85
1900 M	*	*	*	£100
1900 P	*	*	*	£135
1900 S	*	*	*	£125
1901	*	*	*	£85
1901 M	*	*	*	£85
1901 P	*	*	*	£150
1901 S	*	*	*	£120

EDWARD VII

	F	VF	EF	Unc
1902	*	*	*	£85
1902 proof	*	*	£100	£150
1902 M	*	*	*	£90
1902 P	*	*	*	£90
1902 S	*	*	*	£90
1903	*	*	*	£85
1903 M	*	*	*	£90
1903 P	*	*	*	£90
1903 S	*	*	*	£90
1904	*	*	*	£85
1904 M	*	*	*	£90
1904 P	*	*	*	£90
1904 S	*	*	*	£90
1905	*	*	*	£85
1905 M	*	*	*	£90
1905 P	*	*	*	£90

SOVEREIGNS

	F	VF	EF	Unc
1905 S	*	*	*	£90
1906	*	*	*	£80
1906 M	*	*	*	£90
1906 P	*	*	*	£80
1906 S	*	*	*	£90
1907	*	*	*	£80
1907 M	*	*	*	£90
1907 P	*	*	*	£90
1907 S	*	*	*	£90
1908	*	*	*	£80
1908 C (Canada, Ottawa mint) on ground below dragon (F)	*	*	£1600	£2700
1908 M	*	*	*	£90
1908 P	*	*	*	£90
1908 S	*	*	*	£90
1909	*	*	*	£90
1909 C	*	*	£100	£350
1909 M	*	*	*	£90
1909 P	*	*	*	£90
1909 S	*	*	*	£90
1910	*	*	*	£80
1910 C	*	*	£100	£300
1910 M	*	*	*	£90
1910 P	*	*	*	£90
1910 S	*	*	*	£90

GEORGE V

	F	VF	EF	Unc
1911 -	*	*	*	£75
1911 proof	*	*	£150	£275
1911 C	*	*	*	£110
1911 M	*	*	*	£65
1911 P	*	*	*	£65
1911 S	*	*	*	£65
1912	*	*	*	£65
1912 M	*	*	*	£65
1912 P	*	*	*	£65
1912S	*	*	*	£65
1913	*	*	*	£65
1913 C (F)	*	£120	£400	£675
1913 M	*	*	*	£70
1913 P	*	*	*	£70
1913 S	*	*	*	£70
1914	*	*	*	£70
1914 C	*	£100	£225	£350
1914 M	*	*	*	£70
1914P	*	*	*	£70
1914 S	*	*	*	£70
1915	*	*	*	£70
1915 M	*	*	*	£70
1915 P	*	*	*	£70
1915 S	*	*	*	£70
1916	*	*	*	£70
1916 C	*	£2750	£5750	*
1916 M	*	*	*	£70
1916 P	*	*	*	£70
1916 S	*	*	*	£70
1917 (F)	*	£2500	£3750	*
1917 C	*	*	£80	£125
1917 M	*	*	*	£70
1917 P	*	*	*	£70
1917 S	*	*	*	£70
1918 C	*	*	£80	£125
1918 I (Indian mint, Bombay), on ground below dragon	*	*	*	£70
1918 M	*	*	*	£70
1918 P	*	*	*	£70
1918 S	*	*	*	£70
1919 C	*	*	£80	£125
1919 M	*	*	*	£70
1919 P	*	*	*	£70
1919 S	*	*	*	£70
1920 M	*	£1150	£2000	£3000

	F	VF	EF	Unc
1920 P	*	*	*	£70
1920 S			highest	rarity
1921 M	*	£2750	£4750	£6000
1921 P	*	*	*	£75
1921 S	*	£350	£750	£1375
1922 M	*	£1750	£4250	£7500
1922 P	*	*	*	£75
1922 S	*	£2500	£6000	£8500
1923 M	*	*	*	£75
1923 S	*	£2500	£5000	£7500
1923 SA (South Africa, Pretoria Mint) on ground below dragon	*	£1250	£1750	£3000
1924 M	*	*	£60	£90
1924 P	*	*	*	£75
1924 S	*	£450	£800	£1200
1924 SA	*	*	£2000	£3000
1925	*	*	*	£75
1925 M	*	*	*	£75
1925 P	*	*	£120	£175
1925 S	*	*	*	£75
1925 SA	*	*	*	£70
1926 M	*	*	*	£75
1926 P	*	£100	£200	£1000
1926 S	*	£5000	£8000	£12500
1926 SA	*	*	*	£65
1927 P	*	*	£125	£350
1927 SA	*	*	*	£70
1928 M	*	£800	£1300	£1900
1928 P	*	*	£85	£150
1928 SA	*	*	*	£70
1929 M	*	£400	£975	£1500
1929 P	*	*	*	£70
1929 SA	*	*	*	£70
1930 M	*	*	£100	£175
1930 P	*	*	*	£70
1930 SA	*	*	*	£70
1931 M	*	£100	£175	£300
1931 P	*	*	*	£65
1931 SA	*	*	*	£65
1932 SA	*	*	*	£65

GEORGE VI

	F	VF	EF	Unc
1937 proof only		*	*	£700

ELIZABETH II

	F	VF	EF	Unc
1957	*	*	*	£65
1958	*	*	*	£65
1959	*	*	*	£65
1962	*	*	*	£65
1963	*	*	*	£65
1964	*	*	*	£65
1965	*	*	*	£65
1966	*	*	*	£65
1967	*	*	*	£65
1968	*	*	*	£65
1974	*	*	*	£65
1976	*	*	*	£65
1978	*	*	*	£65
1979	*	*	*	£65
1979 proof	*	*	*	£100
1980	*	*	*	£55
1980 proof	*	*	*	£85
1981	*	*	*	£55
1981 proof	*	*	*	£95
1982	*	*	*	£55
1982 proof	*	*	*	£95
1983 proof	*	*	*	£100
1984 proof	*	*	*	£100
1985 proof	*	*	*	£140
1986 proof	*	*	*	£140
1987 proof	*	*	*	£140
1988 proof	*	*	*	£150
1989 500th anniversary of the sovereign, proof	*	*	*	£250

St James's Auctions

Auctions 4 and 5 will take place in Spring and Autumn 2006 at the De Vere Cavendish Hotel, 81 Jermyn Street, St James's, London SW1

We are currently accepting consignments for these auctions which will be taking place in Spring and Autumn 2006.

If you have consignments which you wish to sell - either individual coins or an entire collection - we shall be accepting lots for Auction 4 until January 31st 2006 and for Auction 5 until July 31st 2006.

Commissions are often negotiable and generous advances can be arranged. If you wish to discuss this further, please contact us at the address below:

St James's Auctions
(Knightsbridge Coins / S C Fenton)
43 Duke Street, St James's
London SW1Y 6DD
Phone: 020 7930 7597 / 7888 / 8215
Fax: 020 7930 7597 / 7888 / 8215
Fax: 020 7930 8214

SOVEREIGNS

	F	VF	EF	Unc
1990 proof … … … … …	*	*	*	£175
1991 proof … … … … …	*	*	*	£175
1992 proof … … … … …	*	*	*	£200
1993 proof … … … … …	*	*	*	£200
1994 proof … … … … …	*	*	*	£200
1995 proof … … … … …	*	*	*	£200
1996 proof … … … … …	*	*	*	£200
1997 proof … … … … …	*	*	*	£200
1998 new portrait proof	*	*	*	£200
1999 proof … … … … …	*	*	*	£250
2000 … … … … … … …	*	*	*	£85
2000 proof … … … … …	*	*	*	£150
2001 … … … … … … …	*	*	*	£85
2001 proof … … … … …	*	*	*	£135
2002 Shield reverse …	*	*	*	£70
2002 Shield reverse, proof	*	*	*	£150
2003 Shield reverse, proof	*	*	*	£80
2003 proof … … … … …	*	*	*	£150
2003 Ingot & sovereign …	*	*	*	£135
2004 Forth Rail Bridge, proof	*	*	*	£345
2004 Forth Rail Bridge	*	*	*	£80
2004 proof Forth Rail Bridge	*	*	*	£135
2005 … … … … … … …	*	*	*	£139
2005 proof … … … … …	*	*	*	£80

Half sovereigns

GEORGE III

	F	VF	EF	Unc
1817 … … … … … …	£80	£125	£300	£500
1818 … … … … … …	£80	£140	£300	£525
1820 … … … … … …	£80	£140	£300	£525

GEORGE IV

Laureate head/ornate shield, date on rev

	F	VF	EF	Unc
1821 … … … … … …	£350	£750	£1650	£2750
1821 proof … … … …	*	*	£1650	£2750
1823 plain shield …	£85	£160	£350	£575
1824 … … … … … …	£75	£120	£300	£550
1825 … … … … … …	£75	£120	£300	£550

Bare head, date on obv/shield, full legend rev

	F	VF	EF	Unc
1826 … … … … … …	£85	£120	£300	£600
1826 proof … … … …	*	*	£800	£1250
1827 … … … … … …	£85	£120	£300	£600
1828 … … … … … …	£85	£120	£325	£650

WILLIAM IV

	F	VF	EF	Unc
1831 proof … … … … …	*	*	£1000	£1750
1834 reduced size …	£110	£200	£575	£950
1835 normal size …	£110	£200	£500	£800
1836 sixpence oberse die … … … … … … …	£750	£1500	£3000	£4000
1836 … … … … …	£125	£275	£575	£850
1837 … … … … …	£110	£225	£575	£850

VICTORIA

Young head/shield rev

	F	VF	EF	Unc
1838 … … … … … …	*	£100	£265	£500
1839 proof only … …	*	*	£850	£1500
1841 … … … … … …	*	£100	£265	£500
1842 … … … … … …	*	£90	£200	£450
1843 … … … … … …	*	£100	£265	£525
1844 … … … … … …	*	£100	£265	£485
1845 … … … … …	£100	£285	£1000	*
1846 … … … … … …	*	£100	£265	£475
1847 … … … … … …	*	£100	£265	£475
1848 … … … … … …	*	£125	£275	£500
1849 … … … … … …	*	£100	£200	£375
1850 … … … … …	£100	£275	£825	*
1851 … … … … … …	*	£90	£200	£375
1852 … … … … … …	*	£90	£200	£400
1853 … … … … … …	*	£80	£180	£300
1854 … … … … … …		Extremely rare		
1855 … … … … … …	*	£90	£175	£325
1856 … … … … … …	*	£90	£175	£325
1857 … … … … … …	*	£75	£200	£375
1858 … … … … … …	*	£75	£200	£375
1859 … … … … … …	*	£75	£175	£325
1860 … … … … … …	*	£75	£175	£325
1861 … … … … … …	*	£90	£175	£325
1862 … … … … …	£300	£825	£2750	*
1863 … … … … … …	*	£90	£160	£300
1863 die no … … … …	*	£80	£200	£400

	F	VF	EF	Unc
1864 die no… …	*	£75	£165	£275
1865 die no… …	*	£75	£165	£300
1866 die no… …	*	£75	£165	£300
1867 die no… …	*	£75	£165	£300
1869 die no… …	*	£75	£165	£300
1870 die no… …	*	£75	£165	£300
1871 die no. …	*	£75	£165	£300
1871 S below shield	*	£150	£600	£1650
1872 die no. …	*	£85	£135	£250
1872 S … … …	*	£190	£550	£1650
1873 die no. …	*	£75	£150	£250
1873 M below shield	*	£200	£700	£1750
1874 die no. …	*	*	*	£250
1875 die no. …	*	*	*	£250
1875 S … … …	*	*	£575	£1750
1876 die no. …	*	*	£125	£250
1877 die no. …	*	*	£110	£225
1877 M … … …	£100	£200	£750	£2250
1878 die no. …	*	*	*	£225
1879 die no. …	*	*	*	£225
1879 S … … …	£100	£200	£750	£2250
1880 … … … …	*	*	£110	£225
1880 die no. …	*	*	£110	£225
1880 S … … …	£100	£175	£700	£2250
1881 S … … …	£100	£175	£700	£2350
1881 M … … …	£100	£175	£700	£2500
1882 S … … …	£200	£600	£2000	£5500
1882 M … … …	*	£120	£500	£2000
1883 … … … …	*	*	£110	£200
1883 S … … …	*	£90	£450	£950
1884 … … … …	*	*	£110	£200
1884 M … … …	£100	£200	£700	£1750
1885 … … … …	*	*	£100	£200
1885 M … … …	£200	£400	£1750	£3500
1886 S … … …	*	£100	£700	£1750
1886 M … … …	£100	£200	£850	£2500
1887 S … … …	*	£90	£700	£1750
1887 M … … …	£100	£400	£1750	£3500

Jubilee head/shield rev

	F	VF	EF	Unc
1887 … … … …	*	*	£60	£100
1887 proof … …	*	*	£250	£400
1887 M … … …	*	£100	£275	£875
1887 S … … …	*	£100	£375	£875
1889 S … … …	*	£150	£450	*
1890 … … … …	*	*	£50	£100
1891 … … … …	*	*	£50	£100
1891 S … … …	*	*	£650	*
1892 … … … …	*	*	£50	£100
1893 … … … …	*	*	£50	£100
1893 M … … …	*	*	£450	£1250

Old head/St George reverse

	F	VF	EF	Unc
1893 … … … … …	*	*	£45	£90
1893 proof … … … …	*	*	£225	£450
1893 M … … … …	£1500	*	*	*
1893 S … … … …	*	£100	£275	£550
1894 … … … … …	*	*	£45	£90
1895 … … … … …	*	*	£45	£90
1896 … … … … …	*	*	£45	£90
1896 M … … … …	*	£100	£200	£350
1897 … … … … …	*	*	£40	£95
1897 S … … … …	*	£90	£250	£375
1898 … … … … …	*	*	£40	£95
1899 … … … … …	*	*	£40	£95
1899 M … … … …	£70	£125	£375	£1375
1899 P proof only … …	*	*	*	ext. rare
1900 … … … … …	*	*	£40	£90
1900 M … … … …	£70	£125	£375	*
1900 P … … … …	£100	£250	£750	*
1900 S … … … …	*	£80	£350	£1275
1901 … … … … …	*	*	£40	£95
1901 P proof only … …	*	*	*	ext. rare

EDWARD VII

	F	VF	EF	Unc
1902 … … … … …	*	*	*	£60
1902 proof … … … …	*	*	£80	£110

1902 matt proof half sovereign

	F	VF	EF	Unc
1902 S	*	*	£125	£400
1903	*	*	*	£65
1903 S	*	*	£100	£350
1904	*	*	*	£65
1904 P	£100	£200	£500	£1200
1905	*	*	*	£65
1906	*	*	*	£65
1906 M	*	*	£300	£900
1906 S	*	*	£175	£400
1907	*	*	*	£65
1907 M	*	*	£175	£400
1908	*	*	*	£65
1908 M	*	*	£175	£400
1908 P	*	£100	£700	*
1908 S	*	*	£175	£350
1909	*	*	*	£65
1909 M	*	*	£200	£450
1909 P	£	*	£150	£650	£1500
1910	*	*	*	£65
1910 S	*	*	£150	£275

GEORGE V

	F	VF	EF	Unc
1911	*	*	*	£50
1911 proof	*	*	£100	£200
1911 P	*	*	£50	£150
1911 S	*	*	*	£95
1912	*	*	*	£45
1912 S	*	*	£50	£80
1913	*	*	*	£40
1914	*	*	*	£40
1914 S	*	*	*	£80
1915	*	*	*	£40
1915 M	*	*	£60	£100
1915 P	*	*	£100	£300
1915 S	*	*	*	£60
1916 S	*	*	*	£60
1918 P	*	£225	£525	£1250
1923 SA proof...	*	*	*	£200
1925 SA	*	*	*	£50
1926 SA	*	*	*	£50

GEORGE VI

	F	VF	EF	Unc
1937 proof	*	*	*	£150

ELIZABETH II

	F	VF	EF	Unc
1980 proof	*	*	*	£60
1982	*	*	*	£60
1982 proof	*	*	*	£60
1983 proof	*	*	*	£60
1984 proof	*	*	*	£60
1985 proof	*	*	*	£80
1986 proof	*	*	*	£80
1987 proof	*	*	*	£80
1988 proof	*	*	*	£80
1989 500th anniversary of the sovereign, proof	*	*	*	£100
1990 proof	*	*	*	£80
1991 proof	*	*	*	£80
1992 proof	*	*	*	£90
1993 proof	*	*	*	£85
1994 proof	*	*	*	£85
1995 proof	*	*	*	£85
1996 proof	*	*	*	£85
1997 proof	*	*	*	£85
1998 new portrait proof	*	*	*	£85
1999 proof	*	*	*	£90
2000	*	*	*	£50
2000 proof	*	*	*	£70
2001	*	*	*	£50
2001 proof	*	*	*	£75
2002 shield reverse				£40
2002 shield reverse, proof				£75
2003				£40
2003 proof				£75
2004				£40
2004 proof				£75
2005 proof				£79
2005				£40

Crowns

CROMWELL

	F	VF	EF
1658	£1450	£2350	£3500
1658 Dutch copy	£1500	£2500	£4250
1658 Tanner's copy	*	£2750	£5000

CHARLES II

	F	VF	EF
1662 1st bust...	£110	£400	£2500
1663 –	£120	£500	£2500
1664 2nd bust	£120	£450	£3000
1665 –	£750	£1500	*
1666 –	£110	£500	£3000
1666 – eleph	£300	£1000	£6000
1667 –	£100	£400	£2250
1668 –	£95	£400	£1850
1668/7 –	£100	£450	£2750
1669 –	£200	£750	*
1669/8 –	£250	£750	£3500
1670 –	£100	£400	£2000
1670/69 –	£400	£700	*
1671 –	£100	£450	£2250
1671 3rd bust	£100	£400	£2000
1672 –	£100	£400	£2000
1673 –	£100	£400	£2000
1673/2 –	£110	£350	£2000
1674 –	£4000	*	*
1675 –	£500	£1250	£5000
1675/4 –	£500	£1250	*
1676 –	£100	£300	£1500
1677 –	£100	£300	£1500
1677/6 –	£100	£300	£1500
1678/7 –	£120	£500	*
1679 –	£100	£300	£1500
1679 4th bust –	£125	£300	£1650
1680 3rd bust –	£140	£500	£1850
1680/79 –	£100	£350	£1750
1680 4th bust –	£110	£300	£1850
1680/79 –	£125	£400	£2000
1681 – elephant & castle ...	£2000	£3500	*
1681 –	£100	£400	£2000
1682 –	£125	£400	£2000
1682/1 –	£100	£400	£2000
1683 –	£175	£500	£2500
1684 –	£115	£450	£2000

JAMES II

	F	VF	EF
1686 1st bust...	£350	£1000	*
1687 2nd bust	£110	£400	£1500
1688 –	£135	£450	£1500
1688/7 –	£110	£425	£1500

WILLIAM AND MARY

	F	VF	EF
1691	£300	£700	£2000
1692	£325	£750	£2000
1692/2 inverted QVINTO... ...	£325	£750	£2000
1692/2 inverted QVARTO ...	£600	£1250	*

WILLIAM III

	F	VF	EF
1695 1st bust...	£95	£300	£1350
1696 –	£95	£300	£1350
1696 – GEI error...	£200	£650	*
1696/5 –	£135	£375	£1500
1696 2nd bust		unique	
1696 3rd bust	£95	£300	£1350
1697	£600	£2000	£10000
1700 3rd bust variety	£95	£300	£1350

ANNE

	F	VF	EF
1703 1st bust VIGO	£200	£500	£2000
1705 –	£450	£1000	£3250
1706 –	£175	£400	£1400
1707 –	£150	£300	£1375
1707 2nd bust	£100	£275	£1250
1707 – E	£100	£275	£1250
1708 –	£100	£300	£1250
1708 – E...	£100	£350	*
1708/7 –	£100	£375	*
1708 – plumes	£175	£300	£1200
1713 3rd bust	£175	£300	£1200

GEORGE I

	F	VF	EF
1716	£200	£450	£2250
1718	£300	£600	£2500
1718/6	£225	£500	£2250
1720	£225	£500	£2250
1720/18	£200	£500	£2250
1723 SS C	£200	£500	£1750
1726 roses & plumes	£500	£1000	£3250

GEORGE II

	F	VF	EF
1732 YH	£225	£425	£1500
1732 – proof	*	*	£3500
1734	£225	£425	£1500
1735	£225	£425	£1500
1736	£225	£425	£1500
1739	£225	£425	£1000
1741	£225	£425	£1000
1743 OH	£200	£400	£1000

1691 William & Mary Crown

	F	VF	EF
1746 – LIMA	£275	£450	£1200
1746 – proof	*	*	£2500
1750	£250	£600	£1500
1751	£275	£625	£1650

GEORGE III

	F	VF	EF	Unc
Oval counter-stamp[1]	£150	£225	£475	*
Octagonal Counterstamp[1]	£350	£500	£1000	*
1804 Bank of England dollar[1]	£100	£150	£375	£600
1818 LVIII	£10	£45	£225	£600
1818 – error edge	£250	*	*	*
1818 LIX	£10	£45	£225	£600

	F	VF	EF	Unc
1819 –	£10	£45	£250	£600
1819 – no edge stops	£50	£140	£375	*
1819/8 LIX	*	£150	£425	*
1819 LIX	£10	£50	£250	£600
1819 – no stop after TUTAMEN	£45	£150	£400	*
1820 LX	*	*	£250	£600
1820/19	£50	£200	£425	*

[1]Beware of contemporary forgeries. The counterstamps are usually on Spanish-American dollars.

GEORGE IV
	F	VF	EF	Unc
1821 1st hd SEC ...	£35	£150	£600	£1500
1821 – prf	*	*	*	£2500
1821 – TER error edge	*	*	*	£3500
1822 – SEC	£60	£200	£650	£1700
1822 – – prf	*	*	*	*
1822 – TER	£50	£175	£600	£1600
1822 – – prf	*	*	*	£3500
1823 – prf	*	*	*	ext.rare
1826 2nd hd prf	*	*	£1750	£3000

WILLIAM IV
	F	VF	EF	Unc
1831 W.W.	*	*	£4750	£7500
1831 W.WYON	*	*	£5750	£8000
1834 W.W.	*	*	£8000	£12000

VICTORIA
	F	VF	EF	Unc
1839 proof	*	*	£2000	£4250
1844 star stops	£25	£100	£750	£1750
1844 – prf	*	* ext.rare		*
1844 cinquefoil stops	£25	£100	£750	£1750
1845	£25	£100	£750	£1750
1845 proof	*	* ext.rare		*
1847	£25	£100	£850	£2000

Victoria 1847 Gothic crown

	F	VF	EF	Unc
1847 Gothic	£325	£475	£1000	£2250
1847 – plain edge ...	*	£550	£1100	£2650
1853 SEPTIMO	*	*	£3500	£5000
1853 plain	*	*	£4000	£6250
1887 JH	£12	£20	£50	£100
1887 – proof	*	*	£200	£450
1888 close date	£15	£25	£80	£170
1888 wide date	£25	£100	£300	£400
1889	£15	£25	£65	£140
1890	£15	£25	£65	£165
1891	£15	£25	£80	£190
1892	£15	£25	£95	£200
1893 LVI	£15	£25	£110	£265
1893 – proof	*	*	£225	£500
1893 LVII	£15	£65	£200	£400
1894 LVII	£15	£30	£125	£300
1894 LVIII...	£15	£30	£125	£300
1895 LVIII...	£15	£30	£125	£300
1895 LIX	£15	£30	£125	£300
1896 LIX	£15	£50	£225	£450
1896 LX	£15	£30	£125	£295
1897 LX	£15	£30	£125	£295
1897 LXI	£15	£30	£120	£295
1898 LXI	£15	£30	£165	£400
1898 LXII	£15	£30	£130	£325
1899 LXII	£15	£39	£125	£295
1899 LXIII...	£15	£30	£125	£325
1900 LXIII...	£15	£30	£125	£325
1900 LXIV...	£15	£30	£120	£325

EDWARD VII
	F	VF	EF	Unc
1902	£20	£50	£95	£150
1902 matt proof	*	*	£95	£150

GEORGE V
	F	VF	EF	Unc
1927 proof	£35	£70	£110	£150
1928	£40	£90	£150	£250
1929	£40	£90	£150	£250
1930	£40	£95	£150	£250
1931	£40	£95	£150	£250
1932	£110	£165	£275	£400
1933	£45	£95	£150	£250
1934	£300	£600	£1350	£2250
1935	£5	£7	£10	£20
1935 rsd edge prf ...	*	*	*	£245
1935 gold proof	*	*	*	£12500
1935 prf in good silver (.925)	*	*	£650	£1250
1935 specimen	*	*	*	£40
1936	£65	£90	£225	£350

GEORGE VI
	F	VF	EF	Unc
1937	*	*	£18	£25
1937 proof	*	*	*	£30
1937 'VIP' proof	*	*	*	£750
1951	*	*	*	£5
1951 'VIP' proof	*	*	*	£425

ELIZABETH II
	F	VF	EF	Unc
1953	*	*	*	£5
1953 proof	*	*	*	£15
1953 'VIP' proof	*	*	*	£250
1960	*	*	*	£5
1960 'VIP' proof	*	*	*	£375
1960 polished dies ...	*	*	£4	£10
1965 Churchill	*	*	*	£1.00
1965 – 'satin' finish ...	*	*	*	£850

For issues 1972 onwards see under 25 pence in Decimal Coinage section.

*George VI 1937
Crown (reverse)*

Double florins

Cromwell 1658 halfcrown

Victoria 1887 halfcrown

VICTORIA

	F	VF	EF	Unc
1887 Roman 1	*	£15	£40	£75
1887 – proof	*	*	£150	£300
1887 Arabic 1	*	£15	£40	£80
1887 – proof	*	*	£125	£285
1888	*	£12	£45	£110
1888 inverted 1	£15	£30	£135	£350
1889	*	£10	£40	£95
1889 inverted 1	£15	£35	£135	£350
1890	*	£12	£50	£110

Three shilling bank tokens

Contemporary forgeries of these pieces, as well as of other George III coins, were produced in quite large numbers. Several varieties exist for the pieces dated 1811 and 1812. Prices given here are for the commonest types of these years.

GEORGE III

	F	VF	EF	Unc
1811	*	£20	£75	£110
1812 draped bust ...	*	£20	£75	£110
1812 laureate head	*	£20	£75	£110
1813	*	£20	£75	£110
1814	*	£20	£75	£110
1815	*	£20	£75	£110
1816	£100	£250	£600	£1200

Halfcrowns

CROMWELL

	F	VF	EF
1656	£1200	£2650	£4500
1658	£800	£1500	£2500

CHARLES II

	F	VF	EF
1663 1st bust	£100	£500	£2500
1664 2nd bust	£125	£600	£3000
1666/3 3rd bust	£750	*	*
1666/3 – elephant	£750	£1750	£6000
1667/4 –	ext.rare		
1668/4 –	£175	£700	*
1669 –	£275	£1100	*
1669/4 –	£200	£750	*
1670 –	£65	£375	£2500
1671 3rd bust var	£65	£375	£2500
1671/0 –	£95	£500	£2750
1672 –	£80	£425	£2500
1672 4th bust	£100	£400	£2500
1673 –	£65	£300	£2500
1673 – plume below	£1750	*	*
1673 – plume both sides ...	ext. rare		
1674 –	£125	£400	*
1674/3 –	£250	£700	*
1675 –	£80	£350	£1750
1676 –	£80	£350	£1750
1677 –	£80	£350	£1750
1678 –	£175	£650	*
1679 –	£80	£350	£1500
1680 –	£150	£450	*
1681 –	£80	£350	£1750
1681/0 –	£150	£400	£1750
1681 – eleph & castle	£2000	£4750	*
1682 –	£100	£425	*
1682/1 –	£150	£600	*
1682/79 –	ext. rare		
1683 –	£70	£350	£1500
1683 – plume below	ext. rare	*	*
1684/3 –	£175	£650	*

James III 1687 halfcrown

JAMES II

	F	VF	EF
1685 1st bust	£110	£475	£2000
1686 –	£110	£475	£1750
1686/5 –	£165	£750	*
1687 –	£110	£475	£1750

	F	VF	EF
1687/6 –	£125	£500	£1750
1687 2nd bust	£125	£500	£1750
1688 –	£100	£400	£1750

WILLIAM AND MARY

	F	VF	EF
1689 1st busts 1st shield ...	£60	£325	£1350
1689 – 2nd shield	£60	£325	£1350
1690 –	£75	£400	£2250
1691 2nd busts 3rd shield ...	£65	£375	£1350
1692 – –	£65	£300	£1350
1693 – –	£60	£325	£1350
1693 – – 3 inverted	£85	£450	£1600
1693 3 over 3 inverted	£80	£375	£1400

William and Mary 1693 Halfcrown

WILLIAM III

	F	VF	EF
1696 large shield early harp	£50	£225	£700
1696 – – B	£60	£225	£750
1696 – – C	£65	£225	£750
1696 – – E	£85	£275	£875
1696 – – N	£125	£375	£1500
1696 – – Y	£60	£225	£800
1696 – – y/E	ext rare	*	*
1696 – ord harp	£100	£450	£1100
1696 – – C	£110	£375	£1250
1696 – – E	£120	£375	£1100
1696 – – N	£120	£350	£1350
1696 small shield	£45	£200	£675
1696 – B	£80	£200	£700
1696 – C	£100	£275	£825
1696 – E	£200	£475	£1000
1696 – N	£70	£275	£850
1696 – y	£110	£275	£825
1696 2nd bust	unique		
1697 1st bust large shield ...	£40	£175	£600
1697 – – B	£65	£275	£700
1697 – – C	£70	£275	£700
1697 – – E	£50	£225	£700
1697 – – E/C	£125	*	*
1697 – – N	£65	£275	£800
1697 – – y	£65	£275	£700

1697 Halfcrown of NORWICH: N below bust

	F	VF	EF
1698 – –	£40	£200	£600
1699 – –	£80	£300	£1000

HALFCROWNS

	F	VF	EF
1700 – –	£40	£125	£575
1701 – –	£50	£150	£650
1701 – eleph & castle	£2250	*	*
1701 – plumes	£200	£575	£2500

ANNE

	F	VF	EF
1703 plain	£700	£1750	£9000
1703 VIGO	£125	£250	£750
1704 plumes	£250	£600	*
1705 –	£125	£325	£1100
1706 r & p	£90	£225	£750
1707 –	£60	£225	£750
1707 plain	£50	£200	£475
1707 E	£50	£200	*
1708 plain	£40	£200	£500
1708 E	£50	£225	*
1708 plumes	£95	£300	£925
1709 plain	£45	£225	£650
1709 E	£400	*	*
1710 r & p	£75	£275	£750
1712 –	£45	£200	£600
1713 plain	£75	£300	£750
1713 r & p	£60	£275	£700
1714 –	£50	£275	£700
1714/3	£125	£515	£900

GEORGE I

	F	VF	EF
1715 proof	*	*	£5000
1715 r & p	£125	£400	£1475
1717 –	£150	£450	£1500
1720 –	£275	£650	£2000
1720/17 –	£125	£450	£1500
1723 SS C	£100	£375	£1375
1726 small r & p	£2500	£4000	£10000

Spanish Half Dollar with George III counterstamp (octagonal)

GEORGE II

	F	VF	EF
1731 YH proof	*	£1750	£3500
1731	£85	£300	£925
1732	£85	£300	£975
1734	£85	£300	£925
1735	£85	£300	£1000
1736	£85	£300	£975
1739	£70	£225	£700
1741	£90	£275	£800
1741/39	£85	£250	£750
1743 OH	£70	£150	£625
1745	£60	£100	£425
1745 LIMA	£50	£125	£500
1746 -	£50	£125	£500
1746 plain, proof	*	*	£1375
1750	£90	£325	£950
1751	£80	£400	£1250

GEORGE III

	F	VF	EF	Unc
Oval counterstamp usually on Spanish half dollar	£125	£250	£400	*

HALFCROWNS

	F	VF	EF	Unc
1816 large head	*	£50	£175	£400
1817 –	*	£50	£175	£400
1817 small head ...	*	£50	£170	£400
1818	*	£50	£185	£425
1819	*	£50	£175	£425
1819/8	*	*	*	*
1820	*	£60	£180	£425

George IV halfcrown of 1821

GEORGE IV

	F	VF	EF	Unc
1820 1st hd 1st rev ...	*	£50	£185	£400
1821 –	*	£50	£185	£400
1821 proof	*	*	£600	£1100
1823	£750	£1750	£5000	*
1823 – 2nd rev	*	£50	£195	£450
1824 – –	£25	£70	£225	£600
1824 2nd hd 3rd rev ...				ext.rare
1825 – –	*	£70	£125	£400
1826 – –	*	£25	£125	£400
1826 – – proof	*	*	£400	£700
1828 – –	*	£35	£225	£600
1829 – –	*	£35	£190	£500

William IV 1831 halfcrown

WILLIAM IV

	F	VF	EF	Unc
1831		Extremely rare		
1831 proof	*	*	£425	£750
1834 ww	£30	£110	£400	£750
1834 *ww* in script ...	£12	£40	£175	£450
1835	£25	£80	£275	£625
1836	£12	£50	£175	£450
1836/5	£30	£85	£375	*
1837	£35	£90	£325	£725

VICTORIA

From time to time halfcrowns bearing dates ranging from 1861 to 1871 are found, but except for rare proofs: 1853, 1862 and 1864, no halfcrowns were struck between 1850 and 1874, so pieces dated for this period are now considered to be contemporary or later forgeries.

	F	VF	EF	Unc
1839 plain and ornate fillets, ww	*	£975	£3500	*
1839 – plain edge proof	*	*	£600	£1000
1839 plain fillets, ww incuse	*	£1250	£3500	*
1840	£15	£75	£375	£650
1841	£75	£225	£1350	£2500
1842	£15	£40	£350	£700
1843	£50	£125	£500	£1100
1844	£15	£40	£325	£600
1845	£15	£40	£325	£600
1846	£20	£50	£300	£600
1848	£75	£175	£800	£1750
1848/6	£75	£200	£750	£1500
1849 large date	£25	£85	£475	£825
1849 small date	£50	£175	£500	£1000
1850	£25	£85	£425	£875
1853 proof	*	*	£800	£1750
1862 proof	*	*	*	£4000
1864 proof	*	*	*	£4000
1874	*	£30	£110	£300
1875	*	£25	£110	£300
1876	*	£35	£130	£350
1876/5	*	£50	£275	£500
1877	*	£25	£110	£300
1878	*	£25	£110	£300
1879	*	£35	£145	£325
1880	*	£25	£120	£300
1881	*	£25	£120	£300
1882	*	£25	£140	£325
1883	*	£25	£110	£325
1884	*	£25	£110	£325
1885	*	£25	£120	£300
1886	*	£25	£110	£300
1887 YH	*	£25	£135	£300
1887 JH	*	£15	£25	£60
1887 – proof	*	*	£85	£150
1888	*	£20	£50	£100
1889	*	£20	£50	£100
1890	*	£25	£55	£120
1891	*	£25	£55	£120
1892	*	£25	£50	£120
1893 OH	*	£20	£30	£120
1893 – proof	*	*	£90	£175
1894	*	£20	£55	£140
1895	*	£20	£50	£125
1896	*	£20	£45	£125
1897	*	£15	£50	£125
1898	*	£20	£50	£135
1899	*	£20	£50	£125
1900	*	£20	£50	£125
1901	*	£20	£45	£125

EDWARD VII

	F	VF	EF	Unc
1902	*	£20	£45	£90
1902 matt proof	*	*	*	£110
1903	£50	£120	£700	£1100
1904	£35	£90	£500	£950
1905 (F)	£150	£500	£1500	£3000
1906	*	£30	£150	£400
1907	*	£40	£150	£425
1908	*	£40	£350	£725
1909	*	£25	£300	£600
1910	*	£20	£110	£300

GEORGE V

	F	VF	EF	Unc
1911	*	£110	£40	£100
1911 proof	*	*	*	£85
1912	*	£14	£60	£150
1913	*	£14	£65	£165
1914	*	*	£20	£70
1915	*	*	£15	£60
1916	*	*	£15	£60

	F	VF	EF	Unc
1917	*	*	£30	£65
1918	*	*	£20	£50
1919	*	*	£20	£50
1920	*	*	£20	£80
1921	*	*	£25	£85
1922	*	*	£20	£85
1923	*	*	£12	£40
1924	*	*	£25	£60
1925	£12	£25	£245	£500

George V 1926 halfcrown

	F	VF	EF	Unc
1926	*	*	£30	£100
1926 mod eff	*	*	£35	£95
1927	*	*	£20	£50
1927 new rev, proof only	*	*	*	£45
1928	*	*	£10	£25
1929	*	*	£10	£20
1930	£7	£35	£125	£300
1931	*	*	£10	£20
1932	*	*	£15	£35
1933	*	*	£9	£20
1934	*	*	£20	£45
1935	*	*	£6	£14
1936	*	*	£6	£12

GEORGE VI

	F	VF	EF	Unc
1937	*	*	*	£12
1937 proof	*	*	*	£18
1938	*	*	£4	£25
1939	*	*	*	£17
1940	*	*	*	£12
1941	*	*	*	£12
1942	*	*	*	£9
1943	*	*	*	£12
1944	*	*	*	£9
1945	*	*	*	£9
1946	*	*	*	£7
1947	*	*	*	£7
1948	*	*	*	£7
1949	*	*	*	£12
1950	*	*	*	£15
1950 proof	*	*	*	£18
1951	*	*	*	£15
1951 proof	*	*	*	£18

ELIZABETH II

	F	VF	EF	Unc
1953	*	*	*	£10
1953 proof	*	*	*	£12
1954	*	*	£3	£25
1955	*	*	*	£7
1956	*	*	*	£7
1957	*	*	*	£4
1958	*	*	£3	£20
1959	*	*	£4	£45
1960	*	*	*	£4
1961	*	*	*	£2
1962	*	*	*	£4
1963	*	*	*	£2
1964	*	*	*	£2
1965	*	*	*	£2
1966	*	*	*	£1
1967	*	*	*	£1

Florins

The first florins produced in the reign of Victoria bore the legend VICTORIA REGINA and the date, omitting DEI GRATIA (By the Grace of God). They are therefore known as 'Godless' florins.

The date of a Victorian Gothic florin is shown in Roman numerals, in Gothic lettering on the obverse for example: mdccclvii (1857). Gothic florins were issued during the period 1851-1887.

VICTORIA	F	VF	EF	Unc
1848 'Godless' proof with milled edge	*	*	*	£1750
1848 'Godless' proof with plain edge	*	*	*	£750

Victoria 1849 'Godless' florin

	F	VF	EF	Unc
1849 – ww obliterated by circle	£25	£50	£150	£325
1849 – ww inside circle	£15	£40	£125	£225
1851 proof only	*	*	*	£7000
1852	£15	£40	£125	£275
1853	£15	£40	£125	£275
1853 no stop after date	£20	£50	£150	£375
1853 proof	*	*	*	£1500
1854	£250	£675	£2500	*
1855	*	£35	£150	£350
1856	*	£50	£165	£375
1857	*	£40	£150	£295
1858	*	£40	£150	£295
1859	*	£40	£150	£295
1859 no stop after date	*	£50	£165	£295
1860	*	£50	£180	£350
1862	£40	£200	£1500	*
1863	£80	£300	£1750	*
1864	*	£40	£150	£295
1865	*	£40	£180	£425
1865 colon after date	*	£50	£250	*
1866	*	£50	£160	£350
1866 colon after date	*	£55	£185	*
1867	£15	£70	£185	£375
1868	*	£50	£200	£450
1869	*	£45	£200	£425
1870	*	£40	£135	£275
1871	*	£40	£140	£325

Victoria 1859 Gothic florin

FLORINS

	F	VF	EF	Unc
1872	*	£35	£135	£250
1873	*	£35	£135	£250
1874	*	£35	£150	£325
1874 xxiv/iii - (die 29) ...	£75	£175	£400	*
1875	*	£45	£150	£300
1876	*	£45	£150	£300
1877	*	£45	£150	£300
1877 no ww	*	*	*	*
1877 42 arcs	*	*	*	*
1878	*	£40	£150	£325
1879 ww 48 arcs ...	*	£40	£150	£325
1879 die no.	*	*	*	*
1879 ww. 42 arcs ...	£12	£40	£150	£300
1879 no ww, 38 arcs	*	£45	£150	£300
1880	*	£40	£150	£300
1881	*	£40	£150	£300
1881 xxri	*	£40	£150	£300
1883	*	£40	£140	£250
1884	*	£40	£140	£250
1885	*	£40	£140	£250
1886	*	£40	£140	£250
1887 33 arcs	*	*	*	*
1887 46 arcs		£40	£165	£350
1887 JH	*	£10	£25	£40
1887 – proof	*	*	*	£120
1888	*	£10	£40	£95
1889	*	£10	£45	£110
1890	£8	£15	£60	£150
1891	£20	£50	£140	£350
1892	£20	£50	£100	£300
1893 OH	*	£12	£45	£90
1893 proof	*	*	*	£120
1894	*	£12	£60	£125
1895	*	£12	£50	£100
1896	*	£12	£45	£100
1897	*	£12	£45	£100
1898	*	£12	£45	£100
1899	*	£12	£45	£100
1900	*	£12	£45	£100
1901	*	£12	£45	£100

Edward VII 1902 florin

EDWARD VII

	F	VF	EF	Unc
1902	*	£12	£40	£75
1902 matt proof	*	*	*	£65
1903	*	£25	£100	£300
1904	*	£32	£125	£325
1905	£35	£125	£475	£900
1906	*	£20	£95	£275
1907	*	£25	£90	£275
1908	*	£30	£170	£475
1909	*	£25	£150	£375
1910	*	£15	£75	£150

GEORGE V

	F	VF	EF	Unc
1911	*	*	£30	£85
1911 proof	*	*	*	£70
1912	*	*	£40	£95
1913	*	*	£60	£145
1914	*	*	£25	£50
1915	*	*	£30	£55
1916	*	*	£20	£65
1917	*	*	£25	£55
1918	*	*	£20	£50
1919	*	*	£25	£55
1920	*	*	£20	£60
1921	*	x	£18	£50
1922	*	*	£18	£45
1923	*	*	£18	£40
1924	*	*	£27	£55
1925	£15	£35	£125	£275
1926	*	*	£30	£80
1927 proof only	*	*		£50

George V 1928 florin

	F	VF	EF	Unc
1928	*	*	£7	£17
1929	*	*	£7	£17
1930	*	*	£10	£35
1931	*	*	£8	£20
1932	£15	£60	£150	£300
1933	*	*	£8	£20
1935	*	*	£8	£17
1936	*	*	£5	£15

GEORGE VI

	F	VF	EF	Unc
1937	*	*	*	£7
1937 proof	*	*	*	£15
1938	*	*	£4	£25
1939	*	*	*	£12
1940	*	*	*	£10
1941	*	*	*	£10
1942	*	*	*	£8
1943	*	*	*	£8
1944	*	*	*	£8
1945	*	*	*	£8
1946	*	*	*	£8
1947	*	*	*	£8
1948	*	*	*	£8
1949	*	*	*	£12
1950	*	*	*	£12
1950 proof	*	*	*	£12
1951	*	*	*	£15
1951 proof	*	*	*	£20

George VI 1949 florin

ELIZABETH II	F	VF	EF	Unc
1953	*	*	*	£6
1953 proof	*	*	*	£10
1954	*	*	*	£45
1955	*	*	*	£5
1956	*	*	*	£5
1957	*	*	*	£45
1958	*	*	*	£20
1959	*	*	*	£35
1960	*	*	*	£3
1961	*	*	*	£3
1962	*	*	*	£2
1963	*	*	*	£2
1964	*	*	*	£2
1965	*	*	*	£2
1966	*	*	*	£1
1967	*	*	*	£1

One and sixpence bank tokens

GEORGE III	F	VF	EF	Unc
1811	£9	£25	£70	£110
1812 laureate bust ...	£9	£25	£75	£120
1812 laureate head	£9	£25	£75	£120
1813	£9	£25	£75	£120
1814	£9	£25	£75	£120
1815	£9	£25	£75	£120
1816	£9	£25	£75	£120

Shillings

1658 shilling of Cromwell

CROMWELL	F	VF	EF
1658	£400	£800	£1650
1658 Dutch copy	*	*	*

Charles II 1671 shilling, plumes below bust

CHARLES II	F	VF	EF
1663 1st bust	£80	£275	£850
1663 1st bust var	£80	£275	£850
1666 –	*	*	*
1666 – eleph	£350	£1250	£3500
1666 guinea hd, eleph ...	£1500	*	*

	F	VF	EF
1666 2nd bust	£1250	*	*
1668 1st bust var	£350	£1250	*
1668 2nd bust	£50	£275	£750
1668/7 –	£90	£350	£875
1669/6 1st bust var ... ...ext. rare		*	*
1669 2nd bust ... ...ext. rare		*	*
1670 –	£85	£400	£1000
1671 –	£95	£425	£1150
1671 – plumes both sides	£425	£875	*
1672 –	£70	£350	£875
1673 –	£70	£400	£1100
1673/2 –	£80	£450	£1375
1673 – plumes both sides	£425	£900	£2500
1674 –	£70	£425	£1150
1674/3 –	£70	£425	£1100
1674 – plumes both sides	£425	£900	£2500
1674 – plumes rev only ...	£425	£900	£2500
1674 3rd bust	£300	£700	£2500
1675 –	£350	£700	£2500
1675/3 –	£350	£700	£2500
1675 2nd bust	£250	£550	*
1675/4 –	£250	£550	*
1675 – plumes both sides	£425	£900	£2500
1676	£65	£325	£875
1676/5 –	£70	£350	£925
1676 – plumes both sides	£425	£900	£2500
1677 –	£60	£350	£875
1677 – plume obv only ...	£500	£1350	£3500
1678 –	£70	£400	£975
1678/7 –	£70	£400	£975
1679 –	£60	£350	£850
1679/7 –	£70	£350	£925
1679 plumes	£425	£900	£2500
1679 plumes obv only ...	£575	£1200	£3500
1680 –	Extremely rare		
1680 plumes	£425	£900	£2650
1680/79 –	£425	£900	£2650
1681 –	£100	£450	£1150
1681/0	£100	£450	£1150
1681/0 – eleph & castle ...	£1750	*	*
1682/1 –	£475	£1200	*
1683 – ... ...Ext rare		*	*
1683 4th bust	£125	£450	£1500
1684 –	£110	£400	£1500

James II 1685 shilling

JAMES II	F	VF	EF
1685	£125	£350	£1375
1685 no stops on rev	£175	£600	£1750
1685 plume on rev	Extremely Rare		
1686	£125	£375	£1250
1686 V/S	£125	£400	£1375
1687	£125	£375	£1250
1687/6	£125	£350	£1250
1688	£125	£375	£1375
1688/7	£125	£400	£1375
WILLIAM & MARY			
1692	£125	£375	£1200
1693	£125	£375	£1150

SHILLINGS

WILLIAM III	F	VF	EF
1695	£20	£80	£450
1696	£20	£65	£300
1696 no stops on rev	£50	£175	£550
1669 in error	£750	*	*
1696 1st bust B	£35	£110	£485
1696 – C	£35	£110	£485
1696 – E	£35	£110	£485
1696 – N	£35	£110	£485
1696 – Y	£35	£110	£485
1696 – Y	£40	£135	£550
1696 2nd bust		unique	
1696 3rd bust C	£145	£375	£850
1696 – E		Extremely rare	
1697 1st bust	£25	£75	£350
1697 – no stops on rev ...	£75	£200	£575
1697 – B	£45	£110	£475
1697 – C	£40	£110	£475

1697 Shilling of BRISTOL: B below bust

	F	VF	EF
1697 – E	£40	£110	£475
1697 – N	£40	£110	£475
1697 – y	£40	£110	£475
1697 – Y	£40	£110	£500
1697 3rd bust	£25	£75	£300
1697 – B	£40	£110	£485
1697 – C	£30	£100	£400
1697 – E	£40	£110	£475
1697 – N	£40	£110	£475
1697 – y	£35	£110	£475
1697 3rd bust var	£20	£80	£300
1697 – B	£30	£90	£450
1697 – C	£120	£275	£725
1698	£35	£110	£475
1698 – plumes	£165	£400	£975
1698 4th bust	£85	£300	£900
1699 –	£90	£300	£900
1699 5th bust	£80	£300	£700
1699 – plumes	£50	£400	£1575
1699 – roses	£50	£400	£1575
1700 –	£30	£70	£250
1700 – no stops on rev ...	£55	£175	£350
1700 – plume	£2000	*	*
1701	£65	£200	£500
1701 – plumes	£120	£325	£1250

Anne 1702 shilling, VIGO below bust

ANNE	F	VF	EF
1702 – 1st bust	£70	£250	£575

	F	VF	EF
1702 – plumes	£75	£275	£625
1702 – VIGO	£60	£200	£475
1703 2nd bust VIGO	£60	£200	£425
1704 –	£385	£1100	£*
1704 – plumes	£80	£300	£675
1705 –	£80	£300	£625
1705 – plumes	£75	£250	£575
1705 – r&p	£70	£225	£475
1707 – r&p	£70	£225	£475
1707 – E	£60	£145	£450
1707 – E★	£90	£275	£600
1707 3rd bust	£25	£120	£300
1707 – plumes	£40	£165	£425
1707 – E	£30	£85	£375
1707 Edin bust E★	£350	*	*
1708 2nd bust E	£80	£250	£625
1708 – E★	£70	£200	£525
1708/7 – E★		Extremely rare	
1708 – r&p	£125	£300	£700
1708 3rd bust	£30	£70	£275
1708 – plumes	£50	£150	£425
1708 – r&p	£80	£285	£600
1708 – E	£85	£275	£575
1708 – E	£110	£300	£700
1708 – Edin bust E★	£80	£200	£550
1709 –	£50	£100	£350
1709 - Edin bust E	£250	£750	*
1709 - Edin bust E ?	£90	£265	£625
1710 – r&p	£45	£175	£375
1710 4th bust prf		Extremely rare	
1710 – r&p	£50	£150	£475
1711 3rd bust	£175	£425	£950
1711 4th bust	£20	£70	£200
1712 – r&p	£30	£125	£365
1713/2 –	£50	£165	£375
1714 –	£35	£125	£350
1714/3 –		**Extremely rare**	

George I 1723 SS C shilling

GEORGE I	F	VF	EF
1715 1st bust r&p	£35	£125	£475
1716 –	£100	£295	£800
1717 –	£35	£125	£475
1718 –	£45	£135	£425
1719 –	£95	£200	£700
1720 –	£45	£125	£475
1720 – plain	£35	£125	£425
1720 – large 0	£35	£125	£450
1721 –	£175	£500	£950
1721 r&p	£35	£100	£500
1721/0 –	£35	£100	£475
1721/19 –	£40	£135	£525
1721/18 –	9 ext.rare		*
1722 –	£35	£145	£485
1723 –	£35	£145	£485
1723 – SS C	£30	£75	£250
1723 - SSC - C/SS	£35	£100	£275
1723 - SSC Fench arms at date...	£125	£400	£1250
1723 2nd bust SS C...	£50	£120	£325
1723 - r&p	£50	£165	£425
1723 - w.c.c	£375	£800	£2250
1724 - r&p	£50	£165	£425
1724 - w.c.c	£375	£800	£2250

	F	VF	EF
1725 – r & p	£50	£165	£425
1725 – no obv stops	£75	£200	£600
1725 – w.c.c.	£425	£825	£2500
1726 – r & p	£500	£1100	*
1726 – w.c.c.	£450	£875	£2250
1727 – r & p	£500	*	*
1727 – – no stops on obv	£450	£1200	*

GEORGE II

	F	VF	EF
1727 YH plumes	£60	£300	£800
1727 – r & p	£50	£150	£525
1728 –	£150	£375	£950
1728 – r & p	£70	£175	£600
1729 – –	£80	£175	£600
1731 – –	£60	£150	£525
1731 – plumes	£120	£375	£975
1732 – r & p	£70	£175	£600
1734 – –	£50	£135	£475
1735 – –	£50	£135	£475
1736 –	£50	£135	£475
1736/5 – –	£70	£175	£575
1737 – –	£50	£135	£475
1739 – roses	£25	£110	£400
1741 – roses	£25	£110	£400

1763 'Northumberland' Shilling

	F	VF	EF
1743 OH roses	£25	£80	£350
1745 – –	£30	£95	£375
1745 – LIMA	£20	£75	£325
1746 – – LIMA	£80	£225	£625
1746/5 – LIMA	£110	£275	£650
1746 – proof	*	£500	£800
1747 – roses	£35	£325	£250
1750 –	£40	£135	£475
1750/6 –	£50	£165	£500
1751 –	£80	£225	£700
1758 –	£15	£40	£75

1728 Young Head Shilling

GEORGE III

	F	VF	EF	Unc
1763 'Northumber-land'	£225	£450	£750	£1150
1786 proof or pattern	*	*	*	£5000
1787 no hearts	£15	£25	£70	£150
1787 – no stop over head	£20	£40	£100	£200
1787 – no stops at date	£20	£50	£150	£250

	F	VF	EF	Unc
1787 – no stops on obv	£250	£600	*	*
1787 hearts	£15	£25	£70	£150
1798 'Dorrien and Magens'	*	£3750	£6000	£8500
1816	*	£5	£50	£90
1817	*	£5	£50	£90
1817 GEOE	£50	£125	£375	£750
1818	£4	£25	£125	£250
1819	*	£4	£65	£110
1819/8	*	*	£90	£200
1820	*	£4	£40	£125

GEORGE IV

	F	VF	EF	Unc
1820 1st hd 1st rev pattern or prf ...	*	*	*	£3500
1821 1st hd 1st rev	£10	£30	£150	£325
1821 – proof	*	*	£400	£700
1823 – 2nd rev	£20	£50	£250	*
1824 – –	£8	£35	£150	£300
1825 – –	£15	£40	£150	£350
1825 2nd hd	£10	£25	£120	£275
1826 –	*	£25	£110	£225

George IV 1824 shilling

	F	VF	EF	Unc
1826 – proof	*	*	£185	£325
1827	£10	£50	£250	£500
1829	*	£40	£175	£400

WILLIAM IV

	F	VF	EF	Unc
1831 proof	*	*	*	£425
1834	£10	£30	£150	£300
1835	£10	£35	£165	£345
1836	£15	£25	£165	£325
1837	£25	£75	£200	£475

William IV 1837 shilling

VICTORIA

	F	VF	EF	Unc
1838	£8	£18	£100	£250
1839	£8	£20	£100	£250
1839 2nd YH	£8	£20	£100	£250
1839 – proof	*	*	*	£475
1840	£12	£35	£135	£300
1841	£12	£35	£135	£300
1842	£10	£20	£80	£225
1843	£12	£30	£125	£275
1844	£8	£20	£80	£210
1845	£8	£20	£85	£250
1846	£8	£20	£80	£210
1848/6	£40	£125	£525	£850
1849	£12	£25	£125	£250

SHILLINGS

	F	VF	EF	Unc
1850	£200	£800	£1500	*
1850/46	£200	£800	£1650	*
1851	£40	£150	£450	£800
1852	£8	£20	£85	£200
1853	£8	£20	£85	£200
1853 proof	*	*	*	£400
1854	£75	£300	£975	*
1855	£8	£20	£80	£200
1856	£8	£20	£80	£200
1857	£8	£20	£80	£200
1857 F:G:	£200	*	*	*
1858	£8	£20	£80	£200
1859	£8	£20	£80	£200
1860	£10	£25	£100	£250
1861	£10	£25	£100	£250
1862	£15	£35	£150	£300

Victoria 1839 shilling

	F	VF	EF	Unc
1863	£15	£50	£300	£650
1863/1	£60	£150	£500	*
1864	£8	£15	£70	£195
1865	£8	£15	£70	£195
1866	£8	£15	£70	£195
1866 BBITANNIAR	*	*	£450	*
1867	£8	£15	£80	£195
1867 3rd YH, die no.	£150	£325	*	*
1868	£8	£20	£90	£195
1869	£12	£30	£90	£225
1870	£10	£25	£90	£200
1871	£8	£20	£80	£185
1872	£8	£20	£80	£185
1873	£8	£20	£80	£185
1874	£8	£20	£80	£185
1875	£8	£20	£80	£185
1876	£10	£25	£85	£185
1877 die no.	£8	£20	£85	£185
1877 no die no	*	*	*	*
1878	£8	£20	£85	£185
1879 3rd YH	£45	£100	£250	*
1879 4th YH	£8	£20	£75	£150
1880	£6	£15	£65	£135
1880 longer line below SHILLING	*	*	*	*
1881	£6	£15	£65	£135
1881 longer line below SHILLING	£6	£15	£60	£135
1881 – Large rev lettering	£6	£15	£60	£125
1882	£10	£35	£95	£200
1883	£6	£15	£60	£135
1884	£6	£15	£60	£135
1885	£6	£15	£60	£135
1886	£6	£15	£60	£135
1887	£7	£25	£100	£200
1887 JH	*	*	£12	£30
1887 proof	*	*	*	£85
1888	*	£6	£40	£70
1889	£40	£100	£300	*
1889 large JH	*	*	£40	£70
1890	*	*	£40	£80
1891	*	*	£40	£80
1892	*	*	£40	£80

Victoria Jubilee Head and Old Head shillings

	F	VF	EF	Unc
1893 OH	*	*	£30	£60
1893 – proof	*	*	*	£100
1893 small obv letters	*	*	£35	£75
1894	*	*	£40	£75
1895	*	*	£35	£65
1896	*	*	£35	£65
1897	*	*	£35	£60
1898	*	*	£35	£60
1899	*	*	£35	£60
1900	*	*	£35	£60
1901	*	*	£30	£50

EDWARD VII

	F	VF	EF	Unc
1902	*	*	£40	£60
1902 matt prf	*	*	£40	£60

Edward VII 1905 shilling

	F	VF	EF	Unc
1903	*	£15	£100	£350
1904	*	£12	£95	£275
1905	£40	£120	£450	£1500
1906	*	*	£50	£150
1907	*	*	£60	£175
1908	£8	£20	£125	£275
1909	£8	£20	£135	£300
1910	*	*	£45	£100

GEORGE V

	F	VF	EF	Unc
1911	*	*	£18	£40
1911 proof	*	*	*	£35
1912	*	*	£25	£65
1913	*	*	£40	£80
1914	*	*	£15	£35
1915	*	*	£15	£35
1916	*	*	£15	£35
1917	*	*	£17	£35
1918	*	*	£15	£30
1919	*	*	£20	£45
1920	*	*	£20	£40
1921	*	*	£25	£50

George V nickel trial shilling, 1924

	F	VF	EF	Unc
1922	*	*	£22	£45
1923	*	*	£18	£40
1923 nickel	*	*	£600	£850
1924	*	*	£25	£45
1924 nickel	*	*	£600	£850
1925	*	*	£30	£75
1926	*	*	£18	£50
1926 mod eff	*	*	£18	£40
1927 –	*	*	£18	£40
1927 new type	*	*	£8	£30
1927 – proof	*	*	*	£20
1928	*	*	*	£12
1929	*	*	£7	£15
1930	*	*	£15	£35
1931	*	*	£7	£15
1932	*	*	£7	£15
1933	*	*	£7	£15
1934	*	*	£10	£28
1935	*	*	£3	£12
1936	*	*	£3	£12

GEORGE VI

	F	VF	EF	Unc
1937 Eng	*	*	*	£6
1937 Eng prf	*	*	*	£8
1937 Scot	*	*	*	£4
1937 Scot prf	*	*	*	£7
1938 Eng	*	*	£5	£20
1938 Scot	*	*	£5	£18
1939 Eng	*	*	*	£8
1939 Scot	*	*	*	£8
1940 Eng	*	*	*	£8
1940 Scot	*	*	*	£8
1941 Eng	*	*	*	£7
1941 Scot	*	*	£2	£8
1942 Eng	*	*	*	£7
1942 Scot	*	*	*	£8
1943 Eng	*	*	*	£7
1943 Scot	*	*	*	£8
1944 Eng	*	*	*	£7
1944 Scot	*	*	*	£7
1945 Eng	*	*	*	£7
1945 Scot	*	*	*	£6
1946 Eng	*	*	*	£6
1946 Scot	*	*	*	£6
1947 Eng	*	*	*	£5
1947 Scot	*	*	*	£5

Reverses: English (left), Scottish (right)

	F	VF	EF	Unc
1948 Eng	*	*	*	£7
1948 Scot	*	*	*	£7
1949 Eng	*	*	*	£15
1949 Scot	*	*	*	£15
1950 Eng	*	*	*	£17
1950 Eng prf	*	*	*	£17
1950 Scot	*	*	*	£17
1950 Scot prf	*	*	*	£17
1951 Eng	*	*	*	£17
1951 Eng prf	*	*	*	£17
1951 Scot	*	*	*	£17
1951 Scot prf	*	*	*	£17

ELIZABETH II

	F	VF	EF	Unc
1953 Eng	*	*	*	£4
1953 Eng prf	*	*	*	£8
1953 Scot	*	*	*	£4

SHILLINGS

	F	VF	EF	Unc
1953 Scot prf	*	*	*	£8
1954 Eng	*	*	*	£4
1954 Scot	*	*	*	£4
1955 Eng	*	*	*	£4
1955 Scot	*	*	*	£4
1956 Eng	*	*	*	£6
1956 Scot	*	*	*	£8
1957 Eng	*	*	*	£3
1957 Scot	*	*	*	£15
1958 Eng	*	*	*	£15
1958 Scot	*	*	*	£3

Reverses: English (left), Scottish (right)

	F	VF	EF	Unc
1959 Eng	*	*	*	£3
1959 Scot	*	*	*	£25
1960 Eng	*	*	*	£2
1960 Scot	*	*	*	£3
1961 Eng	*	*	*	£2
1961 Scot	*	*	*	£10
1962 Eng	*	*	*	£1
1962 Scot	*	*	*	£1
1963 Eng	*	*	*	£1
1963 Scot	*	*	*	£1
1964 Eng	*	*	*	£1
1964 Scot	*	*	*	£1
1965 Eng	*	*	*	£1
1965 Scot	*	*	*	£1
1966 Eng	*	*	*	£1
1966 Scot	*	*	*	£1

Sixpences

CROMWELL

	F	VF	EF
1658		of the highest rarity	
1658 Dutch copy	*	£1650	£3500

CHARLES II

	F	VF	EF
1674	£50	£190	£600
1675	£50	£190	£600
1675/4	£50	£190	£625
1676	£50	£190	£625
1676/5	£50	£190	£625
1677	£50	£190	£650
1678/7	£50	£190	£650

Charles II 1678 sixpence

	F	VF	EF
1679	£50	£185	£650
1680	£60	£285	£800

SIXPENCES

	F	VF	EF
1681	£50	£195	£575
1682	£50	£250	£650
1682/1	£50	£195	£575
1683	£50	£195	£525
1684	£50	£225	£625

James II 1688 sixpence

JAMES II

	F	VF	EF
1686 early shields	£100	£350	£1000
1687 –	£100	£350	£1000
1687/6	£100	£350	£1000
1687 later shield	£100	£350	£1000
1687/6	£100	£375	£1100
1688 –	£100	£375	£1100

WILLIAM AND MARY

	F	VF	EF
1693	£110	£375	£1100
1693 3 upside down	£125	£400	£1100
1694	£140	£400	£1200

William and Mary 1694 sixpence

WILLIAM III

	F	VF	EF
1695 1st bust early harp	£40	£90	£450
1696 - -	£30	£70	£250
1696 - - no obv stops	£35	£90	£350
1696/5	£35	£100	£350
1696 - - B	£30	£70	£300
1696 - - C	£35	£90	£350
1696 - - E	£35	£90	£350
1696 - - N	£35	£100	£350
1696 - - y	£30	£85	£325
1696 - - Y	£40	£100	£350
1696 - later harp	£50	£135	£325
1696 - - B	£50	£175	£425
1696 - - C	£60	£225	£450
1696 - - N	£60	£185	£450
1696 2nd bust	£175	£485	£1200
1696 - - E, 3rd Bust, early harp	Extremely rare		
1696 - - y, 3rd Bust, early harp	Extremely rare		
1697 1st bust early harp	£25	£60	£225
1697 - - B	£40	£100	£325
1697 - - C	£40	£110	£325
1697 - - E	£40	£110	£325
1697 - - N	£40	£85	£325
1697 - - y	£40	£85	£325
1697 2nd bust	£125	£375	£950
1697 3rd bust later harp	£25	£60	£225
1697 - - B	£40	£100	£325
1697 - - C	£60	£125	£400
1697 - - E	£65	£120	£400
1697 - - Y	£55	£120	£400
1698 -	£45	£100	£275
1698 - - plumes	£95	£225	£400
1699 - -	£85	£250	£485
1699 - - plumes	£100	£225	£450

William III 1699 sixpence, plumes

	F	VF	EF
1699 - - roses	£100	£225	£500
1700	£30	£65	£180
1700 plume below bust	£2000	*	*
1701	£30	£65	£200

ANNE

	F	VF	EF
1703 VIGO	£40	£110	£250
1705	£60	£185	£425
1705 plumes	£50	£150	£325
1705 roses & plumes	£45	£150	£400
1707 –	£40	£140	£300
1707 plain	£25	£75	£185
1707 E	£20	£100	£265

Anne 1707 sixpence, E below bust

	F	VF	EF
1707 plumes	£35	£80	£300
1708 plain	£30	£80	£150
1708 E	£35	£80	£325
1708/7 E	£60	£135	£375
1708 E★	£40	£110	£325
1708/7 E★	£60	£135	£350
1708 Edin bust E★	£45	£110	£375
1708 plumes	£45	£125	£350
1710 roses & plumes	£45	£125	£350
1711	£18	£75	£150

George I 1717 sixpence

GEORGE I

	F	VF	EF
1717	£50	£165	£425
1720/17	£50	£165	£425
1723 SS C, Small letters on obv	£25	£75	£200
1723 SS C, large letters on both sides	£25	£75	£200
1726 roses & plumes	£35	£150	£425

GEORGE II

	F	VF	EF
1728 YH	£65	£225	£500
1728 – plumes	£45	£150	£375
1728 – r & p	£25	£100	£295
1731 - -	£25	£100	£295
1732 - -	£25	£100	£295
1734 - -	£35	£110	£350
1735 - -	£35	£110	£350
1736 - -	£30	£110	£325
1739 – roses	£25	£100	£250
1739 - - O/R	£60	£175	£400

	F	VF	EF
1741 – –	£25	£100	£250
1743 OH	£25	£100	£250
1745 – –	£25	£100	£250
1745/3 – –	£30	£110	£325
1745 – LIMA	£20	£75	£150
1746 – LIMA	£20	£75	£150
1746 – plain proof	*	*	£675

George II 1746 sixpence

	F	VF	EF
1750	£35	£135	£325
1751	£35	£175	£400
1757	£8	£20	£50
1757	£8	£20	£50
1758/7	£10	£35	£60

GEORGE III

	F	VF	EF	Unc
1787 hearts	£10	£20	£50	£85
1787 no hearts	£10	£20	£50	£85
1816	£8	£12	£40	£70
1817	£8	£12	£40	£70
1818	£8	£18	£45	£120
1819	£8	£15	£40	£85
1819 small 8	£10	£20	£85	£175
1820	£8	£15	£40	£85
1820 1 inverted	£30	£100	£350	£600

GEORGE IV

	F	VF	EF	Unc
1820 1st hd 1st rev ...	*	*	*	£1,750
(pattern or proof)				
1821 1st hd 1st rev ...	£8	£20	£125	£250
1821 – –				
BBITANNIAR	£90	£175	£500	*
1824 1st hd 2nd				
rev	£8	£20	£100	£225
1825 – –	£8	£20	£100	£225
1826 – –	£20	£60	£200	£475
1826 2nd hd 3rd				
rev	£5	£14	£85	£250

George IV 1825 sixpence

	F	VF	EF	Unc
1826 – – proof	*	*	*	£250
1827	£15	£45	£185	£450
1828	£8	£20	£125	£300
1829	£6	£20	£110	£250

WILLIAM IV

	F	VF	EF	Unc
1831	£6	£20	£95	£225
1831 proof	*	*	*	£300
1834	£6	£30	£100	£225
1835	£6	£20	£100	£225
1836	£15	£35	£165	£300
1837	£12	£30	£165	£300

VICTORIA

	F	VF	EF	Unc
1838	£5	£12	£75	£125
1839	£5	£12	£75	£125
1839 proof	*	*	*	£350

	F	VF	EF	Unc
1840	£5	£10	£70	£150
1841	£5	£10	£70	£185
1842	£5	£10	£80	£150
1843	£5	£10	£70	£150
1844	£5	£10	£70	£150
1845	£5	£10	£70	£150
1846	£3	£10	£70	£150
1848	£15	£90	£400	£700
1848/6	£10	£80	£325	£725
1848/7	£10	£80	£325	£725
1850	£5	£18	£80	£185
1850 5 over 3	£15	£45	£250	£450
1851	£4	£12	£70	£150
1852	£4	£12	£70	£150
1853	£5	£15	£70	£115
1853 proof	*	*	*	£400
1854	£40	£125	£600	*
1855	£4	£12	£70	£140
1856	£4	£12	£70	£145
1857	£4	£12	£70	£145
1858	£4	£12	£70	£140
1859	£4	£12	£70	£140
1859/8	£8	£20	£75	£150
1860	£5	£15	£75	£145
1862	£20	£60	£350	£750
1863	£12	£40	£250	£675
1864	£5	£12	£65	£150
1865	£6	£14	£70	£185
1866	£5	£12	£60	£150
1866 no die no. ...	*	*	*	*
1867	£8	£20	£80	£185
1868	£8	£20	£80	£185
1869	£8	£25	£110	£225
1870	£8	£20	£110	£225
1871	£5	£12	£65	£160
1871 no die no. ...	£5	£12	£65	£160
1872	£5	£12	£65	£150
1873	£5	£12	£65	£150
1874	£5	£12	£65	£150
1875	£5	£12	£70	£150
1876	£6	£20	£80	£195
1877	£5	£12	£65	£135
1877 no die no. ...	£5	£12	£65	£135
1878	£5	£10	£60	£135
1878 DRITANNIAR...	£65	£150	£450	*
1879 die no.	£8	£20	£85	£200
1879 no die no. ...	£5	£10	£60	£135
1880 2nd YH	£7	£15	£60	£130
1880 3rd YH	£3	£8	£40	£95
1881	£4	£10	£40	£80
1882	£8	£20	£75	£175
1883	£4	£10	£35	£80
1884	£4	£10	£35	£80
1885	£4	£10	£35	£80
1886	£4	£10	£35	£80
1887 YH	£4	£10	£35	£80
1887 JH shield rev	£2	£5	£10	£25

1887 Jubilee Head sixpence, withdrawn type

	F	VF	EF	Unc
1887 – proof	*	*	*	£90
1887 – new rev	£2	£5	£10	£25
1888	£3	£5	£15	£45
1889	£3	£7	£15	£45

SIXPENCES

	F	VF	EF	Unc
1890	*	£3	£15	£50
1891	*	£3	£17	£55
1892	*	£3	£17	£55
1893	£250	£650	£1750	*
1893 OH	*	£3	£15	£45
1893 proof	*	*	*	£100
1894	*	£3	£25	£45
1895	*	£3	£25	£45
1896	*	£3	£25	£45
1897	*	£3	£20	£40
1898	*	£3	£20	£40
1899	*	£3	£25	£45
1900	*	£3	£20	£40
1901	*	£3	£20	£40

EDWARD VII

	F	VF	EF	Unc
1902	*	£5	£25	£45
1902 matt proof ...	*	*	*	£40
1903	*	£7	£25	£75
1904	*	£12	£45	£110
1905	*	£8	£30	£90
1906	*	£5	£25	£80
1907	*	£7	£25	£80
1908	*	£8	£35	£95
1909	*	£6	£30	£75
1910	*	£6	£22	£45

GEORGE V

	F	VF	EF	Unc
1911	*	*	£12	£35
1911 proof	*	*	*	£45
1912	*	*	£20	£50
1913	*	*	£30	£50
1914	*	*	£12	£25
1915	*	*	£12	£25
1916	*	*	£12	£25
1917	*	*	£20	£50
1918	*	*	£12	£25
1919	*	*	£12	£30
1920	*	*	£12	£40
1920 debased	*	*	£12	£40
1921	*	*	£10	£30
1922	*	*	£10	£30
1923	*	*	£10	£40
1924	*	*	£10	£30
1925	*	*	£10	£25
1925 new rim ...	*	*	£12	£20
1926 new rim	*	*	£12	£25
1926 mod effigy ...	*	*	£7	£25
1927	*	*	£5	£25
1927 new rev prf ...	*	*	£5	£30
1928	*	*	£5	£17
1929	*	*	£5	£17
1930	*	*	£5	£17
1931	*	*	£5	£17
1932	*	*	£8	£22
1933	*	*	£5	£15
1934	*	*	£6	£20

George V 1929 sixpence

	F	VF	EF	Unc
1935	*	*	£5	£15
1936	*	*	£5	£15

GEORGE VI

	F	VF	EF	Unc
1937	*	*	£1	£5
1937 proof	*	*	*	£10
1938	*	*	£4	£12
1939	*	*	£2	£7
1940	*	*	£2	£7
1941	*	*	£2	£7
1942	*	*	£1	£6
1943	*	*	£1	£6
1944	*	*	£1	£6
1945	*	*	£1	£6
1946	*	*	£1	£6
1947	*	*	*	£5
1948	*	*	£1	£5
1949	*	*	£1	£7
1950	*	*	£1	£7
1950 proof	*	*	*	£10
1951	*	*	£1	£12
1951 proof	*	*	*	£10
1952	*	£5	£20	£50

ELIZABETH II

	F	VF	EF	Unc
1953	*	*	*	£3
1953 proof	*	*	*	£5
1954	*	*	*	£5
1955	*	*	*	£3
1956	*	*	*	£3
1957	*	*	*	£3
1958	*	*	*	£2
1959	*	*	*	£2
1960	*	*	*	£2
1961	*	*	*	£2
1962	*	*	*	£1
1963	*	*	*	£1
1964	*	*	*	£1
1965	*	*	*	£1
1966	*	*	*	£1
1967	*	*	*	£1

Groats (fourpences)

William IV 1836 groat
Earlier dates are included in Maundy sets

WILLIAM IV

	F	VF	EF	Unc
1836	*	*	£40	£70
1836 proof	*	*	*	£525
1837	*	£12	£50	£85

Victoria 1842 groat

VICTORIA

	F	VF	EF	Unc
1838	*	£5	£20	£65
1838 8 over 8 on side	*	£10	£35	£110
1839	*	£8	£25	£70
1839 proof	*	*	*	£200
1840	£2	£10	£30	£70
1840 narrow 0	*	£12	£50	*
1841	£3	£10	£35	£80
1841 I for last 1	*	*	*	*
1842	*	£8	£30	£80

COINS MARKET VALUES

	F	VF	EF	Unc
1842/1	£4	£15	£70	£100
1843	*	£5	£25	£80
1844	*	£8	£35	£80
1845	*	£8	£35	£80
1846	*	£8	£35	£80
1847/6	£25	£50	£250	*
1848	*	£8	£25	£65
1848/6	£15	£65	£250	*
1848/7	£5	£15	£50	£125
1849	*	£8	£25	£70
1849/8	*	£8	£45	£90
1851	£15	£60	£200	*
1852	£40	£100	£300	*
1853	£35	£90	£400	*
1853 proof	*	*	*	£300
1854	*	£8	£25	£60
1854 5 over 3	£5	£10	£40	*
1855	*	£8	£25	£60
1857 proof	*	*	*	£850
1862 proof	*	*	*	*
1888 JH	£5	£10	£30	£65

Silver threepences

Earlier dates are included in Maundy sets

WILLIAM IV

	F	VF	EF	Unc
1834	*	£10	£60	£125
1835	*	£10	£60	£110
1836	*	£10	£60	£125
1837	£10	£20	£75	£150

Victoria threepence of 1848

VICTORIA

	F	VF	EF	Unc
1838	*	£8	£70	£125
1839	*	£10	£100	£175
1840	*	£10	£100	£150
1841	*	£10	£100	£175
1842	*	£10	£100	£175
1843	*	£10	£90	£145
1844	*	£12	£100	£175
1845	*	£5	£45	£100
1846	*	£15	£110	£185
1847	*	*	£400	£800
1848	*	*	£400	£750
1849	*	£12	£100	£175
1850	*	£5	£50	£100
1851	*	£8	£50	£135
1852	£45	£175	£400	*
1853	*	£20	£100	£200
1854	*	£8	£60	£100
1855	*	£12	£100	£175
1856	*	£10	£95	£165
1857	*	£10	£90	£175
1858	*	£8	£50	£125
1858/6	*	£25	£150	*
1859	*	£4	£50	£125
1860	*	£8	£50	£175
1861	*	£4	£60	£110
1862	*	£8	£65	£110
1863	*	£10	£90	£145
1864	*	£8	£65	£125
1865	*	£10	£70	£150
1866	*	£8	£60	£125
1867	*	£8	£60	£125

SILVER THREEPENCES

	F	VF	EF	Unc
1868	*	£8	£65	£120
1868 RRITANNIAR	ext.rare			*
1869	£10	£30	£110	£165
1870	*	£6	£50	£85
1871	*	£7	£60	£100
1872	*	£5	£55	£100
1873	*	£5	£35	£75
1874	*	£5	£35	£65
1875	*	£5	£35	£65
1876	*	£5	£35	£65
1877	*	£5	£35	£65
1878	*	£5	£35	£65
1879	*	£5	£35	£65
1880	*	£6	£40	£70
1881	*	£6	£40	£70
1882	*	£8	£45	£100
1883	*	£5	£30	£60
1884	*	£5	£30	£55
1885	*	£5	£25	£55
1886	*	£5	£25	£50
1887 YH	*	£6	£30	£55
1887 JH	*	£2	£5	£10
1887 proof	*	*	*	£40
1888	*	£2	£7	£25
1889	*	£2	£6	£20
1890	*	£2	£6	£20
1891	*	£2	£6	£20
1892	*	£3	£10	£25
1893	£12	£40	£100	£250
1893 OH	*	*	£4	£20
1893 OH proof	*	*	*	£65
1894	*	£2	£8	£25
1895	*	£2	£8	£25
1896	*	£2	£6	£25
1897	*	*	£5	£25
1898	*	*	£5	£25
1899	*	*	£5	£25
1900	*	*	£5	£25
1901	*	*	£5	£20

EDWARD VII

	F	VF	EF	Unc
1902	*	*	£6	£12
1902 matt proof ...	*	*	*	£15
1903	*	£1.50	£15	£40
1904	*	£6	£25	£65
1905	*	£6	£25	£40
1906	*	£3	£20	£40
1907	*	£1.50	£15	£40
1908	*	£1.50	£12	£35
1909	*	£2	£25	£50
1910	*	£1.25	£10	£25

George V 1927 threepence, acorns on reverse

GEORGE V

	F	VF	EF	Unc
1911	*	*	£4	£17
1911 proof	*	*	*	£30
1912	*	*	£4	£17
1913	*	*	£4	£17
1914	*	*	£3	£15
1915	*	*	£3	£15
1916	*	*	£2	£12
1917	*	*	£2	£12
1918	*	*	£3	£12
1919	*	*	£3	£12

SILVER THREEPENCES

	F	VF	EF	Unc
1920	*	*	£2	£15
1920 debased	*	*	£2	£15
1921	*	*	£2	£17
1922	*	*	£2	£17
1925	*	£1	£6	£23
1926	*	£3	£10	£30
1926 mod effigy ...	*	£1	£6	£25
1927 new rev prf ...	*	*	*	£45
1928	*	£2	£6	£25
1930	*	£1.50	£5	£15
1931	*	*	£1	£7
1932	*	*	£1	£7
1933	*	*	£1	£7
1934	*	*	£1	£7
1935	*	*	£1	£7
1936	*	*	£1	£7

GEORGE VI

	F	VF	EF	Unc
1937	*	*	£1	£2
1937 proof	*	*	*	£10
1938	*	*	£1	£6
1939	*	£1	£3	£10
1940	*	*	£1	£8
1941	*	*	£1	£12
1942	£1	£2	£6	£35
1943	£1	£3	£7	£45
1944	£1.50	£5	£12	£60
1945[2]	*	*	*	*

[1]Threepences issued for use in the Colonies.
[2]All specimens of 1945 were thought to have been melted down but it appears that one or two still exist.

Small silver for Colonies

These tiny coins were struck for use in some of the Colonies – they were never issued for circulation in Britain. However, they are often included in collections of British coins and it is for this reason that prices for them are given here.

TWOPENCES

Other dates are included in Maundy sets.

VICTORIA

	F	VF	EF	Unc
1838	*	£2	£15	£35
1838 2nd 8 like S ...	*	£6	£25	£75
1848	*	£2	£15	£35

THREEHALFPENCES

WILLIAM IV ... ...

	F	VF	EF	Unc
1834	*	£5	£40	£75
1835	*	£5	£65	£150
1835/4	*	£10	£40	£95
1836	*	£5	£35	£60
1837	£10	£25	£100	£250

VICTORIA

	F	VF	EF	Unc
1838	*	£5	£25	£60
1839	*	£3	£25	£60
1840	*	£7	£65	£125
1841	*	£5	£30	£80
1842	*	£5	£30	£80
1843	*	£5	£15	£50

George V threepence

	F	VF	EF	Unc
1843/34	£5	£20	£65	£145
1860	£4	£15	£45	£100
1862	£4	£15	£45	£100
1870 proof	**Extremely rare**			

Maundy sets

EF prices are for evenly matched sets

Charles II 1677 Maundy set

CHARLES II

	F	VF	EF
1670	£90	£200	£450
1671	£90	£200	£450
1672	£90	£200	£475
1673	£90	£200	£450
1674	£90	£200	£450
1675	£90	£225	£475
1676	£90	£225	£475
1677	£90	£200	£450
1678	£95	£250	£500
1679	£90	£225	£475
1680	£90	£200	£450
1681	£95	£250	£500
1682	£95	£225	£475
1683	£90	£200	£450
1684	£90	£225	£475

JAMES II

	F	VF	EF
1686	£95	£275	£550
1687	£90	£275	£550
1688	£95	£275	£550

WILLIAM AND MARY

	F	VF	EF
1689	£300	£550	£1200
1691	£125	£275	£600
1692	£135	£275	£700
1693	£135	£275	£700
1694	£125	£250	£600

WILLIAM III

	F	VF	EF
1698	£95	£250	£550
1699	£100	£275	£600
1700	£100	£275	£600
1701	£95	£250	£575

ANNE		F	VF	EF
1703	… … … … … … … …	£85	£165	£475
1705	… … … … … … … …	£85	£165	£475
1706	… … … … … … … …	£75	£150	£425
1708	… … … … … … … …	£85	£175	£475
1709	… … … … … … … …	£75	£165	£400
1710	… … … … … … … …	£85	£175	£475
1713	… … … … … … … …	£75	£150	£450

GEORGE I
		F	VF	EF
1723	… … … … … … … …	£85	£185	£500
1727	… … … … … … … …	£90	£150	£475

GEORGE II
		F	VF	EF
1729	… … … … … … … …	£60	£150	£375
1731	… … … … … … … …	£60	£150	£375
1732	… … … … … … … …	£55	£150	£300
1735	… … … … … … … …	£55	£150	£300
1737	… … … … … … … …	£55	£150	£300
1739	… … … … … … … …	£55	£150	£300
1740	… … … … … … … …	£55	£150	£300
1743	… … … … … … … …	£55	£150	£375
1746	… … … … … … … …	£50	£150	£275
1760	… … … … … … … …	£70	£195	£325

GEORGE III
		F	VF	EF	Unc
1763	… … … … … …	*	£75	£175	£275
1766	… … … … … …	*	£80	£200	£275
1772	… … … … … …	*	£20	£200	£275
1780	… … … … … …	*	£80	£200	£275
1784	… … … … … …	*	£80	£200	£275
1786	… … … … … …	*	£80	£200	£275
1792 wire type	… …	*	£125	£350	£400

William and Mary 1694 Maundy set

		F	VF	EF	Unc
1795	… … … … … …	*	£60	£110	£250
1800	… … … … … …	*	£60	£110	£250
1817	… … … … … …	*	£65	£110	£250
1818	… … … … … …	*	£65	£110	£250
1820	… … … … … …	*	£65	£110	£250

GEORGE IV
		F	VF	EF	Unc
1822	… … … … … …	*	*	£90	£175
1823	… … … … … …	*	*	£90	£175
1824	… … … … … …	*	*	£90	£175
1825	… … … … … …	*	*	£90	£175
1826	… … … … … …	*	*	£90	£175
1827	… … … … … …	*	*	£90	£175
1828	… … … … … …	*	*	£90	£175
1829	… … … … … …	*	*	£90	£175
1830	… … … … … …	*	*	£90	£175

WILLIAM IV
		F	VF	EF	Unc
1831	… … … … … …	*	£65	£100	£250
1831 proof	… … … …	*	*	*	£400
1832	… … … … … …	*	£65	£100	£250
1833	… … … … … …	*	£60	£90	£225
1834	… … … … … …	*	£60	£90	£225
1835	… … … … … …	*	£60	£90	£225

MAUNDY SETS

		F	VF	EF	Unc
1836	… … … … … …	*	£65	£110	£275
1837	… … … … … …	*	£65	£110	£275

VICTORIA
		F	VF	EF	Unc
1838	… … … … … … … … … … … …			£80	£150
1839	… … … … … … … … … … … …			£85	£150
1839 proof	… … … … … … … …			*	£350
1840	… … … … … … … … … … … …			£85	£150
1841	… … … … … … … … … … … …			£85	£185
1842	… … … … … … … … … … … …			£90	£170
1843	… … … … … … … … … … … …			£90	£165
1844	… … … … … … … … … … … …			£90	£165
1845	… … … … … … … … … … … …			£80	£150
1846	… … … … … … … … … … … …			£95	£200
1847	… … … … … … … … … … … …			£90	£140

George IV 1825

		EF	Unc
1848	… … … … … … … … … … … …	£85	£150
1849	… … … … … … … … … … … …	£95	£200
1850	… … … … … … … … … … … …	£75	£110
1851	… … … … … … … … … … … …	£75	£110
1852	… … … … … … … … … … … …	£80	£125
1853	… … … … … … … … … … … …	£80	£125
1853 proof	… … … … … … … … … …	*	£500
1854	… … … … … … … … … … … …	£80	£150
1855	… … … … … … … … … … … …	£80	£150
1856	… … … … … … … … … … … …	£80	£120
1857	… … … … … … … … … … … …	£80	£120
1858	… … … … … … … … … … … …	£80	£120
1859	… … … … … … … … … … … …	£80	£120
1860	… … … … … … … … … … … …	£80	£110
1861	… … … … … … … … … … … …	£80	£110
1862	… … … … … … … … … … … …	£80	£110
1863	… … … … … … … … … … … …	£80	£110
1864	… … … … … … … … … … … …	£80	£110
1865	… … … … … … … … … … … …	£80	£110
1866	… … … … … … … … … … … …	£80	£110
1867	… … … … … … … … … … … …	£80	£110
1868	… … … … … … … … … … … …	£80	£110
1869	… … … … … … … … … … … …	£80	£110
1870	… … … … … … … … … … … …	£80	£100
1871	… … … … … … … … … … … …	£80	£100
1872	… … … … … … … … … … … …	£80	£100
1873	… … … … … … … … … … … …	£80	£100
1874	… … … … … … … … … … … …	£80	£100
1875	… … … … … … … … … … … …	£80	£100
1876	… … … … … … … … … … … …	£80	£100
1877	… … … … … … … … … … … …	£80	£100
1878	… … … … … … … … … … … …	£80	£100
1879	… … … … … … … … … … … …	£80	£100
1880	… … … … … … … … … … … …	£80	£100
1881	… … … … … … … … … … … …	£80	£100
1882	… … … … … … … … … … … …	£80	£100
1883	… … … … … … … … … … … …	£80	£100
1884	… … … … … … … … … … … …	£80	£100
1885	… … … … … … … … … … … …	£80	£100
1886	… … … … … … … … … … … …	£80	£100
1887	… … … … … … … … … … … …	£80	£100
1888 JH	… … … … … … … … … … … …	£60	£95

MAUNDY SETS

	EF	Unc
1889	£70	£100
1890	£70	£100
1891	£70	£100
1892	£70	£100
1893 OH	£58	£80
1894	£58	£80
1895	£58	£80
1896	£58	£80
1897	£58	£80
1898	£58	£80
1899	£58	£80
1900	£58	£95
1901	£58	£80

EDWARD VII
	EF	Unc
1902	£50	£70
1902 matt proof	*	£65
1903	£45	£65
1904	£45	£65
1905	£45	£65
1906	£45	£65
1907	£45	£65
1908	£45	£65
1909	£55	£90
1910	£55	£90

GEORGE V
	EF	Unc
1911	£50	£80
1911 proof	*	£85
1912	£50	£80
1913	£50	£80
1914	£50	£85
1915	£50	£80
1916	£50	£80
1917	£50	£80
1918	£50	£80
1919	£50	£80
1920	£50	£80
1921	£50	£80
1922	£50	£80
1923	£50	£80
1924	£50	£80
1925	£50	£80
1926	£50	£80
1927	£50	£80
1928	£50	£80
1929	£50	£80
1930	£50	£80
1931	£50	£80
1932	£50	£80
1933	£50	£80
1934	£50	£80
1935	£50	£80
1936	£55	£80

GEORGE VI
	EF	Unc
1937	*	£65
1938	*	£70
1939	*	£70
1940	*	£70
1941	*	£70
1942	*	£70
1943	*	£70
1944	*	£70
1945	*	£70
1946	*	£70
1947	*	£70
1948	*	£70
1949	*	£70
1950	*	£70
1951	*	£70
1952	*	£70

ELIZABETH II
	EF	Unc
1953	£200	£300
1954	*	£90
1955	*	£90
1956	*	£90
1957	*	£90
1958	*	£90
1959	*	£90
1960	*	£90
1961	*	£90
1962	*	£90
1963	*	£90
1964	*	£90
1965	*	£90
1966	*	£90
1967	*	£90
1968	*	£90
1969	*	£90
1970	*	£70
1971	*	£70
1972	*	£70
1973	*	£70
1974	*	£70
1975	*	£70
1976	*	£70
1977	*	£70
1978	*	£70
1979	*	£70
1980	*	£70
1981	*	£70
1982	*	£70
1983	*	£70
1984	*	£70
1985	*	£70
1986	*	£70
1987	*	£70
1988	*	£70
1989	*	£70
1990	*	£70
1991	*	£70
1992	*	£70
1993	*	£70
1994	*	£70
1995	*	£70
1996	*	£70
1997	*	£70
1998	*	£70
1999	*	£85
2000	*	£90
2001	*	£95
2002	*	£110
2002 gold (from set)	*	£900
2003	*	£125
2004	*	£135
2005	*	£150

1925 Maundy (part set)

Nickel-brass threepences

1937 threepence of Edward VII, extremely rare

1937-dated Edward VIII threepences, struck in 1936 ready for issue, were melted after Edward's abdication. A few, however, escaped into circulation to become highly prized collectors' pieces. George VI 1937 threepences were struck in large numbers.

EDWARD VIII	F	VF	EF	BU
1937	*	*	£25000	*

GEORGE VI				
1937	*	*	£1	£4
1938	*	*	£3	£20
1939	*	*	£6	£40
1940	*	*	£2	£15
1941	*	*	£1	£6
1942	*	*	£1	£6
1943	*	*	£1	£6
1944	*	*	£1	£6
1945	*	*	£1	£6
1946	£2	£10	£85	£300
1948	*	*	£4	£6
1949	£2	£10	£80	£275
1950	*	*	£8	£25
1951	*	*	£8	£25
1952	*	*	*	£10

Elizabeth II 1953 nickel-brass threepence

ELIZABETH II				
1953	*	*	*	£3
1953 proof	*	*	*	£8
1954	*	*	*	£5
1955	*	*	*	£5
1956	*	*	£1	£5
1957	*	*	*	£4
1958	*	*	£2	£6
1959	*	*	*	£3
1960	*	*	*	£3
1961	*	*	*	£1
1962	*	*	*	£1
1963	*	*	*	£1
1964	*	*	*	£1
1965	*	*	*	£1
1966	*	*	*	*
1967	*	*	*	*

Copper twopence

George III 1797 'cartwheel' twopence

GEORGE III	F	VF	EF	BU
1797	£20	£75	£275	*

Copper pennies

GEORGE III	F	VF	EF	BU
1797 10 leaves	£5	£35	£175	*
1797 11 leaves	£8	£45	£160	*

1797 'cartwheel' penny

1806	£3	£8	£70	£250
1806 no incuse curl	£3	£8	£70	£250
1807	£3	£8	£70	£250

1806 penny of George III

GEORGE IV	F	VF	EF	BU
1825	£5	£15	£125	£400
1826	£3	£12	£125	£400
1826 thin line down				
St Andrew's cross	£5	£15	£125	£400
1826 thick line	£5	£15	£125	£400
1827	£200	£550	£1750	*

William IV 1831 penny

WILLIAM IV	F	VF	EF	BU
1831	£10	£50	£250	*
1831.w.w incuse ...	£12	£60	£300	*
1831.w.w incuse ...	£15	£75	£350	*
1834	£15	£75	£300	*
1837	£20	£100	£600	*

Victoria 1841 copper penny

VICTORIA	F	VF	EF	Unc
1839 proof	*	*	*	£500
1841	£12	£30	£75	£225
1841 no colon				
after REG	£3	£15	£50	£275
1843	£45	£200	£900	£2300
1843 no colon				
after REG	£30	£125	£800	£2250
1844	£3	£15	£70	£175
1845	£8	£20	£95	£275
1846 DEF far				
colon	£3	£15	£85	£250
1846 DEF close				
colon	£3	£15	£85	£295
1847 DEF close				
colon	£3	£15	£50	£175
1847 DEF far				
colon	£3	£15	£50	£175

	F	VF	EF	BU
1848	£3	£15	£60	£175
1848/6	£15	£35	£250	*
1848/7	£3	£15	£60	£175
1849	£40	£120	£800	*
1851 DEF far colon	£3	£15	£100	£295
1851 DEF close colon	£4	£15	£100	£250
1853 OT	£2	£10	£50	£135
1853 colon nearer F	£3	£10	£60	£175
1853 PT	£2	£10	£60	£200
1854 PT	£2	£10	£60	£150
1854/3	£15	£50	£100	£250
1854 OT	£2	£10	£60	£150
1855 OT	£2	£10	£60	£150
1855 PT	£2	£10	£60	£150
1856 PT	£50	£200	£425	*
1856 OT	£20	£50	£225	£900
1857 OT	£2	£10	£60	£150
1857 PT	£2	£10	£60	£150
1857 small date ...	£2	£10	£75	£225
1858	£2	£10	£50	£150
1858 small date ...	£3	£10	£55	£200
1858/3 now thought to be 1858 9/8 (see below)				
1858/7	£2	£5	£45	£150
1858/6	£15	£35	£100	*
1858 no ww	£2	£5	£45	£150
1858 no ww (large 1 and 5				
small 8s)	£3	£8	£50	£165
1858 9/8?	£12	£25	£60	£175
1858 9/8? large rose	£12	£30	£75	£200
1859	£3	£10	£45	£150
1859 small date ...	£4	£15	£50	£150
1860/59	£200	£600	£1500	*

Bronze pennies

For fuller details of varieties in bronze pennies see English Copper, Tin and Bronze Coins in the British Museum 1558-1958 *by C. W. Peck;* The Bronze Coinage of Great Britain *by M. J. Freeman and* The British Bronze Penny 1860-1970 *by Michael Gouby.*

VICTORIA	F	VF	EF	BU
1860 RB, shield crossed with incuse				
treble lines	*	£15	£55	£225
1860 RB, shield crossed with close double				
raised lines	£8	£20	£65	£250
1860 RB, double lines, but farther apart,				
rock to left of				
lighthouse	£10	£50	£250	£600
1860 RB obv/TB rev	£100	£350	£1250	*
1860 TB obv/RB rev	£100	£350	£1250	*

1860 penny, toothed border on obverse

1860 TB, L.C. WYON on truncation, L.C.W. incuse below

	F	VF	EF	BU
shield	*	£17	£60	£225

	F	VF	EF	BU
1860 TB, same obv but L.C.W. incuse below foot	£45	£125	£475	£1100
1860 TB, as previous but heavy flan of 170 grains		ext. rare		
1860 TB, LC, WYON below truncation, L.C.W. incuse below shield	*	£17	£60	£225
1860 TB, no signature on obv. L.C.W. incuse below shield	*	£25	£100	£225
1861 L.C. WYON on truncation, L.C.W. incuse below shield	£15	£60	£200	£550
1861 same obv. no signature on rev	*	£15	£65	£275
1861 L.C. WYON below truncation, L.C.W. incuse below shield	*	£10	£60	£225
1861 similar, but heavy flan (170 grains)	*	*	*	£1500
1861 same obv but no signature on rev	*	£15	£60	£250
1861 no signature on obv, L.C.W. incuse below shield ... ...·	*	£15	£65	£250
1861-6/8		ext.rare		
1861 no signature either side	*	£12	£55	£225
1862	*	£10	£50	£225
1862 sm date figs ...		ext. rare		
1863	*	£10	£60	£225
1863 slender 3		ext. rare		
1863 die no. (2, 3 or 4) below date		ext. rare		
1864 plain 4	£20	£85	£500	£1500
1864 crossiet 4	£25	£85	£600	£1750
1865	*	£25	£100	£400
1865/3	£15	£75	£400	£1100
1866	*	£12	£70	£250
1867	*	£20	£80	£425
1868	£6	£40	£125	£600
1869	£50	£200	£1350	£2500
1870	£6	£40	£175	£425
1871	£8	£60	£300	£725
1872	*	£12	£65	£250
1873	*	£12	£65	£250
1874 (1873 type) ...	*	£12	£65	£250
1874 H (1873 type) ...	*	£12	£70	£265
1874 new rev, lighthouse tall and thin	*	£20	£70	£250
1874 H as previous	£4	£15	£65	£275
1874 new obv/1873 rev	*	£15	£60	£250
1874 H as previous	*	£15	£60	£250
1874 new obv/new rev	*	£15	£60	£250
1874 H as previous	*	£15	£60	£250
1875	*	£15	£60	£250
1875 H	£30	£125	£600	*
1876 H	*	£15	£85	£275
1877	*	£8	£65	£225
1878	*	£15	£75	£400
1879	*	*	£50	£175
1880	*	*	£70	£275
1881 (1880 obv)	*	*	£70	£275
1881 new obv	*	£15	£80	£375
1881 H	*	*	£55	£250
1882 H	*	*	£45	£175
1882 no H	£75	£300	*	*
1883	*	*	£35	£175
1884	*	*	£35	£150
1885	*	*	£35	£150
1886	*	*	£35	£150
1887	*	*	£35	£150

BRONZE PENNIES

	F	VF	EF	BU
1888	*	*	£30	£150
1889 14 leaves	*	*	£30	£150
1889 15 leaves	*	*	£30	£150
1890	*	*	£30	£150
1891	*	*	£30	£130
1892	*	*	£30	£150
1893	*	*	£30	£150
1894	*	*	£40	£200
1895 2mm	*	£40	£195	£425

Victoria old head penny of 1895

	F	VF	EF	BU
1895	*	*	£15	£55
1896	*	*	£12	£50
1897	*	*	£12	£50
1897 higher horizon	£5	£25	£175	£400
1898	*	*	£15	£55
1899	*	*	£15	£50
1900	*	*	£12	£45
1901	*	*	£10	£25

Edward VII 1902, penny, low horizon

EDWARD VII

	F	VF	EF	BU
1902 low horizon ...	*	£15	£70	£150
1902	*	*	£5	£30
1903	*	*	£15	£45
1904	*	*	£30	£95
1905	*	*	£25	£70
1906	*	*	£15	£55
1907	*	*	£15	£60

BRONZE PENNIES

	F	VF	EF	BU
1908	*	*	£12	£50
1909	*	*	£15	£50
1910	*	*	£12	£45

GEORGE V

	F	VF	EF	BU
1911	*	*	£12	£30
1912	*	*	£12	£35
1912 H	*	*	£60	£175
1913	*	*	£15	£40
1914	*	*	£12	£35
1915	*	*	£12	£35
1916	*	*	£12	£35
1917	*	*	£12	£35
1918	*	*	£12	£35
1918 H	*	£15	£175	£400
1918 KN	*	£20	£250	£700
1919	*	*	£12	£35
1919 H	*	£5	£200	£500
1919 KN	*	£10	£250	£750
1920	*	*	£12	£35
1921	*	*	£12	£35
1922	*	*	£12	£35
1922 rev as 1927 ext. rare		*	*	*
1926	*	*	£20	£60
1926 mod effigy ...	*	£50	£800	£1500
1927	*	*	£7	£25
1928	*	*	£7	£25
1929	*	*	£7	£25
1930	*	*	£10	£25
1931	*	*	£10	£25
1932	*	*	£15	£45
1933			highest rarity	
1934	*	*	£8	£35
1935	*	*	£2	£15
1936	*	*	*	£15

GEORGE VI

	F	VF	EF	BU
1937	*	*	*	£5
1938	*	*	*	£5
1939	*	*	*	£6
1940	*	*	*	£10
1944	*	*	*	£15
1945	*	*	*	£12
1946	*	*	*	£12
1947	*	*	*	£4
1948	*	*	*	£5
1949	*	*	*	£5

George VI 1948 penny

	F	VF	EF	BU
1950	£2	£5	£15	£35
1951	£2	£5	£20	£50

ELIZABETH II

	F	VF	EF	BU
1953	*	£1	£2	£3
1953 proof	*	*	*	£5

	Fair	F	VF	EF
1961	*	*	*	£0.50
1962	*	*	*	*
1963	*	*	*	*
1964	*	*	*	*
1965	*	*	*	*
1966	*	*	*	*
1967	*	*	*	*

Copper halfpennies

All copper unless otherwise stated

Charles II 1675 halfpenny

CHARLES II

	Fair	F	VF	EF
1672	£5	£45	£150	£800
1672 CRAOLVS		Extremely rare *		
1673	£5	£45	£80	£800
1673 CRAOLVS		Extremely rare *		
1673 no stops on reverse	£10	£50	£200	£800
1673 no stops on obverse	£10	£50	£200	£800
1675	£10	£50	£200	£800
1675 no stops on obverse	£10	£60	£200	£800

James II 1685 tin halfpenny

JAMES II

	Fair	F	VF	EF
1685 (tin)	£30	£150	£450	£3000
1686 (tin)	£35	£160	£500	*
1687 (tin)	£30	£150	£450	*
1687 D over D	*	*	*	*

WILLIAM AND MARY

	Fair	F	VF	EF
1689 (tin) ET on right	£450	£900	£1500	*
1689 (tin) ET on left	*	*	*	*
1690 (tin) dated on edge	£30	£120	£400	£2000
1691 (tin) date in exergue and on edge	£30	£120	£450	£2000

	Fair	F	VF	EF
1691/2 (tin) 1691 in exergue 1692 on edge ...	£30	£120	£450	£2000
1692 (tin) date in exergue and on edge ...	£30	£75	£450	*
1694 ...	£5	£25	£150	£800

William and Mary 1694 halfpenny

	Fair	F	VF	EF
1694 GVLIEMVS ...	£150	*	*	*
1694 no stop after MARIA ...	£15	£45	£200	£825
1694 BRITANNIA with last I over A ...	£30	£125	*	*
1694 no stop on reverse ...	£10	£25	£165	£800

WILLIAM III
Type 1 (date in exergue)

	Fair	F	VF	EF
1695 ...	£5	£25	£125	£800
1695 thick flan ...	£25	£75	£185	*
1695 BRITANNIA ...	£5	£25	£125	£800
1695 no stop on reverse ...	£5	£30	£125	*
1696 ...	£5	£25	£125	£800
1696 GVLIEMVS, no stop on reverse ...	£25	£65	£185	*
1696 TERTVS ...	£15	£50	£185	*
1696 obv struck from doubled die ...	£15	£50	£185	*
1697 ...	£5	£25	£80	*
1697 no stops either side ...	£5	£25	£120	*
1697 I of TERTIVS over E ...	£15	£50	£185	*
1697 GVLILMVS no stop on reverse ...	£15	£40	£185	*
1697 no stop after TERTIVS ...	£10	£25	£80	£800
1698 ...	£10	£25	£80	£800

Type 2 (date in legend)

	Fair	F	VF	EF
1698 ...	£5	£25	£150	£800
1699 ...	£5	£15	£150	£700
1699 BRITANNIA ...	£5	£15	£150	£700
1699 GVLIEMVS ...	£5	£25	£150	£850

Type 3 (Britannia's hand on knee, date in exergue)

	Fair	F	VF	EF
1699 ...	£5	£20	£125	£700
1699 stop after date	£10	£25	£150	£825
1699 BRITANNIA ...	£5	£20	£150	£700
1699 GVILELMVS ...	£10	£25	£150	£800
1699 TERTVS ...	£20	£50	£200	*
1699 no stop on reverse ...	£20	£50	£200	*
1699 no stops on obverse ...	£10	£30	£150	£800

COPPER HALFPENNIES

	FAIR	F	VF	EF
1699 no stops after GVLIELMVS ...	£5	£20	£150	£750
1700 ...	£5	£15	£150	£750
1700 no stops on obverse ...	£5	£15	£150	*
1700 no stop after GVLIELMVS ...	£5	£15	£150	*
1700 BRITANNIA ...	£5	£15	£150	£750
1700 no stops on reverse ...	£5	£15	£150	*
1700 GVLIELMS ...	£5	£25	£150	*
1700 GVLIEEMVS ...	£5	£25	£150	*
1700 TER TIVS ...	£5	£15	£150	*
1700 1 of TERTIVS over V ...	£10	£25	£225	*
1701 BRITANNIA ...	£5	£15	£150	*
1701 no stops on obverse ...	£5	£15	£150	*
1701 GVLIELMVS TERTIVS ...	£5	£25	£200	*

GEORGE I
Type 1

	FAIR	F	VF	EF
1717 ...	£5	£30	£200	£550
1717 no stops on obverse ...	£10	£40	£250	£600
1718 ...	*	£35	£200	£600
1718 no stop on obverse ...	£10	£40	£250	£700
1719 on larger flan of type 2 ...	£15	£50	£300	*
1719 – edge grained	£50	£200	*	*

Type 2

	FAIR	F	VF	EF
1719 both shoulder straps ornate ...	£5	£20	£100	£525
1719 – edge grained	£10	£40	*	*
1719 bust with left strap plain ...	£5	£20	£100	£600
1719 – edge grained	£10	£40	*	*
1720 ...	£5	£20	£100	£525
1721 ...	£5	£20	£100	£525
1721/0 ...	£5	£20	£100	*
1721 stop after date	£5	£20	£100	£525
1722 ...	£5	£20	£100	£525
1722 GEORGIVS ...	£5	£20	£100	*
1723 ...	£5	£20	£100	£525
1723 no stop on reverse ...	£5	£20	£100	£550
1724 ...	£5	£20	£100	£450

George II 1729 halfpenny

GEORGE II
Young Head

	FAIR	F	VF	EF
1729 ...	£2	£12	£80	£275
1729 no stop on reverse ...	£2	£12	£90	£300

COPPER HALFPENNIES

	Fair	F	VF	EF
1730	*	£12	£70	£225
1730 GEOGIVS, no stop on reverse ...	£5	£25	£110	£275
1730 stop after date	£5	£25	£85	£275
1730 no stop after REX or on reverse	£5	£25	£110	£325
1731	*	£12	£70	£225
1731 no stop on reverse	*	£25	£100	£275
1732	*	£20	£70	£225
1732 no stop on reverse	*	£25	£100	£300
1733	*	£20	£70	£225
1733 only obverse stop before REX ...	*	£20	£70	£225
1734	*	£12	£70	£225
1734/3	*	£25	£145	*
1734 no stops on obverse	*	£25	£145	*
1735	*	£18	£70	£225
1736	*	£18	£70	£225
1737	*	£18	£70	£225
1738	*	£18	£70	£225
1739	*	£18	£70	£225

Old Head

		F	VF	EF
1740	*	£7	£55	£200
1742	*	£7	£55	£200
1742/0	*	£10	£80	£225
1743	*	£7	£55	£200
1744	*	£7	£55	£200
1745	*	£7	£55	£200
1746	*	£7	£55	£200
1747	*	£7	£55	£200
1748	*	£7	£55	£200
1749	*	£7	£55	£200
1750	*	£7	£55	£200
1751	*	£7	£55	£200
1752	*	£7	£55	£200
1753	*	£7	£55	£200
1754	*	£7	£55	£200

GEORGE III

	F	VF	EF	BU
1770	£1	£40	£150	£350
1771	£1	£40	£150	£300
1771 no stop on reverse	£2	£40	£150	£300
1771 ball below spear head	£2	£40	£150	£300
1772	£2	£40	£150	£300
1772 GEORIVS	£18	£100	£225	*
1772 ball below spear head	£2	£40	£150	£300
1772 no stop on reverse	£2	£40	£150	£300
1773	£2	£40	£150	£300
1773 no stop after REX	£2	£40	£150	£300
1773 no stop on reverse	£2	£40	£150	*
1774	£2	£40	£150	£300
1775	£3	£40	£150	£300
1799 5 incuse gunports	*	£5	£50	£110
1799 6 relief gunports	*	£5	£50	£110
1799 9 relief gunports	*	*	£50	£140
1799 no gunports ...	*	*	£50	£115
1799 no gunports and raised line along hull	*	£5	£55	£150
1806 no berries on olive branch	*	*	£45	£125

	F	VF	EF	BU
1806 line under SOHO 3 berries	*	*	£45	£110
1807 similar but double-cut border bead between B and R	*	*	£45	£120

GEORGE IV

	F	VF	EF	BU
1825	*	£30	£125	£250

George IV 1826 halfpenny

	F	VF	EF	BU
1826 two incuse lines down cross	*	£15	£75	£175
1826 raised line down centre of cross ...	*	£15	£75	£200
1827	*	£12	£75	£185

WILLIAM IV

	F	VF	EF	BU
1831	*	£5	£55	£175
1834	*	£5	£55	£175
1837	*	£4	£50	£175

VICTORIA

	F	VF	EF	BU
1838	*	£3	£25	£100
1839 proof	*	*	*	£250
1839 proof, rev inv	*	*	*	£300
1841	*	£3	£25	£85
1843	£3	£30	£90	£300
1844	*	£5	£40	£100
1845	£18	£40	£450	*
1846	£2	£5	£40	£110
1847	*	£10	£40	£110
1848	*	£5	£40	£110
1848/7	*	£3	£35	£110
1851	*	£3	£25	£100
1851 7 incuse dots on and above shield	*	£3	£25	£100
1852	*	£3	£25	£100
1852 7 incuse dots on and above shield	*	£3	£25	£100
1853	*	£3	£25	£90
1853/2	£10	£25	£85	*
1854	*	£3	£15	£70

Victoria 1853 copper halfpenny

	F	VF	EF	BU
1855	*	£3	£25	£85
1856	*	£3	£35	£100
1857	*	£3	£25	£75

	F	VF	EF	BU
1857 7 incuse dots on and above shield	*	£5	£25	£85
1858	*	£5	£25	£85
1858/6	£2	£10	£35	£85
1858/7	£1	£5	£25	£70
1858 small date	£1	£5	£25	£70
1859	£1	£5	£25	£120
1859/8	£3	£10	£50	*
1860 prog	*	*	*	£6000

Bronze halfpennies

VICTORIA

	F	VF	EF	BU
1860	*	£5	£30	£120
1860 TB 7 berries in wreath	*	£5	£35	£140
1860 TB4 berries in wreath	*	£5	£35	£140
1860 TB similar but centres of four of leaves are double incuse lines	*	£10	£50	£175
1861 obv 4 berries, 15 leaves, raised leaf centres, rev L.C.W. on rock	*	£20	£70	£225
1861 same obv, rev no signature			ext. rare	
1861 same but lighthouse has no vertical lines	*	£15	£50	£185
1861 obv 4 berries, 4 double incuse leaf centres, rev L.C.W. on rock ...	*	£5	£45	£150
1861 same obv, rev no signature	*	£8	£45	£175
1861 obv 7 double incuse leaf centres, rev L.C.W on rock	*	£5	£45	£165
1861 same obv, rev no signature	*	£5	£40	£110
1861 obv 16 leaves, rev lighthouse has rounded top	*	£5	£40	£110
1861 same obv, rev lighthouse has pointed top	*	£5	£40	£110
1861 no signature ...	*	£5	£35	£110
1862 L.C.W. on rock	*	£5	£25	£100
1862 letter (A,B or C) left of lighthouse base ...	£75	£300	*	*
1863	*	£5	£45	£145
1864	*	£6	£45	£200
1865	*	£10	£80	£275
1865/3	£10	£50	£250	£600
1866	*	£8	£60	£200
1867	*	£8	£80	£275
1868	*	£8	£60	£225

Victoria 1889 bronze halfpenny

BRONZE HALFPENNIES

	F	VF	EF	BU
1869	*	£25	£200	£425
1870	*	£5	£55	£165
1871	£10	£45	£200	£475
1872	*	£5	£40	£145
1873	*	£7	£50	£200
1874	*	£15	£75	£300
1874H	*	£5	£40	£145
1875	*	£5	£40	£145
1875H	*	£5	£45	£145
1876H	*	£5	£40	£145
1877	*	£5	£40	£145
1878	*	£15	£60	£265
1879	*	£5	£40	£125
1880	*	£4	£40	£140
1881	*	£4	£40	£140
1881H	*	£4	£35	£140
1882H	*	£4	£35	£140
1883	*	£4	£35	£140
1884	*	£2	£30	£125
1885	*	£2	£30	£125
1886	*	*	£30	£125
1887	*	*	£30	£125
1888	*	*	£30	£125
1889	*	*	£30	£125
1889/8	*	£8	£60	£225
1890	*	*	£25	£90
1891	*	*	£25	£90
1892	*	*	£25	£90
1893	*	*	£25	£90
1894	*	£5	£35	£140
1895 OH	*	*	£3	£50
1896	*	*	£3	£30
1897 normal horizon	*	*	£3	£30
1897 higher horizon	*	*	£3	£30
1898	*	*	£6	£30
1899	*	*	£4	£30
1900	*	*	£15	£20
1901	*	*	£12	£15

EDWARD VII

	F	VF	EF	BU
1902 low horizon ...	*	£5	£50	£100
1902	*	*	£5	£15
1903	*	*	£8	£25
1904	*	*	£10	£30
1905	*	*	£6	£20
1906	*	*	£6	£20
1907	*	*	£6	£20
1908	*	*	£6	£20
1909	*	*	£8	£25
1910	*	*	£8	£25

GEORGE V

	F	VF	EF	BU
1911	*	*	£8	£25
1912	*	*	£8	£25

George V 1912 halfpenny

	F	VF	EF	BU
1913	*	*	£10	£35
1914	*	*	£8	£25
1915	*	*	£8	£25

BRONZE HALFPENNIES

	Fair	F	VF	EF
1916		*	£2	£25
1917	*	*	£2	£25
1918	*	*	£2	£25
1919	*	*	£2	£25
1920	*	*	£2	£25
1921	*	*	£2	£25
1922	*	*	£3	£25
1923	*	*	£2	£25
1924	*	*	£3	£25
1925	*	*	£4	£25
1925 mod effigy ...	*	*	£4	£30
1926	*	*	£4	£25
1927	*	*	£2.50	£20
1928	*	*	£2	£15
1929	*	*	£2	£15
1930	*	*	£2	£15
1931	*	*	£2	£15
1932	*	*	£2	£15
1933	*	*	£2	£15
1934	*	*	£2	£15
1935	*	*	£2	£12
1936	*	*	£2	£10

GEORGE VI
1937	*	*	*	£4
1938	*	*	*	£6
1939	*	*	*	£8
1940	*	*	*	£9
1941	*	*	*	£5
1942	*	*	*	£4
1943	*	*	*	£4
1944	*	*	*	£5
1945	*	*	*	£4
1946	*	*	*	£8
1947	*	*	*	£6
1948	*	*	*	£6
1949	*	*	*	£8
1950	*	*	*	£8
1951	*	*	*	£15
1952	*	*	*	£5

ELIZABETH II
1953	*	*	*	£2
1954	*	*	*	£3
1955	*	*	*	£3
1956	*	*	*	£3
1957	*	*	*	£2
1958	*	*	*	£2
1959	*	*	*	£1
1960	*	*	*	£1
1962	*	*	*	*
1963	*	*	*	*
1964	*	*	*	*
1965	*	*	*	*
1966	*	*	*	*
1967	*	*	*	*

Copper farthings

Copper unless otherwise stated

OLIVER CROMWELL
Patterns only	*	£2000	£5000	£6500

CHARLES II
1671 patterns only	*	*	£350	£700
1672	£1	£25	£125	£500
1672 no stop on obverse	£2.75	£25	£125	£500
1672 loose drapery at Britannia's elbow	£2	£25	£125	£550
1673	£1	£25	£125	£550

Oliver Cromwell copper farthing

	Fair	F	VF	EF
1673 CAROLA	£30	£50	£250	*
1673 BRITANNIA ...	*	*	*	*
1673 no stops on obverse ... ... ext rare	*	*	*	*
1673 no stop on reverse ... ... ext rare	*	*	*	*
1674	*	£25	£125	£550
1675	*	£25	£125	£550
1675 no stop after CAROLVS	*	*	*	*
1676	*	*	*	*
1679	*	£25	£125	£550
1679 no stop on reverse	*	*	*	*
1684 (tin) various edge readings	£25	£125	£450	£2500
1685 (tin)	£30	£150	£500	*

JAMES II
	Fair	F	VF	EF
1684 (tin)		Extremely rare		*
1685 (tin) various edge readings	:£30	£120	£400	£2000
1686 (tin) various edge readings	:£40	£150	£450	£2250
1687 (tin) draped bust, various readings		Extremely rare *		*

WILLIAM AND MARY
	Fair	F	VF	EF
1689 (tin) date in exergue and on edge, many varieties ...	£150	£450	*	*
1689/90 (tin) 1689 in exergue, 1690 on edge	*	*	*	*
1689/90 (tin) 1690 in exergue, 1689 on edge	*	*	*	*
1690 (tin) various types	£40	£100	£400	£2500
1691 (tin) small and large figures	:£40	£100	£400	£2500
1692 (tin)	:£40	£100	£400	£2500
1694 many varieties	£10	£40	£125	£625

WILLIAM III
Type 1, date in exergue
	Fair	F	VF	EF
1695		£25	£125	£600
1695 M over V				
1696		£25	£125	£600
1697		£25	£125	£600

William III 1697 farthing

1698	£25	£100	£350	*
1699	£2	£25	£125	£650
1700	£2	£25	£85	£650

Type 2, date in legend	Fair	F	VF	EF
1698	£5	£35	£125	£650
1699	£5	£35	£125	£650

Anne 1714 pattern farthing

George II 1730 farthing

ANNE

	Fair	F	VF	EF
1714 patterns (**F**) ...	£75	£200	£350	£575

George I 'dump' farthing of 1717

GEORGE I
'Dump Type'

	Fair	F	VF	EF
1717	£30	£100	£275	£600
1718 silver proof ...	*	*	*	£1000

Larger flan

	Fair	F	VF	EF
1719 large lettering on obverse	£3	£10	£90	£450
1719 small lettering on obverse	£3	£10	£100	£475
1719 – last A of BRITANNIA over I	*	*	*	*

George I 1719 farthing

	Fair	F	VF	EF
1719 legend continuous over bust	£20	£60	*	*
1720 large lettering on obverse	£3	£20	£95	£425
1720 small lettering on obverse	£2	£15	£95	£425
1721	£2	£15	£95	£425
1721/0	£10	£30	*	*
1722 large lettering on obverse	£4	£20	£95	£425
1722 small lettering on obverse	£3	£20	£95	£425
1723	£2	£15	£95	£450
1723 R of REX over R	£8	*	*	*
1724	£5	£20	£95	£475

GEORGE II

	Fair	F	VF	EF
1730	*	£10	£45	£185
1731	*	£10	£45	£185
1732	*	£12	£45	£185
1733	*	£10	£40	£185
1734	*	£10	£45	£200
1734 no stops on obverse	*	£10	£50	£250
1735	*	£10	£40	£175
1735 3 over 3	*	£15	£50	£250
1736	*	£10	£40	£175
1736 triple tie-riband	*	£10	£50	£225
1737 sm date	*	£10	£40	£175
1737 lge date	*	£10	£45	£175
1739	*	£10	£40	£150
1739/5	*	*	*	*
1741 Old Head	*	£10	£45	£150
1744	*	£10	£45	£150
1746	*	£10	£45	£125
1746 V over U	*	*	*	*
1749	*	£10	£45	£150
1750	*	£10	£45	£175
1754/0	*	£20	£80	£225
1754	*	£8	£30	£80

GEORGE III

	F	VF	EF	BU
1771	*	£20	£150	£275
1773	*	£5	£100	£225
1774	*	£5	£100	£225
1775	*	£5	£100	£225
1799	*	*	£45	£90
1806	*	£3	£45	£95
1807	*	£4	£45	£90

GEORGE IV

		F	VF	EF
1821	*	£2	£40	£90
1822	*	£2	£40	£90
1823	*	£3	£40	£90
1825	*	£3	£40	£90
1825 D of DEI over U	£2	£7	£65	*
1826 date on rev ...	*	£2	£40	£110
1826 date on obv ...	*	£3	£45	£90
1826 I for 1 in date	*	*	*	*
1827	*	£3	£45	£90
1828	*	£3	£50	£110
1829	*	£5	£50	£135
1830	*	£7	£45	£110

WILLIAM IV

		F	VF	EF
1831	*	£6	£50	£125
1834	*	£6	£50	£125
1835	*	£6	£45	£140
1836	*	£6	£45	£140
1837	*	£6	£50	£140

VICTORIA

		F	VF	EF
1838	*	£3	£30	£90
1839	*	£3	£25	£75

COPPER FARTHINGS

	F	VF	EF	BU
1840	*	£3	£30	£75
1841	*	£3	£30	£75
1842	*	£35	£100	£225
1843	*	£3	£30	£75
1843 I for 1	£40	£200	*	*
1844	£35	£90	£375	*
1845	*	£4	£30	£90
1846	*	£6	£35	£120
1847	*	£3	£30	£90
1848	*	£4	£30	£95
1849	*	£20	£225	*
1850	*	£3	£35	£90
1851	*	£15	£50	£150
1851 D over D	£10	£50	£250	£650
1852	*	£12	£50	£140
1853 w.w. raised	*	£2	£30	£80
1853 ww inc	*	£5	£70	£90
1854 ww inc	*	£3	£30	£70
1855 ww inc	*	£3	£40	£110
1855 ww raised	*	£6	£40	£95
1856	*	£4	£50	£120
1856 R over E	£10	£50	£150	*
1857	*	£3	£30	£85
1858	*	£3	£30	£80
1859	*	£15	£50	£135
1860 proof	*	*	*	£5500

Bronze farthings

VICTORIA	F	VF	EF	BU
1860 RB	*	£2	£15	£75
1860 TB/RB (mule)	£50	£150	£300	*
1860 TB	*	£1	£15	£75
1861	*	£1	£12	£75
1862 small 8	*	£2	£12	£65
1862 large 8	£30	£50	£250	*
1863	£20	£40	£150	*
1864	*	£3	£20	£80
1865	*	£3	£20	£80
1865–5/2	*	£5	£25	£90
1866	*	£2	£18	£70
1867	*	*	£20	£80
1868	*	£1	£20	£80
1869	*	£8	£40	£90
1872	*	£2	£18	£70
1873	*	£3	£20	£70
1874 H	*	£3	£25	£65
1874 H G's over G's			Extremely rare	
1875 5 berries/large date	*	£10	£25	£100
1875 5 berries/small date	£8	£20	£75	£250
1875 4 berries/small date	*	*	*	*
1875 H	*	£2	£10	£65
1876 H	*	*	£25	£95
1877 proof				£3000
1878	*	£2	£10	£60
1879	*	*	£10	£60
1879 large 9	*	£1	£12	£60
1880 4 berries	*	£2	£15	£60
1880 3 berries	*	£2	£15	£60
1881 4 berries	*	£5	£20	£60
1881 3 berries	*	£5	£20	£60

	F	VF	EF	BU
1881 H 3 berries	*	£2	£12	£60
1882 H	*	£1	£12	£60
1883	*	£3	£28	£95
1884	*	*	£10	£38
1886	*	*	£10	£38
1887	*	*	£18	£40
1890	*	*	£10	£38
1891	*	*	£10	£38
1892	*	£7	£28	£85
1893	*	*	£8	£30
1894	*	*	£12	£40
1895	*	£12	£50	£145
1895 OH	*	*	£3	£12

Victoria 1896, Old Head Farthing

	F	VF	EF	BU
1897 bright finish	*	*	£2	£15
1897 black finish higher horizon	*	*	£1	£12
1898	*	*	£2	£15
1899	*	*	£1	£12
1900	*	*	£1	£12
1901	*	*	£1	£10

Edward VII, 1907 Farthing

EDWARD VII				
1902	*	*	£3	£12
1903 low horizon	*	*	£4	£15
1904	*	*	£4	£15
1905	*	*	£4	£15
1906	*	*	£4	£15
1907	*	*	£4	£15
1908	*	*	£4	£15
1909	*	*	£4	£15
1910	*	*	£5	£15

GEORGE V				
1911	*	*	*	£9
1912	*	*	*	£6
1913	*	*	*	£6
1914	*	*	*	£6
1915	*	*	*	£10
1916	*	*	*	£6
1917	*	*	*	£6
1918 black finish	*	*	*	£20
1919 bright finish	*	*	*	£5
1919	*	*	*	£5
1920	*	*	*	£7
1921	*	*	*	£7
1922	*	*	*	£8
1923	*	*	*	£8
1924	*	*	*	£8
1925	*	*	*	£8

COINS MARKET VALUES

	F	VF	EF	BU
1926 modified effigy	*	*	*	£6
1927	*	*	*	£6
1928	*	*	*	£3
1929	*	*	*	£3
1930	*	*	*	£3
1931	*	*	*	£3
1932	*	*	*	£3
1933	*	*	*	£3
1934	*	*	*	£5
1935	*	*	£1.50	£7
1936	*	*	*	£2

George VI 1951 farthing (wren on reverse)

GEORGE VI

	F	VF	EF	BU
1937	*	*	*	£2
1938	*	*	*	£4
1939	*	*	*	£3
1940	*	*	*	£3
1941	*	*	*	£3
1942	*	*	*	£3
1943	*	*	*	£3
1944	*	*	*	£3
1945	*	*	*	£3
1946	*	*	*	£3
1947	*	*	*	£3
1948	*	*	*	£3
1949	*	*	*	£3
1950	*	*	*	£3
1951	*	*	*	£3
1952	*	*	*	£3

ELIZABETH II

	F	VF	EF	BU
1953	*	*	*	£2
1954	*	*	*	£2
1955	*	*	*	£2
1956	*	*	*	£4

Fractions of farthings

COPPER HALF FARTHINGS

GEORGE IV

	F	VF	EF	BU
1828 Britannia breaks legend	£5	£20	£75	£200
1828 Britannia below legend	£8	£35	£125	*
1830 lge date	£5	£25	£85	£225
1830 sm date	£6	£30	£100	*

WILLIAM IV

	F	VF	EF	BU
1837	£15	£75	£250	*

Victoria 1839 half farthing

BRONZE FARTHINGS

VICTORIA

	F	VF	EF	BU
1839	*	£2	£25	£85
1842	*	£2	£25	£85
1843	*	*	£10	£40
1844	*	*	£10	£35
1844 E over N... ...	£3	£12	£75	£250
1847	*	£3	£20	£55
1851	*	£3	£25	£60
1852	*	£3	£25	£60
1853	*	£4	£40	£95
1853 proof				£350
1854	*	£4	£60	£125
1856	*	£5	£50	£110
1856 large date ...	£6	£25	*	*
1868 bronze proof	*			£300
1868 copper-nickel proof	*			£400

COPPER THIRD FARTHINGS

GEORGE IV

	F	VF	EF	BU
1827	*	£10	£40	£100

WILLIAM IV

	F	VF	EF	BU
1835	*	£10	£50	£125

VICTORIA

	F	VF	EF	BU
1844	*	£15	£50	£150
1844 RE for REG ...	£20	£50	£200	*
1844 large G in REG	*	£15	£50	£150

BRONZE THIRD FARTHINGS

VICTORIA

	F	VF	EF	BU
1866	*	*	£15	£40
1868	*	*	£15	£40
1876	*	*	£15	£45
1878	*	*	£15	£40
1881	*	*	£15	£40
1884	*	*	£10	£30
1885	*	*	£10	£30

Edward VII 1902 third farthing

EDWARD VIII

	F	VF	EF	BU
1902	*	*	£8	£25

GEORGE V

	F	VF	EF	BU
1913	*	*	£8	£25

COPPER QUARTER FARTHINGS

VICTORIA

	F	VF	EF	BU
1839	£3	£10	£30	£75

Victoria 1839 quarter farthing

	F	VF	EF	BU
1851	£4	£12	£40	£85
1852	£3	£10	£30	£75
1853	£5	£12	£40	£85
1853 proof	*	*	*	£550
1868 bronze-proof	*	*	*	£300
1868 copper-nickel proof	*	*	*	£425

Decimal coinage

f denotes face value

ELIZABETH II

BRITANNIAS

*A United Kingdom gold bullion coin introduced
in the autumn of 1987 contains one ounce of 22ct gold
and has a face value of £100. There are also half
ounce, quarter ounce and one-tenth ounce versions,
with face values of £50, £25 and £10 respectively. All
are legal tender.*
*The Britannia coins bear a portrait of The Queen on
the obverse and the figure of Britannia on the reverse.*
B.V.

1987-2005 1oz, proof ...	*
1987-2005 inclusive ½oz, proof	*
1987-2005 inclusive ¼oz, proof	*
1987-2005 inclusive ⅒oz, proof	*

(½ and ¼ oz issued only in sets)

*To commemorate the 10th anniversary of the first
Britannia issue, new reverse designs were introduced
for the gold coins as well as a series of 4 silver coins
with denominations from £2 to 20 pence. The silver
coins were issued in Proof condition only for 1997.*

1997. 1oz, ¼oz and ⅒oz issued individually (all coins
issued in 4-coin sets)
1997. 1oz, ¼oz silver coins issued individually (all
coins issued in 4-coin sets)
1998. Gold and silver coins issued with new portrait
of HM the Queen and first reverse design.
2001. New reverse designs introduced for gold
and silver coins. Four coin sets listed in the
appropriate section following.

FIVE POUNDS

1984 gold, BU	£400
1985 – –	£425
1986 – –	£425
1987 – new uncoupled effigy	£425
1988 – –	£425
1989 – BU, 500th anniversary of	
the sovereign	£450
1990 gold, BU	£435
1990 Queen Mother's 90th birthday, gold,	
proof	£600
1990 – silver, proof	£100
1990 – cu-ni, BU	£10
1991 gold, BU	£450
1992 gold, BU	£450
1993 40th Anniversary of The Coronation	
gold, proof	£700
1993 – silver, proof	£32
1993 – cu-ni, BU	£10
1993 gold BU	£475
1994 gold BU	£500
1995 gold BU	£535
1996 Queen's 70th birthday, gold, proof	£645
1996 – silver, proof	£33
1996 – cu-ni, BU	£10
1996 – gold, BU	£575
1997 Golden Wedding, gold, proof	£650
1997 – silver, proof	£32
1997 – cu-ni, BU	£10
1997 – gold, BU	£535
1998 Prince Charles 50th Birthday, gold, proof	£600
1998 – silver, proof	£50

*(Gold versions also listed in FIVE POUNDS section of
milled gold.) In 1984 the Royal Mint issued the first of
an annual issue of Brilliant Uncirculated £5 coins.
These bear the letter 'U' in a circle.*

1998 – cu-ni, BU	£10
1998 – gold, BU	£500
1999 Diana Memorial, gold, proof	£600
1999 – silver, proof	£45
1999 – cu-ni, BU	£10
1999 Millennium, gold, proof	£600
1999 – silver, proof	£33
1999 cu-ni, BU	£10
1999 gold, BU	£500
2000 Millennium, gold, proof	£495
2000 silver with 22 carat gold, proof	£37
2000 cu-ni, BU	£10
2000 Queen Mother commemorative,	
gold, proof	£495
2000 silver, proof	£35
2000 silver, piedfort	£68
2000 cu-ni, BU	£10
2000 gold, BU	£500
2001 Victorian Era anniversary	
gold, proof	£525
gold proof with reverse frosting	£750
silver, proof	£35
silver, proof with reverse frosting	£70
cu-ni, BU	£10
gold, BU	£400
2002 Golden Jubilee, gold, proof	£600
2002 – Silver, proof	£35
2002 cu-ni BU	£10
2002 Sheild reverse, gold, proof	£600
2002 Queen Mother memorial, gold, proof ...	£600
2002 –, Silver, proof	£35
2002 cu-ni BU	£10
2003 BU	£535
2003 proof	£650
2005 BU Trafalgar	£5
2005 BU Nelson	£10

TWO POUNDS

1983 gold, proof	£225
1986 Commonwealth Games (nickel brass)	£4
1986 –, in folder, BU	£6
1986 silver unc	£15
1986 – – proof	£35
1986 gold, proof	£225
1987 gold, proof	£250 f
1988 gold, proof	£250
1989 Bill of Rights (nickel brass)	£4
1989 –, in folder, BU	£6
1989 – silver, proof	£30
1989 Claim of Right (nickel brass)	£4
1989 Bill of Rights (nickel brass)	£4
1989 –, in folder, BU	£6
(For 1989 £2 piedforts see sets)	
1989 500th anniversary of the sovereign,	
gold, proof	£275
1990 gold, proof	£250
1991 gold, proof	£250
1993 gold, proof	£250
1994 Bank of England, gold, proof	£425
1994 –, gold 'mule', proof	£800
1994 –, silver, proof	£30
1994 –, silver piedfort, proof	£60
1994 –, in folder, BU	£8
1994	£4
1995 50th Anniverary of end of Second	
World War, silver, proof	£27
1995 ditto, in folder, BU	£8
1995 –, silver, piedfort, proof	£60
1995 –, gold, proof	£375
1995 50th Anniversary of United Nations,	
gold, proof	£300
1995 –, in folder, BU	£6
1995 –, silver, piedfort, proof	£60
1995 –, proof	£30

1995	£4
1996 European Football, gold, proof	£350
1996 –, silver, proof	£27
1996 –, silver, piedfort	£65
1996 –, in folder, BU	£6
1996	£4
1997 Bimetal, gold, proof	£350
1997 –, silver, proof	£29
1997 –, in folder, BU	£6
1997 silver, piedfort	£60
1997	£4
1998 Bimetal, silver, proof	£29
1998 – silver, piedfort	£50
1998 – proof	£6
1998 –, in folder, BU	£6
1998	£4
1999 Rugby World Cup, gold, proof	£300
1999 – silver, proof	£30
1999 – silver, piedfort	£150
1999 –, in folder, BU	£6
1999	£4
2001 Marconi commemorative,	
gold, proof	£295
2001 – silver, proof	£29
2001 – silver, proof with reverse frosting ...	£29
2001 – silver, piedfort	£50
2001 – in folder, BU	£6

Four different reverse designs representing England, Northern Ireland, Scotland and Wales were issued in sets

2002 Commonwealth Games, gold,proof ...	*
2002 Commonwealth Games, silver,proof ...	*
2002 Commonwealth Games, piedfort	*
2002 Commonwealth Games, BU	*
2002 Shield reverse, gold,proof	£300
2003 DNA Gold ti-metal proof	£295
2003 Silver Bullion Britannia	£14
2003 Silver proof DNA	£30
2003 DNA in folder	£7
2005 Gold proof WWII	£325
2005 Silver proof piedfort WWII	£49
2005 in folder BU WWII	£9

(2001 Gold versions are also listed in TWO POUNDS section of milled gold.)

ONE POUND

1983	£2
1983 Unc, in folder	£5
1983 silver, proof	£35
1983 – – piedfort	£125
1984 Scottish reverse	£2
1984 – Unc, in folder	£5
1984 – silver, proof	£20
1984 – – piedfort	£55
1985 New portrait, Welsh reverse	£4
1985 – – Unc, in folder	£5
1985 – – silver, proof	£22
1985 – – piedfort	£55
1986 Northern Ireland reverse	£5
1986 – Unc, in folder	£5
1986 – silver, proof	£25
1986 – – – piedfort	£60
1987 English reverse	£4
1987 – Unc, in folder	£4
1987 – silver, proof	£30
1987 – – – piedfort	£55
1988 Royal Arms reverse	£5
1988 – Unc, in folder	£5
1988 – silver, proof	£35
1988 – – – piedfort	£55
1989 Scottish rev as 1984,	
silver, proof	£20
1989 – – – silver, piedfort	£50
1990 Welsh reverse as 1985	£5

1990 – silver, proof	£30
1991 Northern Ireland rev as 1986,	
silver proof	£25
1992 English rev as 1987,	
silver, proof	£25
1993 Royal Coat of Arms (reverse as	
1983), silver, proof	£30
1993 – – – piedfort	£65
1994 Scottish Lion, silver, proof	£35
Ditto, Unc. in folder	£5
1994 – silver, piedfort	£55
1995 Welsh dragon, silver, proof	£25
Ditto, Unc in folder, Welsh version	£5
1995 – silver, piedfort	£55
1996 Northern Ireland Celtic Ring	
Unc in folder	£5
Silver, proof	£27
Silver, piedfort	£55
1997 English Lions Unc, in folder	£5
silver, proof	£30
silver, piedfort	£55
1998 Royal coat of arms/reverse as 1983,	
silver, proof	£25
silver, piedfort	£45
1999 Scottish Lion (reverse as 1984)	
new portrait, silver proof	£25
silver proof, reverse testing	£40
silver, piedfort	£45
2000 Welsh Dragon (reverse as 1995)	
new portrait, silver, proof	£25
silver proof, reverse testing	£40
silver, piedfort	£47
2001 Northern Ireland (reverse as 1996)	
new portrait, silver, proof	£25
silver, piedfort	£45
-in folder, BU	£4
2002 English design (reverse as 1997)	
silver, proof	£27
silver, piedfort	£49
in folder, BU	£5
2003 Silver proof	27
2005 Gold proof Menai Bridge	£345
2005 Silver proof piedfort Menai Bridge	£49
2005 in folder BU	£5

2001.Note that the edge inscriptions on £2 and £1 appear either upright or inverted in relation to the obverse. (Sovereign and half sovereign prices are not listed here but in the main listings under milled gold.)

FIFTY PENCE

1969	£1
1970	£1
1973 EEC	£1
1973 – proof	£3
1976-1981	f
1982 rev changed to FIFTY PENCE	
instead of NEW PENCE	f
1983, 1985	f
1992 European Community	£5
1992 – silver, proof	£30
1992 – silver, proof piedfort	£55
1992 – gold, proof	£400
1994 Normandy landing	£2
1994 – silver, proof	£28
1994 – silver, piedfort	£50
1994 – gold, proof	£400
1997 new size (27.3mm diameter)	
silver, proof	£27
silver, piedfort	£46
1997 old and new size,	
silver proofs	£50
1998, 1998	f
1998 European Presidency	£2

1998 – silver, proof	£25
1998 – silver, piedfort	£45
1998 – gold, proof	£250
1998 National Health Service Commemorative	£2
1998 – silver, proof	£25
1998 – silver, piedfort	£45
1998 – gold, proof	£250
1999 Britannia reverse	*
2000 Library Commemorative	£2
2000 –, in folder, BU	£5
2000 –, silver, proof	£25
2000 –, silver, piedfort	£47
2000 –, gold, proof	£250
2003 –, Suffragette, presentation	£5
2004 –, Roger Bannister, gold proof	£265
2004 –, Roger Bannister, silver proof pied fort	£46
2005 –, gold, proof Samuel Johnson	£265
2005 –, silver, proof Samuel Johnson	£26
2005 –, silver proof piedfort Samuel Johnson	£49

TWENTY-FIVE PENCE

1972 Silver Wedding	£1
1972 – silver, proof	£30
1977 Jubilee	£1
1977 – silver, proof	£20
1980 Queen Mother's 80th birthday	£1
1980 – in blister pack	£3
1980 – silver, proof	£50
1981 Royal Wedding	£1
1981 – in folder	£3
1981 – silver, proof	£30
Coronation, Anniv. Silver proof	£35
Coronation, Anniv. folder	£10
Coronation, Anniv	£5
Coronation, Anniv. Gold proof crown	£555

TWENTY PENCE

1982	f
1982 silver, proof piedfort	£50
1983-5, 1987-2003	f

TEN PENCE

1968	£0.25
1969	£0.25
1970	£0.20
1971	£0.20
1973	£0.20
1974-1977, 1979-1981	f
1992 new size (24.5mm diameter)	
silver, proof, piedfort	£40
1992 old and new size, silver, proofs	£30
1992, 1995, 1997-2003 – cu-ni	f

FIVE PENCE

1968-1971	*
1975, 1977-1980, 1987, 1988, 1989	f
1990 silver, proof, old and new	£26
1990 silver, piedfort	£30
1990, 1991, 1992, 1994-1999-2003 – cu-ni ...	f

TWO PENCE

1971	*
1973-1981	f
1985 new portrait, rev changed to	
TWO PENCE instead of NEW PENCE	*
1986-2003	f

ONE PENNY

1971	*
1973-1981	f
1982 rev changed to ONE PENNY	
instead of NEW PENNY	f
1983, 1984	f
1985 new portrait	f
1986-2003	f

HALF PENNY

1971	*
1973-81	*
1982 rev changed to HALFPENNY	
instead of 1/2 NEW PENNY	*
1983	*

Proof and Specimen Sets

Proof or specimen sets have been issued since 1887 by the Royal Mint in official cases. Prior to that date, sets were issued privately by the engraver. Some sets are of currency coins, easily distinguishable from proofs which have a vastly superior finish. The two 1887 sets frequently come on to the market, hence their place in this list. The 1953 'plastic' set, though made up of currency coins, is official. It was issued in a plastic packet, hence the name. Apart from the seats stated, as being uncirculated, currency or specimen, all those in the following listing are proof sets.

GEORGE IV   FDC
New issue, **1826**. Five pounds to farthing (11 coins) £21000

WILLIAM IV
Coronation, **1831**. Two pounds to farthing (14 coins) £18750

VICTORIA
Young head, **1839**. 'Una and the Lion' five pounds plus sovereign to farthing (15 coins) £32500
Young head, **1853**. Sovereign to half farthing, including 'Gothic' crown (16 coins) £26000
Jubilee head, Golden Jubilee, **1887**. Five pounds to Threepence ('full set' – 11 coins) £6250
As above, currency set (unofficial) £1500
Jubilee head, Golden Jubilee, **1887**. Crown to threepence ('short set' – 7 coins) £1200
As above, currency set (unofficial) £250
Old head, **1893**. Five pounds to threepence ('full set') – 10 coins £7500
Old head, **1893**. Crown to threepence ('short set' – 6 coins) £1500

EDWARD VII
Coronation, **1902**. Five pounds to Maundy penny – matt proofs (13 coins) £1650
Coronation, **1902**. Sovereign to Maundy penny – matt proofs (11 coins) £625

GEORGE V
Coronation, **1911**. Five pounds to Maundy penny (12 coins) £3500
Coronation, **1911**. Sovereign to Maundy penny (10 coins) £900
Coronation, **1911**. Halfcrown to Maundy penny (8 coins) £400
New types, **1927**. Crown to threepence (6 coins) £300

GEORGE VI
Coronation, **1937**. Gold set, five pounds to half sovereign (4 coins) £2500
Coronation, **1937**. Silver and bronze set, crown to farthing including Maundy money (15 coins) ... £250
Mid-century, **1950**. Halfcrown to farthing (9 coins) £100
Festival of Britain, **1951**. Crown to farthing (10 coins) £125

ELIZABETH II
Coronation, **1953**. Crown to farthing (10 coins) £85
Coronation, **1953**. Currency ('plastic') set, official, halfcrown to farthing (9 coins) £15
Specimen decimal set, **1968**. 10p, 5p; **1971** 2p, 1p, ¹/₂p in wallet (5 coins) £1
Last £sd coins, **1970**. (sets issued 1971-73). Halfcrown to Halfpenny (8 coins) £18
Proof decimal set, **1971**. (issued 1973), 50p, 10p, 5p, 2p, 1p, ¹/₂p (6 coins) £15
Proof decimal set, **1972**. 50p, Sliver Wedding, 25p, 10p, 5p, 2p, 1p, ¹/₂p (7 coins) £20
Proof decimal sets, **1973, 1974, 1975, 1976**. 50p, to ¹/₂p (6 coins) £12
Proof decimal set, **1977**. 50p to ¹/₂p, plus Jubilee crown (7 coins) £12
Proof decimal set, **1978**. 50p to ¹/₂p (6 coins) £12
Proof decimal set, **1979**. 50p to ¹/₂p (6 coins) £12
Proof decimal set, **1980**. 50p to ¹/₂p (6 coins) £10
Proof gold set, **1980**. Five pounds, two pounds, sovereign, half sovereign (4 coins) £750
Commemorative proof coin set, **1981**. Five pounds, sovereign, Royal Wedding Silver crown,
50p to ¹/₂p (9 coins) £600
Commemorative set, **1981**. Sovereign and Royal Wedding silver crown (2 coins) £125
Proof decimal set, **1981**. 50p to ¹/₂p (6 coins) £10
Proof gold set, **1982**. Five pounds, two pounds, sovereign, half sovereign (4 coins) £800
Proof decimal set, **1982**. 50p to ¹/₂p including 20p (7 coins) £12
Uncirculated decimal set, **1982**. 50p to ¹/₂p including 20p (7 coins) £9
Proof gold set, **1983**. Two pounds, sovereign, half sovereign (3 coins) £325
Proof decimal set, **1983**. £1 to ¹/₂p (8 coins) £18
Uncirculated decimal set, **1983**. £1 to ¹/₂p (8 coins) £14
Proof gold set, **1984**. Five pounds, sovereign, half sovereign (3 coins) £575
Proof decimal set, **1984**. £1 (Scottish rev) to ¹/₂p (8 coins) £16
Uncirculated decimal set, **1984**. £1 (Scottish rev) to ¹/₂p (8 coins) £13
Proof gold set, **1985**. new portrait. Five pounds, two pounds, sovereign, half sovereign (4 coins) £750
Proof decimal set, **1985**. new portrait. £1 (Welsh rev) to 1p (7 coins) in de luxe case £20
Proof decimal set, **1985**. As above, in standard case £16
Uncirculated decimal set, **1985**. £1 (Welsh rev) to 1p (7 coins) £12
Proof gold set, **1986**. Commonwealth Games two pounds, sovereign, half sovereign (3 coins) £350
Proof decimal set, **1986**. Commonwealth Games £2, Northern Ireland £1.50p to 1p (8 coins),
de luxe case £25
Proof decimal set, **1986**. As above in standard case £20
Uncirculated decimal set, **1986**. As above, in folder £12
Proof gold Britannia set, **1987**. One ounce, half ounce, quarter ounce tenth ounce (4 coins) £650
Proof decimal set, **1987**. Quarter ounce, tenth ounce (2 coins) £150

PROOF AND SPECIMEN SETS

Proof gold set, **1987.** Two pounds, sovereign, half sovereign (3 coins) **£325**
Proof decimal set, **1987.** £1 (English rev) to 1p (7 coins) in de luxe case **£23**
Proof decimal set, **1987.** As above, in standing case **£18**
Uncirculated decimal set, **1987.** As above, in folder **£10**
Proof gold Britannia set, **1988.** One ounce, half ounce, quarter ounce, tenth ounce (4 coins) **£650**
Proof gold Britannia set, **1988.** Quarter ounce, tenth ounce (2 coins) **£150**
Proof gold set, **1988.** Two pounds, sovereign, half sovereign (3 coins) **£325**
Proof decimal set **1988.** £1 (Royal Arms rev) to 1p (7 coins) in de luxe case **£26**
Proof decimal set, **1988.** As above, in standard case **£19**
Uncirculated decimal set, **1988.** As above, in folder **£11**
Proof gold Britannia set, **1989.** One ounce, half ounce, quarter ounce, tenth ounce (4 coins) **£700**
Proof gold Britannia set, **1989.** Quarter ounce, tenth ounce (2 coins) **£150**
Proof gold set, **1989.** 500th anniversary of the sovereign. Five pounds, two pounds, sovereign,
  half sovereign (4 coins) **£1100**
Proof gold set, **1989.** 500th anniversary of the sovereign. Two pounds, sovereign, half sovereign (3 coins) **£550**
Proof decimal set, **1989.** Bill of Rights £2. Claim of Right £2,
  £1 (Scottish rev as 1984), 50p to 1p (9 coins) in de luxe case **£35**
Proof decimal set, **1989.** As above in standard case **£30**
Proof silver, Bill of Rights £2. Claim of Right £2. **1989.** (2 coins) **£60**
Proof silver piedfort, **1989.** £2 as above (2 coins) **£80**
Uncirculated. **1989.** As above (2 coins) in folder **£15**
Uncirculated decimal set, **1989.** £1 (Scottish rev as 1984) to 1p (7 coins) **£22**
Proof gold Britannia set, 199**0** **£775**
Proof gold set, **1990.** Five pounds, two pounds, sovereign, half-sovereign (4 coins) **£750**
Proof gold set, **1990.** Two pounds, sovereign, half sovereign (3 coins) **£400**
Proof silver set, **1990.** Five pence (23.59mm diam) and five pence (18mm diam, new size) **£30**
Proof decimal set, **1990.** £1 (Welsh rev as 1985) to 1p including large and small 5p (8 coins) in deluxe case **£30**
Proof decimal set, **1990.** As above, in standard case **£25**
Uncirculated decimal set, **1990.** £1 (Welsh rev as 1985) to 1p including large and small 5p (8 coins) **£20**
Proof gold Britannia set, **1991.** **£700**
Proof gold set, **1991.** Five pounds, two pounds, sovereign, half sovereign (4 coins) **£750**
Proof gold set, **1991.** Two pounds, sovereign, half sovereign (3 coins) **£400**
Proof decimal set, **1991.** £1 to 1p (7 coins) in deluxe case **£30**
Proof decimal set, **1991.** As above, in standard case **£25**
Uncirculated decimal set, **1991.** (7 coins) **£20**
Proof gold Britannia set, **1992.** **£700**
Proof gold set, **1992.** Five pounds, two pounds, sovereign, half sovereign (4 coins) **£750**
Proof gold set, **1992.** Two pounds, sovereign, half sovereign (3 coins) **£400**
Proof silver set, **1992.** Ten pence (large and small size) **£30**
Proof decimal set, **1992.** £1 (English rev as 1987) to 1p (two 50p, new 10p) (9 coins) in deluxe case **£32**
Proof decimal set, **1992.** As above, in standard case **£28**
Uncirculated decimal set, **1992.** **£20**
Proof gold Britannia set, **1993.** **£700**
Proof gold set, **1993.** Five pounds, two pounds, sovereign, half sovereign (4 coins) **£800**
Proof gold set, **1993.** Two pounds, sovereign, half sovereign (3 coins) **£400**
Proof decimal set, **1993.** Coronation Anniversary £5, £1 to 1p (8 coins) in deluxe case **£35**
Proof decimal set, **1993.** As above, in standard case **£30**
Uncirculated decimal set, **1993** (with two 50p, no £5) (8 coins) **£25**
Proof gold Britannia set, **1994.** **£775**
Proof gold set, **1994.** Five pounds, two pounds Bank of England, sovereign, half sovereign (4 coins) **£800**
Proof gold set, **1994.** Two pounds Bank of England, sovereign, half sovereign (3 coins) **£450**
Proof decimal set, **1994.** £2 Bank of England, £1 (Scottish rev), 50p D-Day to 1p (8 coins) in deluxe case **£35**
Proof decimal set, **1994.** As above, in standard case **£30**
Uncirculated decimal set, **1994.** **£14**
Proof gold Britannia set, **1995.** **£850**
Proof godl set, **1995.** Five pounds, two pounds Peace, sovereign, half sovereign (4 coins) **£800**
Proof gold set, **1995.** Two pounds Peace, sovereign, half sovereign (3 coins) **£450**
Proof decimal set, **1995.** Two pounds Peace, £1 (Welsh rev) to 1p (8 coins) in deluxe case **£36**
Proof decimal set, **1995.** As above, in standard case **£29**
Uncirculated decimal set, **1995.** **£12**
Proof gold Britannia set, **1996.** **£900**
Proof gold set, **1996.** Five pounds, two pounds, sovereign, half sovereign (4 coins) **£800**
Proof gold set, **1996.** Two pounds, sovereign, half sovereign (3 coins) **£400**
Proof silver decimal set, **1996.** £1 to 1p (7 coins) **£100**
Proof decimal set, **1996.** 60th Birthday £5, £2 Football, £1 Northern Irish rev) to 1p (9 coins) in deluxe case **£38**
Proof decimal set, **1996.** As above, in standard case **£32**
Proof gold Britannia set, **1997.** **£1000**
Uncirculated decimal sert, **1996.** £2 to 1p (8 coins) **£11**
Proof gold set, **1997.** Five pounds, two pounds (bimetal), sovereign, half sovereign (4 coins) **£800**
Proof gold set, **1997.** Two pounds (bimetal), sovereign, half sovereign **£450**
Proof silver set, **1997.** Proof silver Britannia set, **1997.** Two pounds to 20p **£85**
Proof silver set, **1997.** Fifthy pence (large and small size) **£65**
Golden Wedding £5, £2 bimetal. £1 (English rev) to 1p, with new 50p in deluxe case **£40**
Proof decimal set, **1997.** As above, in standard case **£35**
Uncirculated decimal set, **1997.** As above but no £5 (9 coins) **£11**
Proof gold Britannia set, **1998.** **£1000**
Proof gold set, **1998,** £5 to half sovereign **£900**
Proof gold set, **1998,** £2 to half sovereign **£450**
Proof silver set, Britannia **1998,** £2 to 20p **£100**
Proof decimal set, **1998,** Prince Charles, £5 to 1p in deluxe case **£40**
Proof decimal set, **1998,** as above, in standard case **£33**
Uncirculated decimal set, **1998,** as above but no £5 (9 coins) **£15**
Proof silver set, **1998,** 'EU' and 'NHS' 60p (2 coins) **£50**
Proof gold Britannia set, **1999.** **£1000**

Proof gold set, **1999,** £5, £2 Rugby World Cup, sovereign, half sovereign **£900**
Proof gold set, **1999,** £2 Rugby World Cup, sovereign, half sovereign **£450**
Proof decimal set, **1999,** Diana £5 to 1p in deluxe case **£40**
Proof decimal set, **1999,** as above, in standard case **£35**
Uncirculated set, **1999,** as above but no £5 (8 coins) **£15**
Proof gold, Britannia set, **2000** **£900**
Proof gold, **2000,** £5 to half sovereign **£1000**
Proof gold, **2000,** £2 to half sovereign **£500**
Proof silver decimal set, **2000,** £5 to 1p plus Maundy coins (13 coins) **£245**
Proof decimal set, **2000,** Executive (10 coins) **£70**
Proof decimal set, **2000,** Deluxe (10 coins) **£40**
Proof decimal set, **2000,** Standard (10 coins) **£30**
Proof gold Britannia set, **2001,** new reverse designs **£890**
Proof gold set, **2001,** Five pounds, £2 Marconi commemorative, sovereign, half sovereign **£900**
Proof gold set, **2001,** £2 Marconi commemorative, sovereign, half sovereign **£415**
Proof silver Britannia set, **2001,** new reverse designs, Two pounds to 20p **£90**
Proof decimal set, **2001,** Executive (10) **£75**
Proof decimal set, **2001,** Deluxe (10) **£48**
Proof decimal set, **2001,** Gift (10) **£43**
Proof decimal set, **2001,** Standard (10) **£34**
Uncirculated set, **2001,** as above but no £5 (9) **£14**
Proof gold set, **2002,** £5 to half sovereign, new reverse design **£1100**
Proof gold set, **2002,** £2 to half sovereign, new reverse design **£425**
Proof gold set, **2002,** Golden Jubilee £5, £2 bimetal, £1 (English rev) to 1p plus maundy coins (13 coins) **£2650**
Proof gold set, **2002,** Commonwealth Games £2 (England, N. Ireland, Scotland and Wales) **£1150**
Proof silver set, **2002,** Commonwealth Games £2 (England, N. Ireland, Scotland and Wales) **£98**
Proof gold Britannia set, **2002** **£800**
Proof silver piedfort set, **2002,** Commonwealth Games £2 (England, N. Ireland, Scotland and Wales) **£195**
Proof decimal, **2002,** Executive (9) Golden Jubilee £5, £2 bimetal, £1 (English rev) to 1p **£70**
Proof decimal, **2002,** Delux (9) **£46**
Proof decimal, **2002,** Gift (9) **£40**
Proof decimal, **2002,** Standard (9) **£32**
Uncirculated set, **2002,** As above but no £5 (8) **£14**
Uncirculated set, **2002,** Commonwealth Games £2 (England, N. Ireland, Scotland and Wales) **£15**
Proof gold set, **2003,** £5 to half sovereign **£1000**
Proof gold set, **2003,** £2 to half sovereign (DNA £2) **£425**
Proof decimal set, **2003,** Executive (11) **£69**
Proof decimal set, **2003,** Deluxe (11) **£47**
Proof decimal set, **2003,** Standard (11) **£34**
Uncirculated set, **2003,** (10) **£14**
Proof gold Britannia set, (4) **£800**
Proof gold set, **2005,** £5 to half-sovereign (4) **£995**
Proof gold set, **2005,** £2 to half-sovereign (3) **£450**
Proof decimal set, **2005,** Executive (12) **£75**
Proof decimal set, **2005,** Deluxe (12) **£49**
Proof decimal set, **2005,** Standard (12) **£38**
Uncirculated set, **2005,** (10) **£14**
Gold Proof Britannia set, **2005,** (4) **£935**
Gold Proof Britannia set, **2005,** (3) **£429**
Silver Predfort set (4) **£189**
Proof Gold set, **2004** £2 to half sovereign (3) **£425**
Proof Gold set, **2004,** Entente Cordial (2) **£965**
Proof Gold set, **2004,** D-Day Anniversary, Crowns (3) **£1875**
Proof Gold Britannia set, **2004** (4) **£900**
Proof Gold Britannia set, **2004** (3) **£415**
Proof Silver set, **2004,** Entente Cordial (2) **£69**
Proof Silver set, **2004,** D-Day Anniversary, crowns (3) **£250**
Uncirculated set, **2004,** 'New coin pack', (10) **£9**
Proof Decimal, **2004,** Delux (10) **£40**
Proof Decimal, **2004,** Executive (10) **£65**
Proof Decimal, **2004,** Standard (10) **£29**

Scottish Coins

THE SCOTTISH MINTS
H = A HOARD

Based on a map of actual and supposed mints prepared by Spink and Son Ltd.

The number of mints which have been in operation in Scotland can be seen from the map above. The mints of the first coinage of Alexander III are the greatest number ever working together in Scotland, and it is this area that really attracts the collector of the different mint issues. For this reason, when we deal with this reign later on, we give a price for issues of each mint town, but not for any other reign.

MINT TOWN	KING(S)
ABERDEEN	Alexander III, David II
	Robert III, James I, II, III
AYR	Alexander III
BAMBOROUGH	Henry
BERWICK	David I, Malcom IV,
	William I, Alexander II, III
	Robert Bruce, James III
CARLISLE	David I, Henry
CORBRIDGE	Henry
DUMBARTON	Robert III
DUMFRIES	Alexander III
DUNBAR	William I ?, Alexander III
DUNDEE	William I ?, Alexander III
DUNFERMLINE	William I
FORFAR	Alexander III
FORRES	Alexander III
GLASGOW	Alexander III
INVERNESS	Alexander III
JEDBURGH	Malcom IV
KELSO	Alexander II
KINGHORN	Alexander III
LANARK	Alexander III
LINLITHGOW	James I, II
MONTROSE	Alexander III
PERTH	William I, Alexander III,
	Robert II to James II
RENFREW	Alexander III
ROXBURGH	Alexander III
ST ANDREWS	Alexander III
STIRLING	Alexander III, James I, II
	Mary Stuart

Prices are for the commonest coins in each case. Collectors should expect to pay these amounts and upwards. For further details see The Scottish Coinage, by I. Stewart (Spink, 1967, reprint 1975) and Coins of Scotland, Ireland and The Islands, Spink 2003. Gold coins are indicated. All other coins are silver unless another metal is stated.

DAVID I 1124-53

	F	VF
Pennies	£525	£1100

Four different groups; struck at the mints of Berwick, Carlisle, Roxburgh and Edinburgh **£750** **£1850**

This superb David I penny of Carlisle realised £1,210 in Spink's Douglas auction in 1997

HENRY 1136-52
(Earl of Huntingdon and Northumberland)
Pennies ... ... **£2250** *
Three types; struck at the mints of Corbridge, Carlisle and Barnborough.

MALCOLM IV 1153-65
Pennies ... ... **£5000** *
Five types; struck at the mints of Roxburgh and Berwick.

WILLIAM THE LION 1165-1214
Pennies **£85** **£225**
Three issues; struck at the mints of Roxburgh, Berwick, Edinburgh, Dun (Dunfermline?), Perth

ALEXANDER II 1214-49
Pennies **£825** **£2500**
Mints of Berwick and Roxburgh, varieties of bust.

Halfpenny and farthing of Alexander III and penny of Robert Bruce

ALEXANDER III 1249-86
1st coinage pennies 1250-80
Mints

Aberdeen	£125	£275
Ayr	£200	£525
Berwick	£70	£160
'DUN'	£135	£375
Edinburgh	£85	£200
Forfar	£200	£575
Fres	£225	£600
Glasgow	£175	£450
Inverness	£200	£475
Kinghorn	£225	£675
Lanark	£200	£525
Montrose	£525	£1250
Perth	£85	£185

SCOTTISH COINS

	F	VF
Renfrew	£450	*
Roxburgh	£70	£160
St. Andrews	£135	£400
Stirling	£150	£425
'TERWILANER' (uncertain name)	£575	*

2nd coinage c. 1280 –
Many types and varieties

Pennies	£25	£60
Halfpennies	£75	£250
Farthings	£175	£475

JOHN BALIOL 1292-6
1st coinage (rough surface issue)

Pennies	£100	£275
Halfpennies	£375	£750

2nd coinage (smooth surface issue) £125 £300

Pennies	£135	£300
Halfpennies	£135	£350

Robert Bruce Penny

ROBERT BRUCE 1306-29

Pennies	£475	£1100
Halfpennies	£575	£1350
Farthings		ext. rare

Probably all struck at Berwick.

David II Groat, Edinburgh Mint

DAVID II 1329-71

Nobles (gold)		ext. rare
Groats	£85	£225
Halfgroats	£75	£200
Pennies	£30	£90
Halfpennies	£325	£850
Farthings	£650	*

Three issues, but these denominations were not struck for all issues. Edinburgh and Aberdeen mints.

ROBERT II 1371-90

Groats	£85	£200
Halfgroats	£75	£185
Pennies	£80	£225
Halfpennies	£100	£275

Some varieties. Struck at mints of Dundee, Edinburgh, Perth.

SCOTTISH COINS

ROBERT III 1390-1406 ... ...

	F	VF
Lion or crowns (gold)	£725	£1800
Demy lions or halfcrowns (gold) ...	£625	£1450
Groats	£75	£175
Halfgroats	£125	£350
Pennies	£275	£700
Halfpennies	£275	£675

Three issues, many varieties. Struck at mints of
Edinburgh, Aberdeen, Perth, Dumbarton.

James I Demy or Nine Shilling Piece

JAMES I 1406-37

Demies (gold)	£575	£1250
Half demies (gold)	£725	£1650
Groats	£135	£375
Billon pennies	£150	£400
Billon halfpennies	£375	£900

Mints, Aberdeen, Edinburgh,
Inverness, Linlithgow, Perth, Stirling.

JAMES II 1437-60

Demies (gold) from	£575	£1250
Lions (gold) from	£825	£2000
Half lions (gold) from	Very rare	
Groats	£175	£525
Halfgroats	£525	*
Billon pennies	£175	£525

Two issues, many varieties. Mints: Aberdeen,
Edinburgh, Linlithgow, Perth, Roxburgh, Stirling.

ECCLESIASTICAL ISSUES C 1452-80

Bishop Kennedy copper pennies ...	£75	£175
Copper farthings	£175	£475

Different types, varieties

JAMES III 1460-88

Riders (gold) from	£1100	£2750
Half riders (gold)	£1350	£3500
Quarter riders (gold)	£1650	£4500
Unicorns (gold)	£1000	£2250
Groats ... ...from	£175	£450

*James III groat and
James V one-third groat*

Halfgroats from	£350	£800
Pennies from	£150	£425
Billon placks from	£90	£275
Billon half placks from	£110	£325

	F	VF
Billon pennies from	£100	£275
Copper farthings from	£275	*

Many varieties. Mints: Edinburgh, Berwick,
Aberdeen.

James IV Unicorn

JAMES IV 1488-1513

Unicorns (gold)	£950	£2250
Half unicorns (gold)	£750	£1500
Lions or crowns (gold)	£1350	£3500
Half lions (gold)	£1650	£4750
Pattern angel (gold)	unique	
Groats	£325	£850
Halfgroats	£475	£1200
Pennies (light coinage) ... ...ext rare		*
Billon placks	£30	£90
Billon half placks	£125	£425
Billon pennies	£50	£135

Different types, varieties. Mint: Edinburgh only.

James V 'Bonnet' piece of 1540

JAMES V 1513-42

	F	VF
Unicorns (gold)	£1000	£2750
Half unicorns (gold)	£1500	£4250
Crowns (gold)	£725	£1650
'Bonnet' pieces or ducats (gold) ...	£2250	£5250
Two-thirds ducats (gold)	£2000	£4500
One-third ducats (gold)	£2750	£7000
Groats from	£135	£450
One-third groats	£150	£450

James V groat

Billon placks	£25	£80
Billon bawbees	£25	£75
Billon half bawbees	£75	£200
Billon quarter bawbees	unique	

Different issues, varieties. Edinburgh mint.

Note: from here on all Scottish coins were struck at Edinburgh.

MARY 1542-67

1st Period 1542-58

	F	VF
Crown (gold)	£1350	£3500
Twenty shillings (gold)	£2250	*
Lions or forty-four shillings (gold)	£1350	£2750

Extremely rare Francis and Mary ducat which realised £77,000 at a Spink auction in March 1997

	F	VF
Half lions or twenty-two shillings (gold)	£1000	£2500
Ryals or £3 pieces (gold)	£3250	£6500
1555, 1557, 1558	£3750	£7500
Half ryals (gold) 1555,1557,1558 ...	£2000	£5750
Portrait testoons, 1553		

Mary, Queen of Scots Half Testoon, 1560, Francis and Mary

	F	VF
Non-portrait testoons, 1555-8	£185	£500
– half testoons, 1555-8	£250	£625
Billon bawbees	£35	£100
– half bawbees	£75	£175
– pennies (facing bust)	£225	£675
– pennies (no bust) 1556	£175	£575
– lions, 1555, 1558	£30	£90
– placks, 1557	£40	£125

2nd period (Francis and Mary) 1558-60

	F	VF
Ducats or sixty shillings (gold) ...	ext. rare	
Non-portrait testoons, 1558-61 ...	£200	£475
– half testoons, 1558-60	£225	£550
Twelvepenny groats (Nonsunt) 1558-9	£75	£175
– lions, 1559-60	£25	£75

3rd period (widowhood) 1560-5

	F	VF
Crown (gold) 1562	ext. rare	
Portrait testoons, 1561-2	£1500	£4250
– half testoons, 1561-2	£1650	£5000

4th period (Henry and Mary) 1565-7

	F	VF
Portrait ryals, 1565	ext. rare	
Non-portrait ryals, 1565-7	£325	£825

Mary and Henry 1565 two thirds ryal

	F	VF
– two thirds ryals, 1565-7	£275	£725
– – undated	£800	£2000
– one-third ryals, 1565-6	£275	£675
– testoons, 1565		ext. rare

5th period (2nd widowhood) 1567

	F	VF
_ Non portrait ryals, 1567	£350	£850
– two thirds ryals, 1567	£300	£750
– one third ryals, 1566-7	£375	£900

Mints: Edinburgh, Stirling (but only for some bawbees)

JAMES VI

Before English accession 1567-1603

1st coinage 1567-71

	F	VF
Ryals 1567-71	£300	£750
Two-third ryals –	£250	£650
One-third ryals –	£275	£700

Superb gold £20 piece of 1575 realised £30,800 in Spink auction in March 1997

2nd coinage 1571-80

	F	VF
Twenty pounds (gold)	£18,500	£42,500
Nobles, 1572-7, 1580	£75	£250
Half nobles –	£70	£225
Two merks, 1578-80 –	£1350	£3000
Merks, 1579-80	£1750	£4250

3rd coinage 1580-81

	F	VF
Ducats or sixty shillings 1580	£2750	£6500
Sixteen shillings, 1581	£1750	£4250
Eight shillings, 1581	£1250	£2750
Four shillings, 1581	£1350	£3000
Two shillings, 1581		ext. rare

	F	VF
4th coinage 1582-88		
Lion nobles (gold)	£3000	£6750
Two-third lion nobles (gold)	£3250	£7500
One-third lion nobles (gold)	£3750	£8500
Forty shillings, 1582	£3250	£9000
Thirty shillings, 1582-6	£300	£900
Twenty shillings, 1582-5	£275	£825
Ten shillings, 1582-4	£250	£725

James VI twenty shillings, 1582

	F	VF
5th coinage 1588		
Thistle nobles (gold)	£1450	£3250
6th coinage 1591-93		
Hat pieces (gold) 1591-3	£2750	£6500
Balance half merks, 1591-3	£200	£525
Balance quarter merks, 1591	£375	£900
7th coinage 1594-1601		
Riders (gold)	£725	£1650
Half riders (gold)	£600	£1350
Ten shillings, 1593-5, 1598-1601 ...	£110	£275
Five shillings, 1593-5, 1598-1601 ...	£100	£250
Thirty pennies, 1595-6, 1598-9, 1601	£100	£250
Twelve pennies, 1594-6	£90	£250

James VI Sword and Sceptre piece, 1601

	F	VF
8th coinage 1601-4		
Sword and sceptre pieces (gold) ...	£375	£850
Half sword and sceptre pieces (gold)	£325	£725
Thistle-merks, 1601-4	£75	£200
Half thistle merks –	£65	£175
Quarter thistle-merks –	£45	£150
Eighth thistle-merks, 1601-3	£35	£110
Billon and copper issues		
Billon placks or eight penny groats	£20	£75
Billon half packs	£135	£375
Billon hardheads	£25	£85
Billon saltire placks	£135	£425

	F	VF
Copper twopence 1597	£85	£275
Copper penny 1597	£375	*
After English accession 1603-25		
Units (gold)	£500	£1000
Double crowns (gold)	£625	£1500
Britain crowns (gold)	£425	£900
Halfcrowns (gold)	£400	£875
Thistle crowns (gold)	£375	£800
Sixty shillings	£350	£850
Thirty shillings	£125	£300
Twelve shillings	£135	£325
Six shillings	£375	£900
Two shillings	£35	£110
One shilling	£60	£150

*James VI Gold Unit
(after English accession)*

	F	VF
Sixpences	*	*
Copper twopences	£20	£50
Copper pennies	£65	£175

Charles I Briot Unit, 3rd coinage

	F	VF
CHARLES 1652-49		
1st coinage 1625-36		
Units (gold)	£750	£2000
Double crowns (gold)	£1250	£3250
Britain crowns (gold)	ext. rare	
Sixty shillings	£675	£1750
Thirty shillings	£150	£400
Twelve shillings	£150	£425
Six shillings	£375	£1000
Two shillings	£65	£165
One shillings	£85	£250
2nd coinage 1636		
Half merks	£75	£200
Forty penny pieces	£70	£185
Twenty penny pieces	£70	£175

3rd coinage 1580-81

	F	VF
Units (gold)	£750	£1650
Half units (gold)	£825	£1850
Britain crowns (gold)	£1000	£2750
Britain half crowns (gold)	£425	£900
Sixty shilling	£325	£1000
Thirty shilling	£135	£300

Charles I Twelve Shillings, 3rd coinage; Falconer's issue.

	F	VF
Twelve shillings	£90	£225
Six shillings	£100	£275
Half Merks	£85	£225
Forty pennies	£35	£90
Twenty pennies	£25	£70
Three shillings	£70	£240
Two shillings	£65	£150
Copper twopences (lion)	£20	£50
– pennies –	£375	*
– twopences (CR crowned)	£15	£40
– twopences (Stirling turners) ...	£15	£35

CHARLES II 1660-85
1st coinage
Four merks

	F	VF
1664 thistle above bust	£600	£1250
1664 thistle below bust	£675	£1500
1665	£950	*
1670	£850	*
1673	£650	£1350
1674 F below bust	£600	£1200
1675	£625	£1250

Two merks

	F	VF
1664 thistle above bust	£475	£1000

Charles II silver
two merks 1664

	F	VF
1664 thistle below bust	£325	£850
1670	£575	£1250
1673	£300	£750
1673 F below bust	£425	£950
1674	£350	£850
1674 F below bust	£375	£900
1675	£350	£800

Charles II, Merk 1669

Merks

		F	VF
1664	... ...	£95	£275
1665	... ...	£110	£325
1666	... ...	£225	£575
1668	... ...	£200	£525
1669	... ...	£65	£225
1670	... ...	£65	£225
1671	... ...	£75	£225
1672	... ...	£85	£250
1673	... ...	£75	£225
1674	... ...	£125	£400
1674 F below bust	... ...	£110	£325
1675 F below bust	... ...	£110	£325
1675	... ...	£175	£500

Half merks

		F	VF
1664	... ...	£175	£475
1665	... ...	£150	£425
1666	... ...	£200	£650
1667	... ...	£200	£650
1668	... ...	£150	£425
1669	... ...	£85	£275
1670	... ...	£90	£275
1671	... ...	£100	£300
1672	... ...	£90	£275
1673	... ...	£125	£350
1675 F below bust	... ...	£110	£325
1675	... ...	£125	£350

2nd coinage

Dollars

		F	VF
1676	... ...	£325	£1000
1679	... ...	£325	£1100
1680	... ...	£425	£1250
1681	... ...	£325	£1100
1682	... ...	£300	£950

Half dollars

		F	VF
1675	... ...	£300	£850
1676	... ...	£450	£1250
1681	... ...	£325	£900

Quarter dollars

		F	VF
1675	... ...	£150	£475
1676	... ...	£125	£325
1677	... ...	£125	£350
1678	... ...	£135	£400
1679	... ...	£150	£425
1680	... ...	£125	£350
1681	... ...	£125	£350
1682	... ...	£135	£375

Eighth dollars

		F	VF
1676	... ...	£80	£200
1677	... ...	£85	£225
1678/7	... ...	£175	£525
1679	... ...	£125	£425
1680	... ...	£80	£200
1682	... ...	£125	£425

Sixteenth dollars		
1677	£65	£175
1678/7	£75	£200
1679/7	£100	£375
1680	£75	£200
1681	£65	£175

Charles II 1678 Bawbee

Copper twopence CR"		
crowned	£20	£60
Copper bawbees, 1677-9	£45	£135
Copper turners, 1677-9	£30	£110

JAMES VII 1685-9

	FDC	
Sixty shillings 1688 proof only[1]	FDC	£1600
– gold proof only[1]		Ext. rare
('Struck in 1828, not contemporary)		

Forty shillings		
1887	£225	£750
1688	£250	£800

James VII 1687 ten shillings

Ten shillings		
1687	£135	£475
1688	£200	£650

WILLIAM AND MARY 1689-94

Sixty shillings		
1691	£425	£1350
1692	£375	£1000

Forty shillings		
1689	£250	£750
1690	£200	£625
1691	£200	£500
1692	£150	£475
1693	£135	£450
1694	£200	£600

Twenty shillings		
1693	£350	£1000
1694	£475	£1350

Ten shillings		
1689	*	*
1690	£200	£575
1691	£125	£400
1692	£135	£425
1694	£250	£675

William and Mary 1694 five shillings

Five shillings	F	VF
1691	£135	£450
1694	£100	£325
Copper bawbee 1691-4	£50	£125
Copper bodle 1691-4	£30	£90

WILLIAM II 1694-1702	F	VF
Pistole (gold) 1701	£2500	£6750
Half pistole (gold) 1701	£2250	£6500

Sixty shillings		
1699	*	*

Forty shillings		
1695	£175	£500
1696	£185	£525
1697	£200	£550
1698	£225	£625
1699	£225	£625
1700	£650	£1750

Twenty shillings		
1695	£150	£475
1696	£125	£375
1697	£275	£750
1698	£125	£375
1699	£375	£900

Ten shillings		
1695	£100	£250
1696	£100	£250
1697	£110	£275
1698	£125	£350
1699	£135	£375

Five shillings		
1695	£75	£175
1696	£75	£175
1697	£60	£150
1699	£85	£225
1700	£85	£225
1701	£135	£425
1702	£125	£375
Copper bawbee 1695-7	£65	£275
Copper bodle 1695-7	£45	£150

ANNE 1702-14

Pre-Union 1702-7

Ten shillings		
1705	£150	£350
1706	£175	£425

Five shillings		
1705	£45	£125
1706	£50	£150

Post-Union 1707-14
see under British milled series

JAMES VIII 1688-1766 (The Old Pretender)

Guinea 1716, gold	FDC	£8500
– silver ... ...:	FDC	£1250
– bronze	FDC	£1500
Crown 1709		unique
Crown 1716, silver	FDC	£1650
– gold		ext. rare
– bronze		ext. rare

NB: All the 1716-dated pieces were struck in 1828 from original dies.

Irish Coins

Hammered Issues 995-1661

Prices are for the commonest coins in each case. It should be remembered taht most of the Irish coins of these times are in fairly poor condition and it is difficult to find specimens in VF condition upwards. For more details see The Guide Book to the Coinage of Ireland AD 995 to the present day, *by Anthony Dowle and Patrick Finn (ref. DF in the following lists): Spink's* Coins of Scotland, Ireland and the Islands, *and also Patrick Finn's* Irish Coin Values.

All coins are silver unlesss otherwise stated

HIBERNO-NORSEMEN OF DUBLIN 995-1150

	F	VF
Pennies, imitative of English coins, many types and varieties ...from	£135	£275

Hiberno-Norse penny, c 1015-1035

Hiberno-Norseman of Dublin Penny c1035-1055

JOHN, as Lord of Ireland c 1185-1199

Halfpennies, with profile portrait	£1500	*
Halfpennies, with facing head	£50	£110
Farthings	£275	£700

Different types,varieties, mints, moneyers.

JOHN DE COURCY Lord of Ulster 1177-1205

Halfpenny		unique
Farthings	£575	£1350

Different types,varieties, mints, moneyers.

John as King of England, Rex/Triangle Penny

JOHN as King of England and Lord of Ireland c 1199-1216

Rex/Triangle types

	F	VF
Pennies ... ...from	£45	£100
Halfpennies	£75	£175
Farthings	£575	£1500

Different types,varieties, mints, moneyers.

HENRY III 1216-1272

Pennies (c 1251-1254) ... ...from	£35	£90

Dublin only, moneyers DAVI and RICHARD. many varieties.

Edward I Waterford penny

EDWARD I 1272-1307

Pennies ... ...from	£25	£65
Halfpennies	£40	£125

Edward I Farthing, Dublin

Farthings	£70	£175

Dublin,Waterford and Cork. Many different issues.

EDWARD III 1327-1377

Halfpennies Dublin mint		ext. rare

There were no Irish coins struck for Edward II, Richard II, Henry IV or Henry V.

HENRY VI 1422-1461

Pennies, Dublin mint		ext. rare

Edward IV untitled crown groats

EDWARD IV 1461-1483

Untitled crown groats ... ...from	£325	£850
– pennies	£900	*
Titled crown groats	£1250	*
– halfgroats	£1500	*
– pennies	£1000	*
Cross on rose/-sun groats	£1750	*

	F	VF
Bust/rose-sun double groats	£1350	£4750
– – groats	£1250	*
– – halfgroats	£1250	*
– – pennies	£1000	*
'English style' groats	£85	£225
– halfgroats	£375	£1000
– pennies	£45	£100
– halfpennies	£675	*
Bust/rose groats	£300	£750
– – pennies	£85	£250
copper issues		
Crown/cross farthing	£900	*
– – half farthing	£750	*
PATRICIUS/SALVATOR		
Farthing	£675	£1650
3 crowns/sun half-farthing	£800	*

This is, of course, a very abbreviated listing of the issues of Edward IV which are numerous and complicated, and still pose numismatics many problems. There are also many varieties and different mints.

RICHARD III 1483-1485
	F	VF
Bust/rose-cross groats	£750	£2750
— halfgroat		unique
— penny		ext.rare
Cross and Pellet Penny	£1000	*
Three-crown groats	£375	£800
Different mints, varieties, etc.		

HENRY VII 1485-1509
Early issues
	F	VF
Three-crown groats	£75	£185
— halfgroats	£120	£250
— pennies	£350	£950
— halfpennies		ext. rare
Different mints, varieties, etc.		

LAMBERT SIMNEL (pretender) 1487
	F	VF
Three-crown groats	£750	£2000
Different mints, varieties.		

HENRY VII 1485-1509

Henry VII facing bust Groat, Dublin

Later issues
	F	VF
Facing bust groats	£90	£200
— halfgroats	£900	*
— pennies	£750	*
Crowned H pennies	£900	*

Many varieties. Mainly Dublin. Waterford is extemely rare.

HENRY VIII 1509-1547
	F	VF
'Harp' groats	£50	£140
— halfgroat	£275	£850

Henry VIII harp groats (with initials HA and HI)

These harp coins carry crowned initials, e.g., HA (Henry and Anne Boleyn), HI (Henry and Jane Seymour), HK (Henry and Katherine Howard), HR (Henricus Rex).

Henry VIII portrait groat

Posthumous issues	F	VF
Portrait groats current for 6 pence	£75	£250
— halfgroats ...current for 3 pence	£90	£275
— pennies current for 3 halfpence	£250	£750
— halfpennies current for 3 farthings	£450	£1250
Different busts, mintmarks etc.		

EDWARD VI 1547-1553
	F	VF
Base shillings 1552 (MDLII)	£575	£1750
— contemporary copy	£50	£200

Mary 1553 shilling

MARY 1553-1558
	F	VF
Shillings 1553 (MDLIII)	£500	£2000
Shillings 1554 (MDLIIII)		ext. rare
Groats		**ext. rare**
Halfgroats		ext. rare
Pennies		ext. rare
Several varieties of the shillings and groats.		

PHILIP AND MARY 1554-1558
	F	VF
Base shillings	£225	£750
— groats	£65	£250
Several minor varieties.		

ELIZABETH I 1558-1603
	F	VF
Base portrait shillings	£250	£850
— groats	£100	£350

Elizabeth I 1561 portrait shilling

	F	VF
Fine silver portrait shillings 1561	£150	£575
— groats –	£200	£675
Base shillings arms-harp	£125	£475
— sixpences –	£85	£275
— threepences –	£110	£375
— pennies –	£30	£100
— halfpennies –	£50	£175

JAMES I 1603-1625
Shillings	£70	£225
— Sixpences	£60	£175

Different issues, busts and mintmarks.

CHARLES I 1625-1649
Siege money of the Irish Rebellion 1642-1649
Siege coins are rather irregular in size and shape.

Kilkenny Money 1642
Copper halfpennies (**F**)	£110	£475
Copper farthings (**F**)	£225	£750

Inchiquin Money 1642-1646
(The only gold coins struck in Ireland)
Gold double pistoles		ext. rare
Gold pistoles (**F**)		ext. rare
Crowns	£1650	£4000

Inchiquin shilling

Halfcrowns	£1350	£2750
Shillings	£1350	£2750
Ninepences	£3250	*
Sixpences	£3000	*
Groats (**F**)	£2500	*
Threepences ... ... ext. rare		*

Three issues and many varieties.

Ormonde Money 1643
Crowns (**F**)	£375	£750
Halfcrowns (**F**)	£250	£600
Shillings	£150	£325

Ormonde Money, Halfcrown

Ormonde sixpence

Sixpences (**F**)	£100	£225
Groats (**F**)	£95	£200
Threepences	£95	£200
Halfgroats (**F**)	£275	£675

Many varieties.

Rebel Money 1643
Crowns	£1650	£4000
Halfcrowns	£1500	£3500

Town Pieces 1645-1647
Bandon
Copper farthings (**F**)	£400	*

Kinsale copper farthing

Kinsale
Copper farthings (**F**)	£425	*

Youghal
Copper farthings (**F**)	£450	£1000
Brass twopences		ext. rare
Pewter threepences		ext. rare

IRISH COINS

	F	VF
Cork		
Shillings (F)	£1350	£3000
Sixpences (F)	£600	£1350
Copper halfpennies	£750	*
Copper farthings (F)	£450	*
Elizabeth I shillings countermarked		
CORKE (F)		ext. rare

Youghal farthing

'Blacksmith's' Money 1649
(Based on English Tower halfcrown)

Halfcrown, varieties	£475	£1250

Dublin Money 1649

Crowns	£2500	£6500
Halfcrowns	£1750	£4500

Charles II Armstrong Issue, Farthing

CHARLES II 1660-1685
Armstrong issues 1660-1661

Copper farthings	£25	£80

Charles II to George IV

This series, of which all the issues except Bank of Ireland tokens were struck in base metal, features a large number of varieties, many of which are unpublished, but there is space here for only the main types and best-known variants. A number of rare proofs have also been omitted.

Except for the 'gunmoney' of James II, Irish copper coins are notably hard to find in the top grades, especially the so-called 'Voce populi' issues and specimens of Wood's coinage (which are reasonably common in the lower grades, apart from the rarities).

We have listed some of the 'gunmoney' of James II in only three grades – Fair, Fine and VF. The majority of these hastily produced coins were not well struck and many pieces with little substantial wear are, arguably, not EF in the strictest sense.

Finally, a note on the dating of gunmoney. In the calendar used up to 1723 the legal or civil year commenced on March 25 in Great Britain and Ireland, so December 1689 came before, not after January, February and March 1689. Coins dated March 1689 and March 1690 were struck in the same month.

CHARLES II	Fair	F	VF	EF
St Patrick's coinage				
Halfpenny	£100	£400	*	*
— star in rev legend	£125	£500	*	*
Farthing	£85	£325	£750	*
— stars in rev legend	£100	£350	£800	*
— cloud around				
St Patrick	*	*	*	*
— martlet below king	£100	£375	£850	*
— annulet below king	£100	£375	£850	*

Charles II St Patrick's Farthing

Regal coinage
Halfpennies

1680 large letters				
small cross	£12	£50	£150	*
1680 large letters,				
pellets	£10	£40	£135	£400
1681 large letters	£10	£40	£130	£375
1681 small letters	*	*	*	*
1682 large letters	£15	£60	£175	*
1682 small letters	£10	£40	£125	£375
1683	£10	£40	£135	£350
1684	£25	£100	£325	*

JAMES II
Regular coinage
Halfpennies

1685	£10	£50	£150	£575
1686	£10	£40	£135	£525
1687	£50	£300	*	*
1688	£12	£50	£150	*

Emergency coinage
Gunmoney
Crowns

1690	£20	£65	£150	£375
1690 'chubby'				
horseman, sword				
to E (Sby 6577) ...	£30	£110	£325	*
1690 similar (DF 373)	£45	£135	£350	*

James II Gunmoney Crown

	Fair	F	VF	EF
Large halfcrowns				
1689 July	£15	£60	£135	*
1689 August	£10	£35	£100	*
1689 September	£10	£35	£100	*
1689 October	£8	£30	£90	*
1689 November	£10	£35	£110	*
1689 December	£10	£35	£110	*
1689 January	£10	£35	£120	*
1689 February	£8	£30	£90	*
1689 March	£8	£30	£90	*
1690 March	£8	£30	£90	*
1690 April	£8	£30	£90	*
1690 May	£10	£35	£110	*
Small halfcrowns				
1690 April	£35	£150	*	*
1690 May	£6	£25	£75	£200
1690 June	£8	£30	£85	£225
1690 July	£10	£35	£100	£275
1690 August	£15	£50	£150	£450
1690 September	*	*	*	*
1690 October	£50	£225	£500	*
Large shillings				
1689 July	£8	£25	£65	£175
1689 August	£8	£20	£60	£150
1689 September	£8	£20	£60	£150
1689 October	£8	£25	£65	£175
1689 November	£8	£20	£60	£150
1689 December	£8	£20	£55	£135
1689 January	£8	£20	£55	£135
1689 February	£8	£20	£55	£135
1689 March	£8	£20	£60	£150
1690 March	£8	£20	£60	£150
1690 April	£8	£25	£70	£175
Small shillings				
1690 April	£10	£30	£90	£225
1690 May	£7	£20	£60	£150
1690 June	£7	£20	£60	£150
1690 July	*	*	*	*
1690 August	*	*	*	*
1690 September	£25	£125	*	*

James II

*Gunmoney,
halfcrown, May 1690*

Sixpences	Fair	F	VF	EF
1689 June	£10	£35	£100	£200
1689 July	£8	£30	£90	£175
1689 August	£8	£30	£90	£175
1689 September	£10	£35	£110	£225
1689 October	*	*	*	*
1689 November	£8	£30	£90	£175
1689 December	£8	£30	£90	£175
1689 January	£10	£35	£100	£200
1689 February	£8	£30	£90	£175
1689 March	*	*	*	*
1690 March	*	*	*	*
1690 April	*	*	*	*
1690 May	£20	£60	£150	*
1690 June	*	*	*	*
1690 October	*	*	*	*
Pewter Money				
Crown	£225	£750	£2500	*
Groat	£150	£575	£1500	£2750
Penny large bust	£135	£475	£1000	*
Penny small bust	£110	£375	£850	*

IRISH COINS

	Fair	F	VF	EF

James II Pewter Money, Halfpenny, 1690

	Fair	F	VF	EF
Halfpenny large bust	£70	£225	£625	*
Halfpenny small bust	£60	£175	£475	*

Limerick Money halfpenny

Limerick Money				
Halfpenny	£15	£60	£125	£375
Farthing reversed N	£20	£75	£175	£475
— normal N	£25	£85	£225	*

1693 halfpenny

WILLIAM AND MARY
Halfpennies				
1692	£6	£35	£135	*
1693	£6	£35	£135	*
1694	£8	£40	£150	*

WILLIAM III
	Fair	F	VF	EF
1696 Halfpenny draped bust	£15	£50	£200	*
1696 Halfpenny crude undraped bust	£50	£225	£575	*

GEORGE I
Wood's coinage
	Fair	F	VF	EF
1722 harp left	£15	£55	£200	*
1722 harp right	£8	£35	£135	£425
1723	£6	£20	£80	£325
1723 obv Rs altered Bs	£7	£30	£100	£350
1723 no stop after date	£7	£30	£85	£325
1723/2	£7	£30	£125	*
1723 star in rev legend	*	*	*	*

IRISH COINS

	Fair	F	VF	EF
1723 no stop before HIBERNIA	£7	£30	£80	£325
1724 head divides rev legend	£10	£35	£150	£400
1724 legend continuous over head	£10	£35	£150	*

George I Wood's farthing, 1723

Farthings

	Fair	F	VF	EF
1722 harp left	£40	£150	£675	*
1723 D: G:	£10	£45	£175	£500
1723 DEI GRATIA ...	£6	£25	£100	£250
1724	£10	£35	£140	£375

GEORGE II
halfpennies

	Fair	F	VF	EF
1736	*	£10	£50	£225
1737	*	£10	£50	£225
1738	£1	£15	£60	£250
1741	*	£10	£50	£225
1742	*	£10	£50	£225
1743	£2	£20	£65	£275
1744	£1	£15	£60	£250
1744/43	£2	£20	£65	£275
1746	£1	£15	£60	£250
1747	*	£10	£50	£225
1748	£2	£15	£75	£300
1749	*	£10	£50	£200
1750	*	£10	£45	£195
1751	*	£10	£45	£195
1752	*	£10	£45	£195
1753	*	£12	£50	£225
1755	*	*	*	*
1760	*	£8	£40	£200

Farthings

	Fair	F	VF	EF
1737	£1	£15	£75	£250
1738	*	£10	£60	£225
1744	*	£10	£50	£200
1760	*	£8	£40	£125

George III, Voce Populi Halfpenny 1760

GEORGE III
Voce populi coinage
Halfpennies (1760)

	Fair	F	VF	EF
Type 1 (DF 565) ...	£45	£150	£450	*

	Fair	F	VF	EF
Type 2 (DF 566)	£30	£85	£375	*
Type 3 (DF 567)	£40	£125	£425	*
Type 4 (DF 569)	£30	£85	£325	*
Type 5 (DF 570)	£25	£80	£300	*
Type 6 (DF 571)	£25	£80	£300	*
Type 7 (DF 572)	£30	£85	£350	*
Type 8 (DF 573)	£30	£85	£300	*
Type 9 (DF 575)	£40	£125	£425	*
Type 9, P before head (DF 576)	£25	£80	£300	*
Type 9, P under head (DF 577)	£25	£80	£300	*

Farthings (1760)

	Fair	F	VF	EF
Type 1 loop to truncation	£65	£250	£1250	*
Type 2 no loop ...	*	*	*	*

London coinage
Halfpennies

	F	VF	EF	UNC
1766	*	£35	£100	£250
1769	*	£35	£110	£250
1769 2nd type	*	£50	£120	£300
1775	*	£35	£165	£275
1776	£10	£65	£300	£325
1781	*	£35	£120	£225
1782	*	£35	£100	£225

George III Halfpenny, 1805

Soho coinage

	Fair	F	VF	EF
Penny 1805	£8	£35	£150	£225
Halfpenny 1805 ...	£3	£20	£90	£150
Farthing 1806	£2	£15	£50	£100

Bank of Ireland token coinage

	Fair	F	VF	EF
Six shillings 1804 ...	£50	£85	£250	£600

1804 six shilling Bank of Ireland

IRISH COINS

	F	VF	EF	UNC
Thirty pence 1808	£15	£35	£100	*
Ten pence 1805 ...	£4	£20	£80	£100
Ten pence 1806 ...	£10	£30	£110	£175
Ten pence 1813 ...	£3	£20	£70	£100
Five pence 1805 ...	£3	£20	£70	£100
Five pence 1806 ...	£5	£30	£80	£120

Bank of Ireland ten pence token, 1813

GEORGE IV

	F	VF	EF	UNC
Penny 1822...	£5	£30	£150	£275
Penny 1823...	£5	£35	£165	£300
Halfpenny 1822 ...	£3	£25	£90	£175
Halfpenny 1823 ...	£3	£25	£100	£200

Free State and Republic

Proofs exist for nearly all dates of the modern Irish coinage. However, only a few dates have become available to collectors or dealers and apart from the 1928 proofs, are all very rare. They have therefore been omitted from the list.

TEN SHILLINGS

	F	VF	EF	Unc
1966	*	*	£5	£7.50
1966	*	*	*	£15

HALFCROWNS

	F	VF	EF	Unc
1928	£3	£6	£12	£40
1928 proof	*	*	*	£45

Reverse of halfcrown

	F	VF	EF	Unc
1930	£3	£10	£90	£375
1931	£6	£20	£125	£400
1933	£3	£15	£100	£350
1934	£5	£20	£60	£250
1937	£30	£75	£450	£1250
1939	£3	£6	£15	£60
1940	£3	£5	£10	£50
1941	£4	£6	£20	£60
1942	£4	£6	£20	£55
1943	£70	£150	£700	*
1951	*	£1	£5	£40
1954	*	£1	£5	£40
1955	*	£1	£5	£30
1959	*	£1	£5	£20
1961	*	£1	£5	£25

	F	VF	EF	Unc
1961 mule (normal) obv/pre-1939 rev)	£8	£20	£250	*
1962	*	*	*	£5
1963	*	*	*	£5
1964	*	*	*	£5
1966	*	*	*	£3
1967	*	*	*	£3

1937 florin

FLORINS

	F	VF	EF	Unc
1928	£2	£4	£8	£30
1928 proof	*	*	*	£40
1930	£3	£6	£70	£350
1931	£3	£10	£100	£350
1933	£8	£30	£125	£425
1934	£12	£45	£275	£700
1935	£3	£10	£90	£300
1937	£3	£25	£165	£500
1939	£2	£4	£10	£40
1940	£2	£5	£12	£40
1941	£2	£5	£20	£60
1942	£2	£5	£12	£45
1943	£2500	£5000	£8000	*
1951	*	*	£3	£25
1954	*	*	£3	£25
1955	*	*	£3	£20
1959	*	*	£3	£20
1961	*	£3	£6	£35
1962	*	*	£3	£18
1963	*	*	£3	£18
1964	*	*	*	£5
1965	*	*	*	£5
1966	*	*	*	£5
1968	*	*	*	£5

SHILLINGS

	F	VF	EF	Unc
1928	*	£3	£8	£25
1928 proof	*	*	*	£30
1930	£5	£15	£70	£300
1931	£3	£10	£50	£225
1933	£3	£10	£50	£225
1935	£2	£5	£40	£100
1937	£5	£25	£225	£775
1939	*	£3	£6	£35
1940	*	£3	£8	£30
1941	£2	£5	£8	£30
1942	£2	£5	£8	£28
1951	*	£1	£3	£20
1954	*	*	£3	£15
1955	*	*	£3	£18
1959	*	*	£6	£25
1962	*	*	*	£5
1963	*	*	*	£4
1964	*	*	*	£5
1966	*	*	*	£4
1968	*	*	*	£4

SIXPENCES

	F	VF	EF	Unc
1928	*	£1	£3	£20
1928 proof	*	*	*	£25
1934	*	£1	£8	£50
1935	*	£3	£12	£80
1939	*	£1	£5	£35

	F	VF	EF	Unc
1940	*	£1	£5	£25
1942	*	*	£5	£25
1945	£2	£8	£35	£125
1946	£5	£12	£70	£350
1947	£1	£6	£25	£90
1948	*	£2	£8	£30
1949	*	*	£5	£30
1950	£2	£15	£35	£125
1952	*	£1	£4	£18
1953	*	£1	£4	£18
1955	*	£1	£4	£18
1956	*	*	£3	£12
1958	*	£1	£5	£40
1959	*	*	£2	£7
1960	*	*	£2	£7
1961	*	*	£2	£7
1962	*	*	£3	£30
1963	*	*	*	£3
1964	*	*	*	£3
1966	*	*	*	£3
1967	*	*	*	£3

1968 sixpence

	F	VF	EF	Unc
1968	*	*	*	£2
1969	*	*	*	£3

THREEPENCES

	F	VF	EF	Unc
1928	*	£1	£3	£12
1928 proof	*	£1	£3	£15
1933	£2	£5	£45	£175
1934	*	£3	£15	£60
1935	£2	£5	£25	£100
1939	£1	£5	£50	£185
1940	*	*	£10	£30
1942	*	*	£5	£35
1943	*	*	£8	£65
1946	*	*	£5	£30
1948	*	£2	£15	£80
1949	*	*	£5	£30
1950	*	*	£2	£6
1953	*	*	£2	£5
1956	*	*	£1	£4
1961	*	*	*	£3
1962	*	*	*	£3
1963	*	*	*	£3
1964	*	*	*	£3
1965	*	*	*	£3
1966	*	*	*	£3

1967 threepence

	F	VF	EF	Unc
1967	*	*	*	*
1968	*	*	*	*

PENNIES

	F	VF	EF	Unc
1928	*	*	£3	£15
1928 proof	*	*	*	£35
1931	*	£2	£10	£45

	F	VF	EF	Unc
1933	*	£3	£15	£75
1935	*	*	£6	£30
1937	*	*	£9	£50
1938 (unique?)	*	*	*	*
1940	£2	£6	£90	£400
1941	*	£1	£6	£30
1942	*	*	£3	£15
1943	*	*	£5	£20
1946	*	*	£3	£15
1948	*	*	£3	£15
1949	*	*	£3	£15
1950	*	*	£3	£15
1952	*	*	£2	£7
1962	*	*	£2	£3
1963	*	*	*	£2
1964	*	*	*	£2
1965	*	*	*	£1
1966	*	*	*	£1
1967	*	*	*	£1
1968	*	*	*	£1

HALFPENNIES

	F	VF	EF	Unc
1928	*	£3	£6	£25
1928 proof	*	*	*	£25
1933	£1	£10	£40	£290
1935	*	£5	£25	£175
1937	*	*	£15	£55
1939	£4	£10	£30	£125
1940	*	£10	£35	£150
1941	*	*	£5	£15
1942	*	*	£2	£20
1943	*	*	£3	£15
1946	*	*	£5	£55
1949	*	*	£3	£8
1953	*	*	*	£4
1964	*	*	*	£2
1965	*	*	*	£2
1966	*	*	*	£2
1967	*	*	*	£1.50

FARTHINGS

	F	VF	EF	Unc
1928	*	*	£3	£10
1928 proof	*	*	*	£15
1930	*	*	£5	£15
1931	£1	£3	£8	£25
1932	£1	£3	£10	£30
1933	*	£2	£5	£20
1935	*	£5	£12	£40
1936	*	£6	£15	£45
1937	*	£2	£5	£20
1939	*	*	£3	£12
1940	*	£3	£6	£30
1941	*	£1	£3	£7
1943	*	£1	£3	£7
1944	*	£1	£3	£7
1946	*	£1	£3	£7
1949	*	£2	£5	£10
1953	*	*	£3	£7
1959	*	*	£1	£4
1966	*	*	£2	£6

DECIMAL COINAGE
50p, 10p, 5p, 2p, 1p, ½p
All issues face value only.

SETS

	F	VF	EF	Unc
1928 (in card case)	*	*	FDC	£200
1928 (in leather case)	*	*	FDC	£275
1966 unc. set	*	*	*	£10
1971 specimen set in folder	*	*	*	£5
1971 proof set	*	*	*	£9

The Anglo-Gallic Series

Chronological table of the Kings of England and France in the period 1154-1453

Henry II 1154-89
He was Duke of Normandy and Count of Anjou, Maine and Touraine. Through his marriage in 1152 with Eleanor of Aquitaine he became Duke of Aquitaine and Count of Poitou. He relinquished both these titles to his son Richard who in 1169 did homage to Louis VII of France. In 1185 he forced Richard to surrender Aquitaine and Poitou to ELEANOR who later – during Richard's absence – actually governed her provinces.

Richard I (Coeur de Lion) 1189-99
After his homage to the French King, he was, in 1172, formally installed as Duke of Aquitaine and Count of Poitou. Although his father forced him in 1185 to surrender Aquitaine and Poitou to his mother he retained actual government. Later Eleanor ruled in his absence.

John 1199-1216
He lost all provinces of the Angevin Empire except Aquitaine and part of Poitou.

Henry III 1216-72
In 1252 he ceded Aquitaine to his son Edward.

Edward I 1272-1307
He governed Aquitaine since 1252. In 1279 he became Count of Ponthieu in the right of his wife, Eleanor of Castile. When she died in 1290 the county went to his son Edward.

Edward II 1307-27
He was Count of Ponthieu as from 1290. In 1325 he relinquished the county of Ponthieu and the Duchy of Aquitaine to his son Edward.

Edward III 1327-77
He was Count of Ponthieu and Duke of Aquitaine as from 1325. At the outbreak of the war in 1337 he lost Ponthieu which was restored to him in 1360. In 1340 he assumed the title of King of France, which he abandoned again in 1360 as a result of the Treaty of Calais. He then obtained Aquitaine in full sovereignty and consequently changed his Aquitanian title from Duke (dux) to Lord (dominus) as the first one implied the overlordship of the French King. He gave Aquitaine as an apanage to his son, the Prince of Wales, better known as Edward The Black Prince, b.1330, d.1376, who was Prince of Aquitaine from 1362 till 1372, although he actually ruled from 1363 till 1371. In 1369, after war broke out again Edward reassumed the French title, which was henceforth used by the Kings of England until the Treaty of Amiens in 1802.

Richard II 1377-99
The son of The Black Prince succeeded his grandfather, Edward III, as King of England and as Lord of Aquitaine.

Henry IV 1399-1413
He adopted the same titles Richard II had, whom he ousted from the throne.

Henry V 1413-22
From 1417 until 1420 he used the title 'King of the French' on his 'Royal' French coins. After the Treaty of Troyes in 1420 he styled himself 'heir of France'.

Henry VI 1422-61
He inherited the title 'King of the French' from his grandfather Charles VI. He lost actual rule in Northern France in 1450 and in Aquitaine in 1453.

Louis VII 1137-80

Philip II (Augustus) 1180-1223

Louis VIII 1223-26
Louis IX (Saint Louis) 1226-70
Philip III 1270-85

Philip IV 1285-1314

Louis X 1314-16
Philip V 1316-22
Charles IV 1322-28

Philip VI (de Valois) 1328-50

John II (The Good) 1350-64

Charles V 1364-80

Charles VI 1380-1422

Charles VII 1422-61

'All Kings of England in the period 1154-1453 had interests in France. They were Dukes or Lords of Aquitaine, Counts of Poitou or Ponthieu, Lords of Issoudun or they were even or pretended to be, Kings of France itself, and, in those various capacities, struck coins. These coins, together with the French coins of their sons, and of their English vassals, are called Anglo-Gallic coins'.

So starts the introduction of the Bourgey-Spink book by E.R. Duncan Elias on this series. We would also like to thank Messrs Bourgey and Spink for allowing us to use some of the illustrations from the book, as well as the chronological table of the Kings of England and France during the period.

The Anglo-Gallic Coins by E.R.D. Elias is still available from Spink and Son Ltd, London (see Some Useful Books on page 11).

Henry II
Denier,
Aquitaine

HENRY II 1152-68	F	VF
Denier	£50	£135
Obole	£100	£275

RICHARD THE LIONHEART 1168-99
Aquitaine

Denier	£40	£125
Obole	£45	£135

Poitou

Denier	£40	£85
Obole	£60	£165

Issoudun

Denier	£200	*

ELEANOR 1199-1204

Denier	£50	£125
Obole	£275	*

Edward I
Denier au lion,
during his
father's
lifetime

EDWARD I
During the lifetime of his father 1252-72

Denier au lion	£30	£75
Obole au lion	£45	£120

After succession to the English throne 1272-1307

Denier au lion	£75	£225
Obole au lion	£150	*

Edward I
Obole au lion,
after succession

Denier á la croix longue	£65	£165
Denier au léopard, first type	£30	£75
Obole au léopard, first type	£50	£125
Denier á la couronne	£250	*

The coinage of PONTHIEU (Northern France) under the Edwards

Edward I	F	VF
Denier	£95	£225
Obole	£75	£200
Edward III		
Denier	£150	*
Obole	£250	*

EDWARD II

Gros Turonus Regem	ext. rare	
Maille blanche	ext. rare	
Maille blanche Hibernie	£35	£90

EDWARD III
Gold coins

Ecu d'or	£1100	£2750
Florin	£2750	£7250
Léopard d'or, 1st issue	ext. rare	
Léopard d'or, 2nd issue	£1000	£2500

Edward III Léopard d'or, 2nd issue

Léopard d'or, 3rd issue	£950	£2350
Léopard d'or, 4th issue	£1250	£3250
Guyennois d'or, 1st type	£2750	£7000
Guyennois d'or, 2nd type	£1500	£3750
Guyennois d'or, 3rd type	£950	£2250

Silver coins

Gros aquitainique au léopard	£150	£475
Gros tournois à la crois mi-longue	£250	£675
Gros tournois à la croix longue	£100	£275
Sterling	£75	£200
Demi-sterling	£125	£375
Gros au léopard passant	£475	*
Gros à la couronne	£135	£375
Gros au châtel aquitainique	£175	£475
Gros tournois au léopard au-dessus	£70	£200
Gros à la porte	£70	£200
Gros acquitainique au léopard au-dessous	£225	*
Blanc au léopard sous couronne	£60	£135
Gros au léopard sous couronne	£200	£575
Gros à la couronne avec léopard	£165	£400
Sterling à la tête barbue	£325	£800
Petit gros de Bordeaux	ext. rare	
Gros au lion	£125	£325
Demi-gros au lion	£250	*
Guyennois d'argent (sterling)	£100	£225
Gros au buste	£1000	*
Demi-gros au buste	£450	£1200

Black coins

Double à la couronne, 1st type	£85	*
Double à la couronne, 2nd type	£75	£225
Double à la couronne, 3rd type	£125	*
Double au léopard	£65	£175
Double au léopard sous couronne	£30	£90
Double guyennois	ext. rare	
Denier au léopard, 2nd type	£25	£80
Obole au léopard, 2nd type	ext. rare	
Denier au léopard, 3rd type	£30	£100
Denier au léopard, 4th type	£30	£90

THE ANGLO-GALLIC SERIES

	F	VF
Obole au léopard, 4th type	£30	£90
Denier au lion	£40	£125

N.B. Some issues of the deniers au léopard of the 2nd and 3rd type are very rare to extremely rare and therefore considerably more valuable.

The coinage of BERGERAC
Henry, Earl of Lancaster 1347-51

	F	VF
Gros tournois à la croix longue ...	700	£1650
Gros tournois à la couronne	£625	*
Gros au châtel aquitainque	£650	£1500
Gros tournois au léopard au-dessus	£375	£800
Gros à la couronne	ext. rare	
Gros à fleur-de-lis	ext. rare	
Gros au léopard passant	ext. rare	
Double	£950	*
Denier au léopard	£625	*

Henry, Duke of Lancaster 1351-61

	F	VF
Gros tournois à la couronne avec léopard	£700	*
Gros au léopard couchant	£700	*
Sterling à la tête barbue	£575	*
Gros au lion	ext. rare	

EDWARD THE BLACK PRINCE 1362-72
Gold Coins

	F	VF
Léopard d'or	£925	£2400
Guyennois d'or	£1250	£2750
Chaise d'or	£1200	£2750
Pavillon d'or 1st issue	£1000	£2400
Pavillon d'or 2nd issue	£975	£2250
Demi-pavillon d'or	ext. rare	
Hardi d'or	£925	£2250

Edward the Black Prince
Hardi d'or of Bordeaux

Silver Coins

	F	VF
Gros	£675	£1850

Edward the Black Prince Demi-Gros

	F	VF
Demi-gros	£75	£200
Sterling	£60	£135
Hardi d'argent	£40	£100

Edward the Black Prince Hardi d'argent

Black Coins

	F	VF
Double guyennois	£100	£275
Denier au lion	£45	£125
Denier	£50	£135

RICHARD II 1377-99
Gold Coins

	F	VF
Hardi d'or	£1350	£3750
Demi-hardi d'or	ext. rare	

Silver Coins

	F	VF
Double Hardi d'argent	£650	£1750
Hardi d'argent	£45	£120

Black Coins

	F	VF
Denier	£75	£225

HENRY IV 1399-1413
Silver Coins

	F	VF
Double Hardi d'argent	£425	£1200

Henry IV Double Hardi d'argent

	F	VF
Hardi d'argent...	£35	£110
Hardi aux genêts...	£165	£500

Black Coins
	F	VF
Denier	£50	£135
Denier aux genêts	£125	£350

HENRY V 1413-22
Gold Coins
	F	VF
Agnel d' or	£2750	£7500
Salut d' or	£3750	£12000

Silver Coins
	F	VF
Florette, 1st issue	£75	£175
Florette, 2nd issue	£125	£300
Florette, 3rd issue	£50	£135
Florette, 4th issue	£60	£150
Guénar	£275	£850
Gros au léopard	£325	*

Black Coins
	F	VF
Mansiois		ext. rare
Niquet	£35	£100
Denier tournois	£65	£150

HENRY VI 1422-53
Gold Coins
	F	VF
Salut d' or	£350	£700
Angelot	£850	£2250

Henry VI Salut d'or, Paris Mint

Silver Coins
	F	VF
Grand Blanc aux ècus	£50	£125
Petit Blanc	£75	£225
Trésin...		ext. rare

Henry V Grand Blanc, Paris Mint

Black Coins
	F	VF
Denier Parisis, 1st issue	£50	£125
Denier Parisis, 2nd issue	£50	£125
Denier tournois	£60	£135
Maille tournois	£60	£135

N.B. The prices of the saluts and grand blancs are for the mints of Paris, Rouen and Saint Lô; coins of other mints are rare to very rare and consequently more valuable.

Island Coinages

CHANNEL ISLANDS

From the date of their introduction onwards, proofs have been struck for a large number of Channel Islands coins, particularly in the case of Jersey. Except for those included in the modern proof sets these are mostly at least very rare and in the majority of cases have been omitted from the list. A number of die varieties which exist for several dates of the earlier 19th century Guernsey eight doubles have also been excluded. For further information in both cases the reader is referred to The Coins of the British Commonwealth of Nations, Part I, European Territories by F. Pridmore, published by Spink and Son Ltd.

GUERNSEY

	F	VF	EF	BU
TEN SHILLINGS				
1966	*	*	*	£2
THREEPENCE				
1956	*	*	*	£2
1959	*	*	*	£2
1966 proof only ...	*	*	*	£2
EIGHT DOUBLES				
1834	*	£12	£40	£250
1858	*	£12	£40	£250
1864	*	£15	£50	*
1868	*	£10	£40	*
1874	*	£10	£40	*
1885 H	*	*	£12	£60
1889 H	*	*	£10	£50
1893 H	*	*	£10	£50
1902 H	*	*	£10	£25
1903 H	*	*	£10	£25
1910 H	*	*	£12	£30
1911 H	*	£15	£40	£75
1914 H	*	*	£7	£20
1918 H	*	*	£10	£25
1920 H	*	*	£5	£12
1934 H	*	*	£5	£15
1934 H prooflike ...	*	*	*	£100
1938 H	*	*	*	£5
1945 H	*	*	*	£5
1947 H	*	*	*	£4
1949 H	*	*	*	£4
1956	*	*	*	£1
1959	*	*	*	£1
1966 proof only ...	*	*	*.	£3
FOUR DOUBLES				
1830	*	*	£30	£175
1858	*	*	£35	£250

Guernsey 1864 four doubles

	F	VF	EF	BU
1864	*	£5	£45	*
1868	*	£5	£45	*

	F	VF	EF	BU
1874	*	*	£45	*
1885 H	*	*	£8	£30
1889 H	*	*	£5	£25
1893 H	*	*	£4	£20
1902 H	*	*	£4	£20
1903 H	*	*	£4	£20
1906 H	*	*	£4	£20
1908 H	*	*	£4	£20
1910 H	*	*	£3	£20
1911 H	*	*	£3	£20
1914 H	*	*	£3	£20
1918 H	*	*	£3	£20
1920 H	*	*	*	£15
1945 H	*	*	*	£5
1949 H	*	*	*	£6
1956	*	*	*	£2
1966 proof only ...	*	*	*	£2
TWO DOUBLES				
1858	*	£30	£100	£300
1868	*	£30	£100	£275
1874	*	£30	£100	£225
1885 H	*	*	£6	£20
1889 H	*	*	£4	£15
1899 H	*	*	£4	£15
1902 H	*	*	£5	£15
1903 H	*	*	£5	£20
1906 H	*	*	£4	£20
1908 H	*	*	£4	£25
1911 H	*	*	£4	£20
1914 H	*	*	£4	£25
1917 H	*	£10	£30	£100
1918 H	*	*	£2	£10
1920 H	*	*	£3	£10
1929 H	*	*	£2	£6
ONE DOUBLE				
1830	*	*	£20	£60
1868	*	£40	£100	£275
1868/30	*	£40	£100	£275
1885 H	*	*	£4	£10
1889 H	*	*	£2	£5
1893 H	*	*	£2	£5
1899 H	*	*	£2	£5
1902 H	*	*	£2	£5
1903 H	*	*	£2	£5
1911 H	*	*	£2	£8
1911 H new type ...	*	*	£2	£8
1914 H	*	*	£3	£8
1929 H	*	*	£1	£2
1933 H	*	*	£1	£2
1938 H	*	*	£1	£2

ISLAND COINAGES

SETS

1956 proof	... ...	**£25**
1966 proof	... ...	**£8**
1971 proof	... ...	**£7.25**

For coins post 1971 refer to the Standard Catalogue of World Coins published by Krouse Publications annually. Many commemorative pieces in various metals have been struck and therefore a full list of the complete coinage is beyond the scope of this publication.

JERSEY

CROWN	F	VF	EF	BU
1966	*	*	*	£1
1966 – proof	*	*	*	£3

1/4 OF A SHILLING

	F	VF	EF	BU
1957	*	*	*	£2
1960 proof only	*	*	*	£5
1964	*	*	*	£0.30
1966	*	*	*	£0.75

1/12 OF A SHILLING

	F	VF	EF	BU
1877 H	*	*	£7	£65
1881	*	*	£9	£60
1888	*	*	£8	£50
1894	*	*	£7	£40
1909	*	*	£8	£55
1911	*	*	£5	£30
1913	*	*	£5	£30
1923	*	*	£5	£30
1923 new type	*	*	£7	£25
1926	*	*	£5	£25
1931	*	*	£2	£25
1933	*	*	£3	£15
1935	*	*	£2	£15
1937	*	*	*	£5
'1945' (George VI)[1] ...	*	*	*	£3
'1945' (Elizabeth II)[1] ...	*	*	*	£2
1946	*	*	*	£4
1947	*	*	*	£3
1957	*	*	*	£0.40
1960	*	*	*	£0.20
1964	*	*	*	£0.15
1966	*	*	*	£0.15

The date 1945 on one-twelfth shillings commemorates the year of liberation from German occupation. The coins were struck in 1949, 1950, 1952 and 1954.

1/13 OF A SHILLING

1841	*	*	£60	£165
1844	*	*	£70	£175
1851	*	*	£75	£185
1858	*	*	£70	£175
1861	*	*	£70	£175
1865 proof only	*	*	*	£650
1866	*	*	£20	£70
1870	*	*	£25	£70
1871	*	*	£25	£70

1/24 OF A SHILLING

1877 H	*	*	£4	£45
1888	*	*	£4	£35
1894	*	*	£4	£30
1909	*	*	£3	£30
1911	*	*	£3	£30
1913	*	*	£3	£25
1923	*	*	£2	£20
1923 new type	*	*	£2	£20
1926	*	*	£2	£20
1931	*	*	£1	£10
1933	*	*	£1	£10
1935	*	*	£1	£10
1937	*	*	£1	£5
1946	*	*	£1	£5
1947	*	*	£1	£5

1/26 OF A SHILLING

1841	*	*	£45	£125
1844	*	*	£50	£150
1851	*	*	£45	£125
1858	*	*	£45	£125
1861	*	*	£40	£95
1866	*	*	£20	£85
1870	*	*	£20	£75
1871	*	*	£22	£75

1/48 OF A SHILLING

1877 H	*	£25	£75	£150

1/52 OF A SHILLING

1841	*	£40	£150	£300
1841 proof	*	*		£575
1861 proof only	*	*	*	£600

DECIMAL COINAGE

SETS		BU
1957	... ...	£30
1960	... ...	£15
1964	... ...	£10
1966 (4 coins) proof	... ...	£4
1966 (2 crowns)	... ...	£7
1968/7 1 decimal coins	... ...	£2
1972 Silver Wedding (5 gold, 4 silver coins)		£400
1972 - - proof	... ...	£450
1972 - - (4 silver coins)	... ...	£25

For coins post 1972 refer to the Standard Catalogue of World Coins published by Krouse Publications annually. Many commemorative pieces in various metals have been struck and therefore a full list of the complete coinage is beyond the scope of this publication.

MALCOLM BORD

GOLD COIN EXCHANGE

16 CHARING CROSS ROAD,
LONDON WC2H 0HR
TELEPHONE: 020 7240 0479
FAX: 020 7240 1920

As one of London's leading dealers in most branches of Numismatics we are able to offer you unrivalled advice when it comes to both the buying or selling of coins or whether you wish to buy or sell coins or medals, we will endeavour to offer the most competitive price.

REMEMBER

That any offer we make is not subject to commission and we offer immediate payment.

A comprehensive selection of coins and medals is always available for viewing at our showroom.

Knightsbridge Coins

WE ARE ALWAYS KEEN
TO PURCHASE COINS —
ESPECIALLY **BRITISH,
AMERICAN** AND
AUSTRALIAN
IN CHOICE
CONDITION, EITHER SINGLY OR IN
COLLECTIONS. WE ARE HAPPY TO TRAVEL
TO VIEW COLLECTIONS.

WE ALSO BUY
BANKNOTES, AND WE
CAN ARRANGE
VALUATIONS FOR
INSURANCE OR PROBATE
PURPOSES. IF YOU HAVE

COINS AND YOU ARE THINKING OF
SELLING, PLEASE DO NOT HESITATE TO
CONTACT US AT THE ADDRESS BELOW.

**KNIGHTSBRIDGE COINS,
43 DUKE STREET, ST. JAMES'S,
LONDON SW1Y 6DD, UK
TELEPHONE: (0207) 930 7597/8215
FAX: (0207) 930 8214**

ISLE OF MAN

Contemporary forgeries of several of the earlier Isle of Man coins exist.

COPPER AND BRONZE 1709-1839

Isle of Man, Halfpenny, proof in Silver, 1733

Isle of Man, Penny, 1786

PENNIES	F	VF	EF	Unc
1709	£20	£120	£250	*
1733	£30	£90	£250	*
1733 proof	*	£100	£200	*
1733 silver	*	*	£400	*
1758	£20	£40	£200	*
1758 proof	*	*	*	*
1758 silver	*	*	£600	*
1786	£10	£20	£125	£250
1786 plain edge proof	*	*	£300	£500
1798	£15	£40	£150	£250
1798 bronzed proof	*	*	£150	£250
1798 AE gilt proof ...	*	*	£700	£1250
1798 silver proof	*	*	*	*
1813	£10	£25	£125	£200
1813 bronzed proof ...	*	*	£150	£250
1839	*	£15	£50	£125
1839 proof	*	*	*	£500

HALFPENNIES	F	VF	EF	UNc
1709	£40	£100	£500	*
1733	£25	£120	£200	£350
1733 proof	*	*	£150	£400
1733 silver	*	*	£325	£500
1758	£20	£50	£125	£300
1758 proof	*	*	*	*
1786	£20	£50	£165	£250
1786 plain edge proof	*	*	£250	£425
1798	£10	£40	£165	£250
1798 proof	*	*	£175	£300
1798 AE gilt proof ...	*	*	*	£600
1813	£8	£30	£100	£200
1813 proof	*	*	£150	£250
1839	*	*	£35	£125
1839 proof	*	*	*	*
FARTHINGS				
1839	£10	£25	£45	£125
1839 proof	*	*	*	£300

For coins post 1965 refer to the standard catalogue of world coins published by Krouse Publications annually.

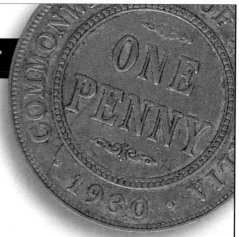

British Paper Money

THE prices listed here are only intended as a guide to values of English bank-notes. Notes with the current Chief Cashier, Andrew Bailey are generally available at a little above face, notes prior to that tend to increase in value, especially the very early notes.

Top condition is the most important factor in banknote pricing although it is quite possible to collect a more attractive selection in lower grades; some notes for example are never seen in better then Very Fine. The prices quoted here, recently updated are for EF and VF, a premium can be expected for first class notes - this is especially relevant to notes of John Bradbury and to a lesser extent, N. F. Warren Fisher.

We have not listed banknotes prior to 1914 as these are all scarce and only available in grades up to Very Fine. The past year has continued to show a healthy demand for material at every level, the emphasis still remaining on quality followed by rarity. The hobby continues to grow at a sensible pace, the shortage of good material being the only drawback.

Reference numbers are according to Vincent Duggleby's *English Paper Money*. 6th edition published by Pam West in October 2002. NEW EDITION OUT SOON.

TREASURY NOTES

Signed by John Bradbury

First Issue

			VF	EF
T8	10s	Red on white. Six digits	£350	£800
T9	10s	Red on white. Prefix 'No'	£300	£550
T10	10s	Red on white. Five digits	£500	£900
T1	£1	Black on white. Prefix large letters A., B. or C.	£700	£1400
T2	£1	Black on white. As previous but no full stop after serial letter	£1000	£2400
T3	£1	Black on white. Six digits	£400	£850
T4	£1	Black on white. Large serial number, 'dot' and five digits	£850	£1900
T5	£1	Black on white. Large serial number, 'dash' and five digits	£650	£1300
T6	£1	Black on white. Double prefix letters	£600	from £1200
T7	£1	Black on white. Small type face serial number	£2200	£4000

(Serial number with prefix 'No' are referred to as 'dot' if 'No' is followed by a full stop and 'dash' when a dash is used).

Second issue

			VF	EF
T12	10s	Red on white. Five digits	£300	£500
T13	10s	Red on white. Six digits	£300	£500
T11	£1	Black on white.	£250	£400
T15	10s	Red on white. Arabic overprint	£500	£1100
T14	£1	Black on white. Arabic overprint	£3200	*

Third issue

			VF	EF
T16	£1	Green and brown on white	£60	£160
T17	10s	Green and brown on white Black serial no. with 'dot'	£200	£400

			VF	FF
T18	10s	Green and brown on white		
		Black serial no. with 'dash'	£200	£400
T19	10s	Green and brown on white		
		Red serial no. with 'dot'	£900	*
T20	10s	Green and brown on white		
		Red serial no. with 'dash'	£200	£400

Signed by Norman Fenwick Warren Fisher First issue (overall watermark)
T25	10s	Green and brown on white, 'dot'	£120	£240
T26	10s	Green and brown on white, 'dash'	£100	£200
T24	£1	Green and brown on white	£50	£120

Second issue (boxed watermark)
T30	10s	Green and brown on white	£90	£200
T31	£1	Green and brown on white 'dot'	£50	£100
T32	£1	Green and brown on white, sq. 'dot'	£100	£190

Third issue (Northern Ireland)
T33	10s	Green and brown on white	£90	£190
T34	£1	Green and brown on white 'dot'	£45	£95
T35	£1	Green and brown on white, sq. 'dot'	£120	£200

Unissued notes prepared during the Great War (all extremely rare)
T21	5s	Deep violet and green on white (Bradbury)		*
T22	2s 6d	Olive-green and chocolate on white	from £7000	
T23	1s	Green and brown on white	from £7500	
T27	5s	Violet and green on white (Warren Fisher)	from £3000	
T28	2s 6d	Olive-green and chocolate on white	from £4500	
T29	1s	Green and brown on white	from £4500	

BANK OF ENGLAND NOTES
Cyril Patrick Mahon 1925-29

			EF	UNC
B210	10s	Red-brown	£100	£180
B212	£1	Green	£65	£140
B215	£5	Black on white	£300	£500

Bank of England £1 serial no. 2 sold at auction by Spink and Son Ltd several years ago for £56,000.

John Bradbury 5 shillings.

Basil Gage Catterns 1929-34

			EF	UNC
B223	10s	Red-brown	£60	£140
B225	£1	Green (prefix: letter, number, number; e.g.E63)	£50	£50
B226	£1	Green (prefix: number, number, letter)	£100	£175
B228	£5	Black on white	£180	£300

Kenneth Oswald Peppiatt 1934-49

B236	10s	Red-brown (prefix: number, number, letter) 1st period	£45	£80
B251	10s	Mauve 2nd period	£35	£70
B256	10s	Red-brown (prefix: number, number, letter) 3rd period	£100	£170
B262	10s	Red-brown (metal filament) 4th period	£40	£80
B238	£1	Green (prefix: number, number, letter) 1st issue	£25	£45
B248	£1	Pale blue (prefix:A-D) 2nd issue	£20	£45
B249	£1	Blue (shades) 2nd issue	£9	£20
B258	£1	Green (prefix: number, number, letter) 3rd issue	£35	£65
B260	£1	Green (metal filament) 4th issue	£16	£28
B241	£5	Black on white, one straight edge, three deckled	£120	£260
B255	£5	Black on white, straight edges, metal filament, thick paper	£110	£190
B264	£5	Black on white, straight edges, metal filament, thin paper	£110	£180

Unissued notes of the 1939-45 War (very rare)

B253	5s	Olive-green on pale pink background	from £4000	
B254	2s 6d	Black on pale blue background	from £4000	

Percival Spencer Beale 1949-55

B265	10s	Red-brown (prefix: number, number, letter)	£30	£50
B266	10s	Red-brown prefix: letter, number, number, letter	£22	£45
B268	£1	Green	£10	£20
B270	£5	Black on white	£90	£180

Leslie Kenneth O'Brien 1955-62

			EF	UNC
B271	10s	Red-brown (prefix: letter, number, number, letter)	£12	£25
B272	10s	Red-brown (prefix: number, number, letter)	£60	£140
B286	10s	Red-brown, Queen's portrait	£3	£6
B273	£1	Green	£6	£12
B281	£1	Green (prefix: letter, number, number) Queen's portrait	£3	£6
B282	£1	Green (prefix: number, number, letter). Queen's portrait		
B283	£1	Green 'R' variety (letter R found in white space above lower BANK OF ENGLAND panel on reverse	£3	£5
			£260	£400
B284	£1	Green (prefix: letter number, number, letter). Queen's portrait	£12	£20
B275	£5	Black on white	£90	£180
B277	£5	Blue, pale green and orange (solid symbols)	£20	£65
B279	£5	Blue, pale green and orange (symbols for £5 white)	£20	£65

Jasper Quintus Hollom 1962-66

			EF	UNC
B295	10s	Red-brown (prefix: number, number, letter)	£3	£6
B294	10s	Red-brown (prefix: letter, number, number, letter)	£2	£5
B288	£1	Green	£3	£6
B292	£1	Green, 'G' variety ('G' in same position as 'R' as B283)	£4	£10
B297	£5	Blue	£16	£35
B299	£10	Multicoloured	£25	£45

John Standish Fforde 1966-70

			EF	UNC
B309	10s	Red-brown (prefix: number, number, letter)	£2	£5
B310	10s	Red-brown (prefix: letter, number, number, letter)	£2	£5
B311	10s	Red-brown (prefix: letter, number, number) Replacement	£5	£12
B301	£1	Green	£4	£8
B303	£1	Green 'G' variety	£4	£10
B312	£5	Blue (prefix: letter, number, number)	£16	£35
B314	£5	Blue (prefix: number, number, letter)	£16	£35
B316	£10	Multicoloured	£20	£45
B318	£20	Multicoloured	£150	£250

John Brangwyn Page 1970-1980

			EF	UNC
B322	£1	Green (prefix: letter, letter, number, number)	£2	£5
B324	£5	Blue	£20	£45
B332	£5	Multicoloured (prefix: letter, number, number). 1st series	£12	£22
B334	£5	Multicoloured, L on reverse signifies lithographic printing	£12	£22
B326	£10	Multicoloured	£20	£40

				EF	UNC
B330	£10	Multicoloured A-series		£18	£40
B328	£20	Multicoloured		£35	£80

David Henry Fitzroy Somerset 1980-1988

				EF	UNC
B341	£1	Green		£2	£5
B346	£10	Multicoloured (prefix: letter, letter, number, number)		£30	£50
B350	£20	Multicoloured		£40	£80
B352	£50	Olive green, brown, grey		£70	£140

George Malcolm Gill (1988-1991)

				EF	UNC
B353	£5	Blue		£9	£20
B354	£10	Brown		£15	£28
B355	£20	Multicoloured		£40	£80
B356	£50	Multicoloured		£75	£100
B357	£5	Multicoloured (Series E) AO1		£12	£25
B358	£20	Multicoloured		£30	£45

G.E.A. Kentfield (1991-)

				EF	UNC
B360	£50	Multicoloured		£18	£35
B362	£5	Multicoloured		£8	£16
B366	£10	Multicoloured		£15	£25
B372	£20	Multicoloured		£25	£45
B375	£50	Multicoloured		£60	£95

M.V. Lowther (1999-2004)

				EF	UNC
B378	£5	Multicoloured		f	£6
B380	£10	Multicoloured		f	£14
B382	£20	Multicoloured		f	£26
B383	£50	Multicoloured		f	£65
B391	£5	Multicoloured		f	£6
B389	£10	Multicoloured		f	£14
B389	£10	Multicoloured	The "Co"	f	£12
B385	£20	Multicoloured	And "Co"	f	£24

A.Bailey (2004-)

Bailey signed notes exist in £5, £10 and £20. A £50 is expected.

* Exist but no price can be quoted. f - still face value unless special prefix number, i.e. AO1. Prices on modern notes for EF or/and UNC

A recently dicovered extraordinarily rare Bank of England £100 of 1790 sold at auction by Spink in 2000 for £44,000